To Dad, Mam, Sharon, Brian, Terri-Ann, David and Dearbhla
for shaping me

To Sam, Matisse and Tiernan
for completing me

To anyone who has been touched by cancer,
may my story give you strength and hope

CONTENTS

	A Note from the Writer	ix
1	Finding Out	1
2	Dublin	11
3	Melbourne	29
4	Beyond Football	47
5	'There Must be Some Mistake'	76
6	Getting My Head Around It	88
7	Under the Knife	112
8	White Coats	132
9	Inside the Brain	164
10	The Other Half	176
11	Fatherhood	196
12	Nature vs Science	208
13	Smoke and Mirrors	237
14	Precious Stones	254
15	Challenges	275
16	Peace	300
17	Reprieve	316
	Postscript	328
	Afterword by Sam Stynes	330
	Picture Credits	338
	Acknowledgements	340

A NOTE FROM THE WRITER

I first met Jim Stynes when we were both 18-year-old students at the now defunct teachers' college in Glenferrie Road, Melbourne. There must have been shared lectures along the way, but most of the memories from those days are of playing pool, table tennis matches, kicking the footy on the college lawn, organising parties and talking about girls.

We were both playing football in the VFL under-19s at the time – Jim was with Melbourne, I was with St Kilda – and one day we lined up against each other in the ruck. We had to look away at centre bounces because we kept wanting to burst into laughter.

One of my fondest memories is of travelling to Dublin and celebrating my 23rd birthday with the Stynes family, before driving through the north and west of the country with Jim, his brother Brian and friends. We became great mates. I was a groomsman at his wedding and he was godfather to my two oldest children.

When Jim was diagnosed with cancer in 2009, his family

and friends were stunned but we all felt certain that he would overcome the disease, just like he had met every other challenge in his remarkable life. Jim knew that the media would be fascinated with how he dealt with cancer and decided to make that journey very public, but on his terms. He hoped that his story might help others who had cancer, particularly those who did not have the support or the resources or the resolve that he did.

Months later on a bleak and wintry afternoon, Jim became emotional as he lay in a darkened room in Epworth Hospital and spoke about the diary notes he had been diligently keeping on his laptop. He hoped to publish the story of his journey and wanted to know if I could help him turn those notes into a book.

After that, we tried to catch up once a week, sometimes discussing life and its meaning, other times just hanging out and talking sparingly because his health was poor or his memory failing. As was Jim's way, he would push and prod to make sure the book was the best it could be. To that end, Jim's family, friends and medical team were gracious and generous in making sure the whole story emerged.

I feel blessed to have spent that time with Jim.

Warwick Green

1

FINDING OUT

'Hey, what is that?'

Not necessarily what you expect to hear from your wife during an affectionate hug.

'What is what?' I replied, maybe a little more tersely than I should have.

'You've got this lump on your back,' Sam said. 'Just here.' She prodded at a spot just next to my spine, that annoying place where you can never quite reach to scratch an itch.

I didn't know what it was, and I was dismissive. It was probably just a fatty knot. Scar tissue. A war wound from my football days. Since retiring, I'd had a couple of operations to remove bone spurs from my ankles. Maybe this was the backbone equivalent.

Sam wasn't so easily brushed aside. 'Well, you should get it checked out.'

'Yeah, I will,' I said, with a total lack of conviction.

Over the next few months of 2008, the lump wasn't mentioned again. It was not something I could see or feel, and besides, I had more important things to get on with.

I

That June, I had taken on the busy role of president of the Melbourne Football Club, the AFL team I had played 264 games for between 1987 and 1998. My other passion was Reach, the youth organisation I had founded with a mate, Paul Currie, in 1994. I also had business interests to attend to, with Pacific Early Learning Group's childcare centres, as well as property management. And somewhere in among all of that, I found time to devote to my wife, Sam, our daughter, Matisse, who was seven, and son, Tiernan, three. By the end of 2008, then, I couldn't wait to leave behind the stresses of life and sit on the beach down at Rye with the kids.

January 2009 was sweltering, with temperatures occasionally hitting the forties. Matisse and Tiernan spent the evenings splashing about in the shallows of Port Phillip Bay while I looked on, usually trying to avoid the temptation of checking my mobile phone messages.

On one of those evenings, our friends and business partners Hugh and Catherine Ellis were there with their two daughters. Life was good. I stripped off my T-shirt and reached for a towel.

'Is it just me, or can you guys see that thing on his back?' Sam asked.

Our friends agreed. 'Yeah, there is something. You should really get that looked at, Jim.'

So when, a few weeks later, I found myself standing next to one of Melbourne's club doctors, Karl Fried, while the footballers were training, the words 'you should really get that looked at' popped into my head.

Karl examined my back and was concerned enough to write a referral for me to see a specialist. I slipped the referral into my diary and added it to my mental checklist. It remained there for weeks. Eventually, I thought I might have lost it.

More weeks passed. One morning in May I was walking back to my car after a meeting in the leafy Melbourne suburb of Malvern. My stomach was rumbling, and since I wasn't rushing to another appointment, the idea of a sandwich appealed. While wandering up Wattletree Road, I realised that I was in front of the rooms of Graeme Southwick.

A keen follower of the Melbourne footy club, Graeme is a plastic and reconstructive surgeon. Many in the wider public will remember his work after the Bali bombings in 2002, which killed 202 people, eighty-eight of whom were Australian. Graeme was in Indonesia at the time on a three-day break after a medical conference. Amid the chaos at Sanglah Hospital in the forty-eight hours after the bombs went off, he worked tirelessly, treating dozens of burns and blast victims.

I had come to know Graeme during my playing days. For him, sitting in the Members' Stand at the MCG on a Saturday afternoon was something of an escape. But whenever one of his beloved Demons was forced off the field with a gash or a bloodied head, he could be relied upon to duck down into the rooms and quickly stitch us up, always with the most delicate threadwork. Graeme once told me how he'd missed most of the 2000 AFL Grand Final, in which Melbourne faced Essendon. He had rushed to the rooms in the first quarter to assist our teenage forward Brad Green, who had taken a nasty knock to the throat, only to find himself flanked by a concussed Troy Simmonds, who'd been knocked senseless by a hit from Essendon's Michael Long. It had been an ugly bump.

That reminded me: the lump. Maybe Graeme could examine it. I rifled through my diary, looking in vain for the referral, before deciding that I should pop inside and ask anyway.

At reception, while it was patiently explained to me that Graeme's every moment over the next few days was crammed with appointments, the man himself appeared through a doorway, following one of his patients.

'Big Jimmy!' he said. 'What brings you here? When are we going to get the Demons off the bottom of the ladder and winning again?'

I explained why I had come, and after quickly checking his schedule Graeme flashed a grin and mouthed a hushed plea to the exasperated receptionist – 'I know, but just give me a couple of minutes' – before ushering me through to his rooms.

'Right, let's have a look then.' As he gently poked around the region near my spine, Graeme explained that the lump was elongated, almost oval-shaped. He was surprised to find out that I had ignored it for so long.

I later learned that it is not unusual for such a lump to be diagnosed as a lipoma, which is a benign soft-tissue tumour. Lipomata are soft to the touch, and are generally painless.

But Graeme was not prepared to discuss any scenarios. 'I'm going to give it a quick ultrasound, Jimmy.'

After doing so, Graeme examined the results. 'Hmm,' he said, before escorting me back out to the front desk. He turned to the receptionist, saying, 'I want to book him in for exploratory surgery.'

Then, to me, Graeme said, 'It needs to be in the next few days, Jim. Make sure you clear an hour in your diary. I want to get this out in one go.'

Denial can be a powerful defence mechanism. As a footballer, I had employed it throughout my career to overcome injuries and to conquer self-doubts. Yet still it seems extraordinary to me, when I look back on it now, that when I pulled up in the car at Wattletree Road a few days later, I hadn't even remotely considered that I might have cancer.

Inside the rooms, Graeme explained that he also wanted to remove a couple of moles from my body – one from my neck, another from my ear. To my mind, the lump on my back was just a larger, more inconvenient blemish that needed to be cut out in the same way.

I lay on my stomach, waiting for the local anaesthetic to kick in, and listened to the banter between Graeme and his assistants. It was a bit like being at the dentist: you need to take your mind somewhere else to make the time tick over more rapidly.

After about forty minutes, I was becoming slightly

uncomfortable. 'Graeme, I'm starting to feel what you're doing back there. I think I might need some more anaesthetic.'

They ramped up the pain relief and resumed. I was fine, but after a while I began to feel the instruments again. Now I was becoming edgy. It wasn't so much that I felt pain, it was more a sense that Graeme was *in* my body, not working on the surface. It felt like he was in deep – about as deep as you could possibly imagine a surgeon being inside your body.

I remember thinking at one point, *This might be worse than I first thought* . . . But not long after that Graeme began to stitch me up. He rested a hand on my shoulder, exhaled in a way that suggested relief, and said, 'Right, we're all done.'

In that moment, my doubts disintegrated in a wave of positivity. It's always been my natural inclination to take an optimistic approach. So as I stood up and leaned across to grab my shirt, I thought, *Okay, it's all good.* The lump was out. I barely registered being told that it would now be sent away to be tested.

By that evening, I had banished the whole episode from my mind. The only reminders were the jolts of pain that occasionally flashed through my back. But my thoughts were elsewhere.

There were the final details of a Reach youth camp in Sydney that weekend to organise. Furthermore, Melbourne's 'home' game that Saturday night was being played 1700 kilometres away. Instead of running onto the MCG, the boys would be taking on St Kilda at the Gold Coast. There was plenty to get on with. My only thought about the day's surgery was that it was going to be annoying having to answer questions about the couple of visible scars where the moles had been removed.

Of course, Sam had wanted to know how the exploratory surgery had gone and was keen to have a look at my back. Despite the unwieldy dressing on the wound, I assured her that the surgery had done its job – it had just taken longer than expected.

I did tell Sam about the nervous moment I'd experienced. 'They were all chatting away and happy,' I said, 'but at one point they went quiet. It just felt like the mood in the room changed.' But I was convinced that all would be fine now.

A few days later, Graeme phoned me. 'Can we get you in here? How about Monday?'

I found an empty space in my diary. 'No problem,' I said, 'but why the appointment?'

'It's a follow-up,' Graeme replied. 'We can discuss it on Monday, Jim. Oh, and ask Sam to come along too.' He hung up.

I stopped and frowned, biting my lip. That last sentence hung in the air, making me a little apprehensive. My mind began to wind over. There was a conversation going on inside my head between positivity and negativity. *Maybe that lump could be cancer. But even if it is, it must be a one-off and it's been removed now. So why does Sam need to be there to hear that?*

It could be some test they want to do – maybe they need her to drive me home. There would be no answers until Monday.

Sitting in the waiting room, I still didn't get it. Sam and I had been ushered to a small private ante-room. At one point, Graeme's top half appeared around the door frame, apologising for keeping us waiting. 'Bear with me – I'll just be a moment.'

While I began to grumble about medical types never being on time, Sam had picked up in an instant that the usually jovial doctor had seemed uncommonly tense. 'He looks worried,' she said.

Graeme reappeared soon afterwards and shepherded us into two comfortable chairs in his office. He did not mess around with niceties, but he did seem to be choosing his words very carefully.

'I'm going to explain the situation,' he began. 'But, Jim, what I'm about to tell you might not sink in very well – your mind might go someplace else. Sam, you will need to listen carefully.

'The results of the biopsy are back. The lump that we removed was a malignant tumour. It is cancer, but at this time we are not sure which type. We've had several specialists examine it but it is unclear what we're dealing with.'

As Graeme had warned, I heard the word 'cancer' and not a lot more. I experienced an intense rush, like some kind of surreal adrenaline. It was as though my whole body had released a chemical that just washed right up through me to my face, and I could barely move a muscle. My legs went like jelly and there was no way I could have stood up.

Now I understood why some people drop to the floor when they hear devastating news. It was weird – I had always wondered what it would like to be told something so momentous and life-changing. I had asked people what it felt like, but I had never thought it would happen to me.

Sam's instinct was to put her hand on my knee. My immediate thought was, *Well, at least it's not her.*

I had my face down in the palms of my hands as Graeme explained that I would now need to undergo a series of scans to determine the precise nature of my condition. In the best-case scenario, the cancerous growth had all been cut out. If that were the case, the scans would show nothing else and the doctors would monitor me every few months to ensure there were no new problems.

Graeme asked if I needed a cup of tea or a drink of water. I don't know why, but I just started to laugh. Maybe his question was a trigger that started me thinking about how particular I was with food and drink, about what I put in my body. *How dare this happen to me? I'm not sick or unhealthy. I never even get colds.* Then it occurred to me that cancer is not choosy. Cancer is not rational – it doesn't make sense.

In those split-seconds, while Sam and Graeme allowed me to absorb the news, my mind hurtled through the consequences, careering wildly from one thought to another. The thought of dying was incomprehensible, but a tiny pragmatic part of me was raising the possibility and it scared the crap out of me. My brain flashed up the reality of my two little kids growing up without their dad, and I determined that it simply could not happen. Through Reach I had met so many young people scarred by that reality. I wanted to watch my children grow into beautiful, unique adults. Then I thought about Sam, sitting next to me. I wondered how she would be reacting and considered what it was going to mean for her.

I composed myself, gave Sam's hand a squeeze, and willed myself to concentrate. 'Okay . . . Where do we go from here, doc? What do I need to do?'

2

DUBLIN

'Spanish dancer' – I think that's what they used to call it when I was kid growing up in south Dublin. My knowledge of cancer was roughly a nickname and a vague understanding that it was a disease which could kill you. I had never seen anyone really close to me go through a struggle with cancer. I had older relatives who had succumbed to it, but that had never really sunk in. As a young boy, my impression was that they had died of old age.

As a child, I lived a blessed life. I never got sick. I was healthy, resilient and surrounded by a large, loving family. When I was a toddler I was always on the go and always hungry – Mam and Dad reckon that if I had been born forty years later, I would have been diagnosed with Attention Deficit Hyperactivity Disorder. I used to race around constantly, and I was known to throw the odd tantrum if my parents tried to quieten me down – particularly in the church, according to Dad, because I must have sensed that they would have to sit tight, grit their teeth and give in to me. There was one phase where I spent months literally bouncing off the walls at home on a space-hopper, those inflatable orange bouncers with horns for handles. Mam even took me to a doctor, who prescribed Valium. But after seeing what it did to me for a couple of days, Mam decided to flush the medicine down the toilet. Instead, she used to get me out of the house whenever possible to burn off energy.

I was the oldest of six children. After me came Sharon, Brian, Terri-Ann, David and Dearbhla. We lived in Ballyroan Crescent, a quiet and narrow street, where council workers were always patching up the cracks in the concrete road surface. The houses all looked pretty similar. Mostly, they were plain-looking double-storey homes, with a driveway to the garage and trimmed hedges on the brick front fence.

The area was full of young families, including many boys my age, and we would spend the evenings playing in the street until our mothers called us in to dinner or dragged us off to bed. We usually played soccer, because it was easy to organise and didn't require many players. Even though it was illegal to play matches on the street, we always found a way – despite occasional visits by the local police, usually after we had dented a car or shattered a light.

Everyone in the neighbourhood knew everyone else's kids. There was my right-hand man, Chippy, as well as Farreller, Mackie, Matt, Pricey, Kegs, Tiny and Lono, and we used to wander in and out of each other's houses like they were our own. One birthday, I pestered Dad to join me as I walked around the neighbourhood delivering invitations to my party. After knocking at the door of one house, we heard a voice float down from upstairs: 'Don't open the bleeding door if it's that Jim Stynes.' I think they were sick of me always hanging around.

My father, Brian, worked for a telecommunications company; Gaelic football and gardening were two of his passions. There was always so much going on in our house that it was chaotic, and Dad used to seek refuge in the back garden. He had split the space in half – roses, gooseberries and raspberries grew on one side, while a vegetable patch was on the other.

Dad was an old-fashioned head of the family. He would bark at us, criticise us and always push us and challenge us to do better. He could be blunt and did not suffer fools. With a sharp comment he could simultaneously identify the humour and the reality of a situation. It was like he was saying, 'Here's a little one-liner – but understand that I know what's going on and I'm on to you.' He could seem negative but his words and actions always came from love and a desire for his children to improve themselves. And while it was acceptable for him be critical, if anyone outside the family dared to say a bad word about us, he would defend us fiercely and doggedly. Not that he would admit it, but beneath his gruff exterior Dad was a bit of a softy who could get quite emotional.

My mother, Teresa, was an altogether different personality. Mam is the eternal optimist and the most non-judgemental person I have ever come across. She has an impossibly tender and sweet nature, and sees the good in every person, every situation. She listens with a sense of genuine interest and wonderment when people tell her about themselves, and has no interest in looking for their faults. When I had children of my own, I marvelled even more at Mam's ability to always nurture and encourage. Her devotion to caring for her family was an inspiration. 'Mother Teresa', we used to call her, after the Catholic nun who so selflessly gave her life to serving the poor in India. Mam has always been undaunted by any challenge, and optimistically approaches any problem believing a solution can be found.

Through my parents' different expressions of love, I came to have two very strong forces working within me. Where Dad taught me to push, Mam showed me how to caress. It helped me to develop a tough and enduring spirit, and a desire to succeed. Yet it also allowed me to see the importance of compassion and empathy. And one principle that both taught me was that you cannot compromise your integrity.

The other influential figure from my childhood was the heroic figure of my uncle Joe. I have always been intensely proud of my Irish heritage, and he was a larger-than-life figure who contributed significantly to that pride. Joe, who was actually my great-uncle, was a champion sportsman, a political activist and a thrilling part of the family folklore.

Dad was one of nine kids; his father, Peter, was a barman who worked in the heart of Dublin, right next to O'Connell Bridge. The family lived above the pub on third floor, overlooking the River Liffey, all of the boys in one room and all the girls in the other.

Peter and his brother Joe had both played Gaelic football for county Kildare, before moving to Dublin to look for work during the tough economic times after World War I. Uncle Joe had been sworn into the Irish Republican Army in 1920 as the campaign to gain independence from the British intensified; he fought in the same battalion as the famous freedom fighter Michael Collins.

Later that year, Uncle Joe was a steward at Croke Park on the November afternoon that would go down in infamy as 'Bloody Sunday'. While Tipperary played a football match against Dublin, the British Army raided the ground and opened fire on the crowd, killing fourteen, including Tipperary player Michael Hogan. Joe, aged just seventeen, was carrying concealed handguns for the IRA. He was handed an overcoat, dissolved into the crowd and scaled the concrete wall to escape.

After the signing of the Anglo-Irish Treaty in 1921, Joe was among those who remained staunchly opposed to the proposed breakup of the country into north and south. While staying out of the grasp of the Irish Free State authorities, he managed to play several games of football for Dublin. However, during training with the team at Croke Park in 1922, just three days before the All-Ireland final, he was arrested. They bundled Joe off to the Curragh internment camp, where he remained for a year. He was not given the benefit of a trial and was only released as part of an armistice at the birth of the Irish republic.

Uncle Joe returned to playing football and continued his opposition to the Anglo-Irish Treaty. He was a star forward in the Dublin team that won the 1923 final, which was in fact played in 1924, due to political unrest. That match was against fierce rival Kerry, and twenty-nine extra trains were put on to bring fans from the south to a packed Croke Park. Dubs won the match 1-5 to 1-3, and Joe, the star forward, kicked the last two points.

Within a few years he had migrated to New York, but he still regularly returned to Ireland. That is how I got to know him, some five decades later. Every September he would return home to Dublin, ostensibly to watch the All-Ireland football final at Croke Park. There were times when he would stay with us in Rathfarnham; he would get my bed while I slept on the floor. Dad would drive him around town. He'd get to the races at the Curragh and always had meetings in Northern Ireland. Sometimes I'd tag along, and it was always a thrill. I was in awe of Joe as a sporting hero, but his daring republican background also appealed to my rebellious nature. He was a charismatic and magnetic figure who held court wherever he went.

Uncle Joe had become an accountant with Cartier jewellers, but he was also secretary to the prisoners' dependence fund in New York. Now, exactly what that title entailed is a bit unclear to me. I know there was a lot of fundraising, some distribution of funds and support, and some small-time gun smuggling.

I remember hearing the story of the day Joe's wife, Bridget, had some women over for afternoon tea at their home in Queens. One of them sat on the sofa and was shifting about, having trouble getting comfortable. She went to fluff one of the pillows, and her discomfort quickly became anxiety when she realised that the sofa was in fact being used as a hiding place for a sub-machine gun. The matter should have ended that night, when Joe told Bridget that it was probably best not to ask too many questions about IRA business. But the problem was that one of the other women starting gossiping around the neighbourhood about how Bridget's Joe had a machine gun hidden in the living room.

Sure enough, word spread and a few days later Joe was paid a visit. He had a sack put over his head and was driven to a secluded spot. The mobsters said he had to hand over his machine gun and any other weapons he might have, or he would not see his wife again.

Joe said he would willingly do so, but that the mobsters would have to deal with the repercussions of taking weapons from the IRA. The goons told him there had been a misunderstanding and apologised. Joe had the sack put back over his head, was driven home and never heard about the incident again.

Having an uncle who had played in an All-Ireland final and become this revered figure helped me with my self-belief. It helped me dare to dream that I could make something of myself too. I continued to stay in contact with Joe, and visited him in New York at the end of 1990, while I was on my way home from Melbourne to Dublin. A few weeks later he died, aged eighty-eight. An Irish-American newspaper ran an obituary on its front page, with a tribute from Sinn Fein's leader, Gerry Adams.

Apart from these powerful role models, the biggest influence on my life was sport. Not only was it an outlet for my excess energy, it was tremendous for my self-esteem. I was not a great student – I did reasonably well at maths but found many of the other subjects difficult, mainly due to my inability to sit still and concentrate for prolonged periods. If I had to read, my mind would drift by the time I got to the end of the page, and I would need to read passages over and over for them to sink in. I had to force myself to study, and persevere until it made sense.

Not so sport. More likely, you would have had to force me to stop. I would be the first in line for anything that involved a ball or a competition or a race. Sport was in my blood. My sisters, Mam and my maternal grandmother all excelled at *camogie*, the women's equivalent of hurling. Mam was a fine athlete and had taken up cross-country running – with some success – at the age of forty-four; she later became an angel-faced assassin on the golf course.

On my paternal side it was Gaelic football. Dad had played competitive football until his mid-forties. His routine was to eat a steak and a tomato two hours before each match. He began his playing career with the local parish team St Agnes, before joining the Civil Service Club, a team of government workers mainly from rural areas.

Coincidentally, Dad was in the team that played the first match against an Australian touring team, the Galahs, in late 1967. The Australian team was captained by Ron Barassi, the Melbourne Football Club's greatest champion and a man who would be central to a pivotal moment in my life. Australia was supposed to begin its tour with a match against All-Ireland champions Meath at Croke Park. But, concerned that they had never played under compromise Gaelic rules, they managed to organise the match against Civil Service at Island Bridge, near the Liffey.

The Australian footballers were a strange lot to my father, who once told me, 'They all seemed like giants. They wore these strange sleeveless guernseys – we thought it was just so they could show off their muscles.' The Civil Service team led late in the match before being overrun by a team that contained some of the greatest names to have played Australian football. Apart from Barassi, the team included such champions as Royce Hart, Alex Jesaulenko, Bob Skilton, John Nicholls, Bill Barrot and Barry Davis. After their two-point win over Civil Service, the Galahs went on to thump Meath 25–13 in front of a crowd of more than 23000 at Croke Park.

Dad was also a successful juniors coach for many years and was the first to take our local club, Ballyboden St Enda's to a championship. He coached me too, and he was a hard taskmaster. Some teammates used to believe that he was too harsh on his sons – that he singled out Brian, David and me and made an example of us. He would shout curses at us from the sidelines, and when it got too much I would fire off expletives back at him. At times, I did wonder if there was any pleasing him. The saving grace was that while our relationship at the football club was as coach and player, he would not let that be destructive to our father–son relationship at home. If I was struggling, he was always there for advice, or to help me practise my skills down at the park. That proved to me that he genuinely cared. I knew that his love for me was uncompromising – but so was his will to win.

My first recollection of playing organised sport was at age nine, when I played in the under-11s for the local football club, Ballyboden St Enda's. At about the same age, I had some success in cross-country running; in fact, my excitement at winning medals and sashes had Dad worried that I would choose running over football. He had nothing to fear, though. I preferred the camaraderie, the cooperation and the social aspect of team sports.

It helped that we enjoyed a few triumphs along the way. While I was at Ballyroan Boys' National School, our team played off for the schools' title in successive years, winning the first one. I was also selected in the combined Dublin under-12s team, which provided my first taste of media coverage: a newspaper photograph of me scoring a goal, with a caption underneath that read, 'Shane O'Brien drives the ball past the Cork defence'. I carefully corrected the name before pasting the article into my scrapbook.

I can distinctly remember an instance not long after that match when Dad chipped me about not doing my homework, lecturing me about the importance of study. 'I don't need to worry about that,' I declared, 'because I'm going to be a football player.'

'You might well be, son, but you can't make a living out of it.'

I was crestfallen. 'What about the money all those Manchester United and Liverpool players are being paid?' I asked. I had often seen the headlines in the newspapers.

'Oh, that's a different game altogether,' Dad replied. 'There's no money in Gaelic football.'

Even years later, Dad said he could recall the sight of my bottom lip dropping and my shoulders sagging.

Through my teenage years I became consumed by football. I somehow managed to play at least two games a week, as well as rugby at De La Salle College. I also ran with the Pearces club. I took an interest in most sports and even found time to play basketball and squash.

But there was one sport that had me stumped. At about age sixteen, I sat down one evening to watch a film on television. There were men in strange jerseys running around, playing with some kind of rugby ball. It seemed to be a game they had invented for the movie.

I turned to my father. 'What's this, then, Dad?'

He looked up from his paper. 'It's Australian football.'

The scenes were from a film called *The Club*, and from the glimpses of match footage it showed, the game seemed to share quite a few similarities with Gaelic football. I was bemused that the crowd cheered whenever a player caught the ball – especially because he stopped, rather than playing on and beating his man. *What's the big deal about that?* I thought.

I had no idea that I was already on a path towards a life spent immersed in Australian football.

My first major step in that direction came when I was selected in the Dublin squad for the 1984 minors' (under-18) championships. I made the team as one of the two midfielders. I was happy with my form until I let myself down with a poor showing in the Leinster final, which is effectively the All-Ireland quarter-final.

The match was a curtain-raiser for the Dublin senior team's game and was watched by more than 60000 people – and I produced one of the worst performances of my life. It was played on a Sunday, but because my parents had gone away for the weekend my siblings and I had held a huge party at our place on the Friday night. By the time my team took the field I was physically and mentally drained.

Dublin won, however, and I had four weeks to redeem myself before the semi-final against Derry City. When the team was announced a few days before the match, I found I had been relegated to the interchange bench. It was devastating, because I believed I was good enough to be in the starting line-up, but I knew it was hard to argue my case after I'd produced such a lame effort in the previous match.

I immediately realised that there were two important

lessons I had to take from the experience, though. I vowed never again to put myself in a position where poor preparation affected my performance. Also, I took on board Dad's advice that 'the ability to respond to adversity is what separates great footballers from good footballers'. Had I chosen to complain or adopt a negative attitude, my life might have taken a completely different path from that moment on. Instead, I remained positive and trained hard, and I was rewarded with an unexpected development.

At our final training session, the morning before the match, the boy who had taken my place in the team flew to catch a ball and landed heavily on his back. The following day, the coach decided ten minutes before the match that the boy was not fit enough to start the game. He walked over to me and snapped, 'You're in!'

I made the most of my chance by being the best afield in our win over Derry, and I was part of the Dublin team that went on to defeat Tipperary in the All-Ireland final before a packed house at Croke Park.

After the final, a Christian Brother named Tom McDonald told me about a training camp where players would try out for scholarships with an Australian football team called the Melbourne Demons. Brother McDonald, who was the head of a Dublin college and coach of the Leinster schools' minor team, explained that the weekend camp would be held at a north Dublin college in two weeks' time.

I knew that several of my Dublin teammates had been asked to attend the camp, and also that a few of them had been part of an Irish schoolboys team that had toured Australia the previous year. *I've got to at least consider this*, I was thinking, but I also had a nagging doubt. I knew Dad wouldn't be too impressed about the prospect of me trying to run off to Australia.

I had spent the whole Irish summer trying to get a place at tertiary college to study primary-school teaching. After missing out on third-round offers, I had jagged a place at St Patrick's in Drumcondra when another student pulled out of the course at the last moment. Now, just one week into my studies, I was planning to spend a weekend trying out for a football scholarship that would take me to the other side of the world.

I broke the news to Dad. 'You are not going to that trial,' he fumed.

'Come on, Dad,' I pleaded. 'I have to go. They've hand-picked players. Besides, they'll probably give us some free sports gear.'

It was a desperate appeal to my father's enthusiasm for anything that might save him money. I could recall times when he had jammed open the turnstile at the football, pleading ignorance while the kids rushed in and the attendants cried foul.

'All right,' he finally relented. 'But whatever you do, make sure you don't get picked.'

The camp was conducted by Melbourne's coach, Ron

Barassi – the same man who had captained the Australian team in my father's day – and match-committee chairman, Barry Richardson, a former champion footballer for Richmond.

I had several advantages on that camp. One was that we went out to the pub on the first evening, and while I showed some restraint, several of the other boys reported for duty the next morning struggling with hangovers. Secondly, being almost two metres tall helped because I knew that Melbourne was keen on finding players with height. And thirdly, my background in playing several seasons of rugby meant that the oval-shaped Australian football was not as alien to me as it was to most of the other boys. Furthermore, when it came to completing the drills that the Melbourne duo set out for us, I couldn't suppress my competitive instinct. You can imagine my dilemma, then, when at the end of the camp, on the Sunday morning, the Australians offered the two places to me and a Dublin teammate, James Fahey.

I was eighteen years old, and I was looking at the world and thinking, *I want a piece of it*. I had always dreamed of going to the United States to be paid to play Gaelic football. This sounded like a viable alternative – and a real adventure. On the other hand, my life in Dublin had just started to fall into place. There was college, the prospect of progressing through the football ranks with Dublin, and I had a serious girlfriend, Aislinn.

I weighed all of this up in my head before eventually – and reluctantly – summoning the courage to go to a payphone and dial home.

'Now, what did I say?' Dad exploded down the line.

'But what they're offering looks awful good, Dad . . . '
I began.

'Well, you're not going! Stay there and I'll come and pick
you up.'

Dad was coaching me in an under-21 game that afternoon,
and on the way I tried to discuss the two-year scholarship
with him. Whenever I would outline a few details, he would
interrupt me: 'You're not going.' Then he would sit there
with his jaw clenched tight. The only sound that followed
was Dad's breathing through his nose.

Eventually, he made a statement that was delivered with
all the authority of a closing argument. 'All your pieces are
coming into play, Jim, and now you want to run off and live
in Van Diemen's Land.'

A few days later, there was a knock at the door. My three-
year-old sister, Dearbhla, answered it and then came running
into the kitchen. 'There's a man and he sounds funny,' she
said. It was the Australian accent of Melbourne's general
manager, Dick Seddon, who was standing outside the front
door with Barry Richardson.

While Dad looked on begrudgingly, Mam offered the
strangers tea and listened to them state their case about
why I should make the move to the other side of the world.
Seddon was smooth and charming, and had an answer to
every question. Yes, they could organise for me to enrol in a

teachers' course in Melbourne – and they would cover the fees. Yes, they agreed with Mam that my Catholic faith was vitally important; they would pay my board and place me with a family of practising Catholics. And James Fahey would be living just around the corner.

They assured Dad that I would receive a weekly stipend of $60, as well as a lump sum of $500 for clothes and other living expenses. Match payments would be $50 a game with the under-19 team. These were mind-blowing figures to an eighteen-year-old who had been earning $10 a week doing a morning paper round on his bicycle.

Richardson, who had played in three premierships and coached Richmond for a couple of years, answered all of Dad's football questions. Some time later, as I led the two men to the front door, I was thinking how well the meeting had gone.

We passed the staircase, where Sharon, the next oldest kid, with whom I was very close, was sitting with her friends and our two youngest siblings. She later told me that as my parents walked past, Mam had whispered to Dad, 'He's going, you know.' To which he had hissed back, 'Sure he's not going, woman – you've been brainwashed.'

As the Australians walked to their car, Mam turned to me and said, 'Don't take it as a no. Da and I will have a talk about it.'

Melbourne was after an answer by the end of the week, with a view to getting me on a plane within a month. When Seddon and Richardson returned a few days later, they brought along Brother McDonald. 'The boy wants to go,' he told my father. 'If you don't let him go, he'll regret it. And you'll regret it because he'll always wonder what would have been if you'd let him go.' Dad knew he was right.

A couple of weeks later, James Fahey and I were on a plane to Melbourne, via New York. I sat there in a daze, thinking about how much I would miss my younger brothers and sisters, and wondering how quickly they would grow up while I was away. I realised that I still saw myself as one of the kids. But there was a whole new world beyond the clouds outside my window, and I was about to step into it.

3

MELBOURNE

From the moment James and I arrived in Australia, I was outside my comfort zone. It began at Melbourne airport as we waited patiently at the luggage carousel for our bags to appear. A niggling anxiety arose as, one by one, everybody else from the flight collected their cases and backpacks and wandered off. Eventually, no new luggage appeared through the chute. Empty-handed, we walked through the terminal with Melbourne's junior development officer, Rod McNabb, out the sliding glass doors and into a searing heat that neither James nor I had experienced before. It was November 1984 – we expected spring weather. But the temperature was in the high thirties, and the northerly wind seemed to blast away every last drop of moisture and energy from our bodies.

Rod drove us to our respective northern-suburbs homes, in Ivanhoe and Rosanna, which gave us our first insight into the difference between Australian and Irish perspectives of distance. Living 'just around the corner' from each other turned out to be about four or five kilometres away – enough to get you halfway across town in Dublin. The point was reinforced the following day, when Rod took us to a junior football clinic 'a short drive' up the highway, at Woodend.

We drove for what seemed like hours, past acres of dry brown grass; that evening, James and I were convinced that we had been to the Australian outback. We looked up our journey in an atlas and were dumbfounded to find that we had barely gone beyond the outskirts of Melbourne. I flicked through the pages and realised that Ireland was about a third the size of the state of Victoria.

My homesickness in those first few days was acute, but it was eased by the fact that I was boarding with the caring and welcoming Caddy family, who had a similar outlook on life to my own family. They were Catholic and also had six children, although they ranged in age from fifteen to twenty-eight. Had Melbourne not placed me with the Caddys, I might not have made it beyond Christmas before wanting to return home.

I began to come to terms with other differences between Ireland and Australia. My accent was the subject of great mirth. I often had to repeat myself, and I couldn't believe it when people asked if I was Scottish, American or even Scandinavian. I would get baffled looks when I referred to people as 'yer man' (your man) or 'yer woon' (your woman), and some friends took great delight in tallying the different ways I used the term 'bollocks' in conversation. There was 'a load of bollocks' (nonsense), 'what a bollocks' (an idiot), 'he's made a bollocks of it' (a mess) and 'I'm bollocksed' (tired), to list just a few.

One of the aspects of life in Melbourne that I found most enlightening was the diversity of its people. It was not just that I had the chance to mix with Greeks, Italians and Asians, it was also that some of my narrow thinking about religion was exposed. In Dublin, it was a startling revelation when Dad mentioned that there was a Protestant family living in our street. He wouldn't reveal which house they had, just in case anyone thought to goad them. But in Melbourne most people seemed to barely know or even care which denomination they were, let alone to find anyone else's religion an issue.

In Dublin one of the first things people would want to find out about you was your religion; in Melbourne it was which footy team you barracked for.

Any footballer who has had a reasonably long AFL career can break that journey into four distinct phases, and in this regard I was no different.

First of all, you soak up vast amounts of learning and rapidly improve your game as you try to break into the team. Secondly, you overcome a few setbacks as you seek to establish yourself and develop into an essential member of the team. In the third stage, you're less worried about personal ambition and accolades, and become consumed with improving the team and your teammates. And lastly, you have to come to terms with the fact that your career is ending; you have to deal with the void that creates and set out on a new path as a 'former player'.

Each of these stages is an opportunity to strengthen your character, and each makes you a more rounded and resilient person.

The first phase of my Australian football career was clearly unconventional. James and I had some vague idea that we would be feted as young star recruits, but in fact for the first couple of months Melbourne pretty much left us to our own devices. The under-19 squad had not yet begun pre-season training when we arrived, and our tertiary courses didn't start until February, so we spent hours almost every day running, doing gym work and kicking the ball around, in the hope that we'd get ourselves thoroughly prepared for the season ahead.

The first day of official pre-season training with the Melbourne under-19s was on 14 January 1985 at an oval next to what is now Rod Laver Arena. It was forty-two degrees. As our large group of teenage footballers trained that afternoon, a dark, smoky haze seemed to engulf the city – and that meant bushfires. We could taste the tiny flakes of ash that fell from the sky. We later learned that 111 fires had erupted around Victoria that day, taking three lives and destroying hundreds of houses and farms. It took two weeks to bring them under control.

As we trained, I felt like my head was being microwaved. I was dismayed to learn that the man in charge had issued instructions that no player was allowed to have a swig of water between training drills. His name was Ray Jordon but he was known as 'Slug'. He stood there hollering abuse in a harsh voice that reminded me of the boxing trainer Mickey Goldmill, the character played by Burgess Meredith in the *Rocky* movies.

My father may have been a tough taskmaster and capable of delivering a tongue-lashing, but throughout that first season Slug took the coaching rants to another level. He would stand on the outer wing and scream a mixture of instructions and insults at me during games, berating and belittling me in front of the other players. He often hauled me from the field for the slightest error. Although he was about thirty centimetres shorter than me, Slug was in the habit of calling me a such-and-such leprechaun and doing an atrocious imitation of my accent, which made him sound like a Pakistani.

Yet for all his sarcasm and criticism, Slug spent considerable time advising and mentoring me between games, and organising individual tuition for me. Without his ruthlessly and relentlessly driving me on in that first season, I would not have played at AFL level. I began the year not even knowing that the ball was returned to the centre after a goal, and I ended it placing second in the team's best-and-fairest award behind another ruckman, Steve O'Dwyer.

I returned to Ireland that Christmas reasonably pleased with what I had achieved in the first year of my scholarship. I had resolved to break into the senior team to play at least one match the following year. But I had underestimated the pull of home.

Shortly before I returned, my girlfriend, Aislinn, had

written to tell me that she was seeing someone else. I began to think about staying in Ireland in an effort to win her back. There was another shock for me at the airport when I realised that my youngest sister, Dearbhla, barely recognised me; she was too shy to talk to me until we reached home. Part of me did not want to return to Australia in 1986, but even at that age I had an obstinate determination that meant once I set out to achieve something, I had to see it through.

During the next two seasons, I would reach that goal of breaking into the Melbourne team. But that period also included two well-documented episodes that tested what my father had described as 'the ability to respond to adversity'.

Midway through 1986, after several reserve-grade games in which I'd mainly come off the interchange bench, the Demons decided to loan me to Prahran, a club in the second division of the Victorian Football Association. Effectively, this meant I was playing two tiers below Melbourne's senior side. The idea was for me to get more game time, and Melbourne's managers assured me that they would honour their contractual obligations. I could keep training once a week with the club, with a view to being invited back for preseason training in 1987.

Despite this, I felt embarrassed. In my mind, it was clear that I was going to be sent back to Ireland a failure, without having been given a decent chance. I knew nothing about Prahran, which was being coached by a former Melbourne player, Greg Hutchison, but it would prove to be a massive stepping-stone in my career.

Over the next twelve games, including finals, I gained the confidence that comes with being regarded as an important part of the team. I also began to believe that I could play Australian football. It gave me the confidence to believe I could make it at the elite level. Furthermore, the Prahran boys were fun and had a sense of camaraderie, and although I was only there for three months, some of them became mates for life. I won an award as best player in the finals series and was runner-up in the club champion award, and those twelve games rekindled Melbourne's interest in me. They had also stirred within me a passion for Australian football.

I went into the 1987 season on a mission. My two-year football scholarship had lapsed, and although Prahran wanted me back, I was determined to make the grade with Melbourne. I decided that if I was cut from the Demons' list, I would return to Dublin. I was desperate to play at the highest level, and I knew my chance would come if I persisted.

John Northey had taken over as Melbourne's senior coach the previous year, and the 1987 pre-season was the most arduous physical activity I had experienced. On one weekend we had to run up and down the 720-metre Mount Buninyong, then front up on Monday morning for a ten-kilometre team run. A couple of days later I played a round of golf, and my thighs were so sore that I had to walk backwards up any slopes on the course. I hated running downhill from that day on. But Northey himself took part in many of the pre-season runs that summer, and the bonds that were forged among the young playing group were strong.

I began the 1987 season playing in the reserves but got my chance early in the year. In those days, the night series and the season proper ran concurrently, and in early April I was selected for a night match against Geelong at Waverley Park. I played reasonably well in our five-goal win. Coincidentally, we were scheduled to play the Cats again the following Saturday, although this time in Geelong, and I held my place in the team as a back-up ruckman to dual Brownlow medallist Peter Moore. I managed just five possessions from limited game time and was dropped.

Yet I could see opportunities starting to open up. My third senior game was in the night series grand final at Waverley, which we won by four points against Essendon. Towards the end of the season, Moore retired, which created opportunities in the ruck position, and I managed to string together five or six decent games. Melbourne also went on a winning streak and pinched the last finals berth with a fifteen-point win over Footscray at the Western Oval in the last round of the season – it was the match in which my teammate Garry Lyon broke his leg and had to be carried off on a stretcher.

It was the first time in twenty-three years that Melbourne had made the finals, and promised to be a fairy-tale finale to the sixteen-year career of Demons' idol and captain Robert Flower, who had never played a final in his previous 269 games.

As it turned out, we comfortably won our first two finals, putting us through to a Preliminary Final against the reigning premier, Hawthorn. That week the club arranged for my parents and those of fellow Gaelic football recruit Sean Wight to fly out from Ireland. They arrived on the Thursday evening and were seated in the Waverley Park stand that Saturday to watch their first game of Australian football – my thirteenth at league level.

For most of the match, it looked like Melbourne might cause an upset and progress to the Grand Final against Carlton. We led by twenty-two points at half time and three-quarter time, having played desperate, skilful and attacking football. In the fourth quarter, however, Melbourne tightened up.

We were generally an inexperienced group, and I believe our concentration drifted because of the prospect of reaching a Grand Final. We became defensive-minded at times and lost our composure, and we wasted several opportunities to kick crucial goals. The vastly experienced Hawks persisted, improvised and took risks. They also had a lucky break midway through that last quarter when a shot by John Kennedy was given as a goal, although I saw the ball clearly deflect off the point post.

It is fair to say, though, that Hawthorn created its own luck. The match ended with the Hawks sweeping the ball downfield after a kick-in. Chris Langford charged through the middle and drove a long pass to a leading Gary Buckenara with seconds to play. As Buckenara reached for the mark, he was pushed in the back by Rod Grinter, which earned him a free kick on the fifty-metre arc. What happened next was the most dramatic moment of my football career, and one that would have an enormous effect on my life.

The siren was blaring as Buckenara went back to take his shot, but nobody could hear it because of the roaring crowd. I was running back towards our goal-line, but then I saw Hawthorn winger Robert DiPierdomenico creating a loose man further afield, so I cut between Buckenara and Grinter to pick 'Dipper' up. Umpire David Howlett then correctly paid a fifteen-metre penalty, bringing Buckenara to a more comfortable kicking distance from goal. Buckenara duly converted to give the Hawks a two-point win.

Over the years, people have suggested that I didn't know the rule or was running over to my parents in the crowd, but the simple fact is that it was a costly lapse in concentration. I was devastated. I trudged off the field, unable to look my teammates in the eye, hoping that nobody would realise it was me who had given away the penalty. As I entered the changing rooms, Northey spotted me across the room. He raised his hand and bellowed, 'Don't you ever effing do that again!'

It was the lowest I had ever felt in my life. I had made a horrendous mistake in front of a crowd of 70000, including my family and friends, and a television audience of millions. In that one instant I went from one of Australian football's success stories to an abject failure.

To make matters worse, at the after-match function I was seated next to Flower, the man whose career had ended as Buckenara's goal sailed through. He set me out on the path to redemption by saying, 'Don't worry about it, Jimmy – there's nothing you can do about it now. But it's important that you learn something from the experience.'

As I left the ground that evening, I happened to share a lift with Northey, who said, 'I can't believe we missed all those chances.' It was his way of saying that I shouldn't hold myself wholly responsible for the loss.

After the match, Dad had found me in the rooms and told me to keep my chin up. It became clear to me that he did not understand what had happened. When I explained the situation, he groaned. 'Oh, so that's why no one is talking to me.' He understood the depth of my anguish and staunchly stood by me. When he was later asked about the incident by the media, he responded, 'If I had made only one mistake in an entire game, I would feel a hero.' Dad could never listen to a discussion about that match without leaping to my defence. His loyalty and support meant so much to me.

These three key men went out of their way to ease my pain, but for weeks I grieved over that moment. I kept worrying about what other people thought of me. Exacerbating the situation was that when people raised the mistake, they would often link it to my being a 'stupid Irishman'. I felt like I had let down not only myself, my family and my team, but also my country.

It came as a blessed relief, then, when I spent a few weeks travelling with a couple of friends, Alison and Elana, through Western Europe on my way back to Ireland. We set out from Italy and wound our way up to Paris. It was so therapeutic being in an environment where nobody knew the slightest thing about Australian football or fifteen-metre penalties.

We celebrated our last night on the Continent with a

huge night out in Paris; I barely managed a thirty-minute nap before heading off to the airport. I carted my enormous hangover and about forty kilograms of luggage onto two Metro trains before jumping on an airport bus, where I noticed someone staring at me. As I closed my eyes and willed my headache to go away, I heard the man ask, 'Excuse me, but aren't you the guy who ran across the mark?' I could not believe it. We began to chat and it turned out that he was an Australian. He hadn't been home for over a year, yet he knew all about the Buckenara goal.

I scrambled onto the plane to London, where I was to catch a connecting flight to Dublin. As tired and seedy as I was, my chance meeting with the Aussie guy haunted me. I had more time to contemplate its significance when I got to Heathrow and found myself stranded; a delay in customs meant that I'd missed my connecting flight.

It dawned on me that I could not hide from that very public mistake. More importantly, I could not run away from myself. My opinion of myself mattered more than how others saw me. There was no point trying to blame anyone else. It was my fault, my blunder, and I had to take responsibility for it.

As I sat at Heathrow, waiting for my flight that morning, I contemplated one of John Northey's favourite sayings: 'Make sure you don't have any regrets when you leave football.' It rang true. Normally, after a disappointing game, I could return the following week and try to make amends. But because the Preliminary Final had been the last match of the season, I was left with this gnawing regret. I made a commitment to myself not to be remembered as the man who had cost Melbourne a place in a Grand Final. Instead, I wanted to be known as a man who had made a mistake, learned from it and gone on to reach greater heights. I also realised how important playing Australian football had become to me. To that point, I had seen it as just a challenge, but I now realised how passionate I was about the game. I wanted to succeed.

From that day on, I built a relentless belief in myself as footballer, and a flinty determination to succeed. I began to go into every game treating it as though it was my last. On the training track, whenever I was exhausted or hurting I would visualise playing in front of a full crowd at the MCG. I'd tell myself that it was worth the hard work to give me the best chance to make it on that stage.

For the next eleven seasons, I did everything in my power to forge a playing career with Melbourne that measured up to the premises put forward by my two great early mentors: Dad's belief that I'd be judged by how I responded to adversity, and John Northey's advice that I should end my career with no regrets. These were also adages that could be applied to life.

I ended up playing 264 matches for Melbourne between 1987 and 1998. There are several achievements of which I am proud, some obvious, others less so.

I took great satisfaction in bouncing back from that

football career low point in the Preliminary Final and producing a solid season in 1988. I managed to have at least ten
disposals in every game that year, and Melbourne progressed
to the premiership decider against Hawthorn. Unfortunately,
the Hawks, who were in their sixth consecutive Grand Final,
gave us a football lesson that day.

I am proud of the fact that I won four Melbourne best-
and-fairest awards. They were a reflection that I had been
judged by those within the club to have performed well.

Winning the Brownlow Medal was special for me, but not
just because it is the sport's highest individual honour. What
pleased me most about that 1991 season was that I had to
overcome insecurity early in the year about my position in
the team and my future at the club. Going into the season,
Northey had preferred Steve O'Dwyer in the ruck, so I was
tried in a variety of other positions. In one practice match
I floundered while playing as a centreman on Richmond's
Craig Lambert, and in the opening round I was used as a
centre-half forward and even at full-back on West Coast's
Peter Sumich.

Before Melbourne's Round 2 match against Fitzroy, I was
called before the selection committee and asked to explain
why I should not be dropped. My belief was that I was a
ruckman being played out of position, and they agreed that
Steve and I would share the role that Saturday. As it turned
out, Steve missed most of that game and much of the latter
half of the season through injury, and I got the opportunity
to fill the ruckman's role.

There were other important aspects of winning the Brownlow that season. Firstly, my parents flew out for the vote count; they were as proud as I had ever seen them when I was declared the winner. Secondly, I managed to mention the fathers of two close mates – Phil Healy and Michael Scott – during my acceptance speech. Both men were struggling with cancer at the time, and they reported back that their dads had got a boost from hearing their names on national television. Thankfully, Scottie's father, John, who had a grapefruit-sized tumour in his bowel, made a full recovery.

The other football honour that gave me great delight was being selected at representative level. I had the honour of playing for Victoria on the day the great Ted Whitten did his emotional farewell lap of the MCG. I also had the distinction of being selected for both Australia and Ireland in the International Rules matches, which meant I got to play against and alongside some of my boyhood idols, such as county Kerry legend Jack O'Shea and Dublin coach Kevin Heffernan.

That is the indomitable facet of team sport: that you share it with others. It is why two of my most precious football memories are of running onto the field with my brothers. When I left for Australia, Brian, then thirteen, vowed to follow me. He eventually did, and when we played a couple of games together for Melbourne in 1992, it made my heart sing. So too when, one Christmas, Brian and I played alongside our younger brother, David, for our Dublin club, Ballyboden St Enda's.

One aspect of my football career that is often mentioned

is the record streak of 244 consecutive matches. The previous best was 204 games in a row by Richmond's Jack Titus more than fifty years earlier. I didn't chase that record – it just happened. Yet it became an achievement I was pleased to have associated with my name because it is equated with resilience, one of the great qualities a man can possess.

When I was a boy, my father had impressed upon me the need not to miss games, if at all possible. When he coached me as a junior he would say things like, 'It's only a bit of pain,' and, 'You're no good to me on the sidelines.' Like most AFL footballers, I would play with niggles or when my body was nowhere near 100 per cent healthy, and generally that was unknown to the public. Usually, I was able to use those injuries as a way of focusing on playing well; I was also motivated by my desire not to let the team down. It became a sort of badge of honour to be able to play well when I had injuries, some of which were expected to keep me out of the team.

Of all those occasions, I believe there was only one time when I played hurt and did not carry my weight – when I took the field with a strained knee ligament in 1994. Against that, there were times when I managed to perform well despite injury, such as in 1993 when I managed to play the weekend after I severed cartilage in my ribs; the doctors had told me it would mean six to eight weeks on the sidelines. Towards the end of my career, I had a degenerative ankle injury that required me to go into each match with a pain-killing injection, which usually wore off by half time.

Essentially, my ability to play with injury spoke to my

strength as a footballer, which was the ability to hang in there – to keep going and keep going and keep going. I was able to be resilient, to persist, to be mentally strong. Reading the play was not necessarily a strength of mine, particularly in Australian football; as I hadn't grown up with the sport, that did not come instinctively to me. But persistence helped me to get the best out of myself. That is why my best quarters were invariably the third and fourth, when other players were getting tired or slack, or losing focus.

In the 1990s, most people were just happy to get through pre-season training runs and maybe record an impressive time. But I would always find myself wanting to win the runs. I stopped to think about it one day, and asked myself, 'Why am I like this? I hate the fact that it puts me under so much pressure.' But I realised that wanting to be the best I could possibly be was simply part of my makeup.

Thankfully, there came a time late in my football career when I understood that it was an experience to be enjoyed and savoured. Earlier in my career I was so intense, so determined to concentrate for every second of a match, that I never did that. I decided to try to take everything in each time I ran out to play on the MCG. I knew that I could not play AFL football forever, and that one day would be the last day, whether I knew it or not.

So every time I ran down the MCG race, I would soak up the atmosphere. I would look around the stands, marvel at the thousands of faces, the wave of sound, the colours. And then I would get my mind back on the job. It meant that when football did end I could fully appreciate what an amazing opportunity and experience I had been afforded.

My one great disappointment was that I never played in a Premiership, but I left the game in 1998 without regret. I knew that I had done all I could in the pursuit of that dream.

4

BEYOND FOOTBALL

Leaving football with no regrets was one of the reasons I felt well equipped to cope with that transition to the last and most important phase of an AFL footballer's career – setting out as a former player. I was fortunate that Reach had been going for almost five years by then, and it had become strong and vibrant enough as an organisation to become an outlet for all my time and energy. Having that passion and affinity for working with teenagers, helping empower and inspire them to be all they could be, provided the buzz and excitement that had come from playing sport at the elite level.

Reach became an enormous influence on my life, and I know it has shaped and inspired many others. Many successful business leaders who initially offered to help found that they were simultaneously learning a lot about themselves.

Reach is a non-denominational, not-for-profit organisation that works with kids from any background, aged ten to eighteen, within and outside of the school system. Put very simply, our aim is to improve young people's self-belief and resilience, and to help them to get more from life. There is a bit of a misconception that Reach is a program that helps troubled teens. It can be, but it can also be there for the girl who is hating what it's like to be fifteen, or the boy who wishes his parents would stop screaming at each other every night. We want to inspire and empower young people to be all they can be, to challenge their view of the world and offer a different way of thinking. By doing this, Reach might help a troubled teen get back on track, or it might prevent another from going off the rails in the first place. And it might help both find the greatness within them.

In a practical sense, these objectives are achieved through programs. In 2010, more than 57000 young Australians attended Reach programs at 580 metropolitan and regional schools and communities across the country. The activities include school programs, workshops, event days and weekend camps. These are run by staff, volunteers and supporters, with a safety net of social workers and psychologists in the background.

At its core, though, Reach's success can be attributed to the fact that the central philosophy is all about young people inspiring young people. A massive part of that is the Reach Crew, a dynamic group of leaders aged between fifteen and twenty-five. Unquestionably, they give the organisation its energy – they are its lifeblood. They stop it from being preachy, and keep it contemporary and relevant. And they ground all those involved, offering a reminder that no matter what issues there might be relating to future directions, logistics or funding, the prime reason for Reach's existence must always be what is best for the kids.

We try to surround ourselves with reminders of this ideology at our headquarters, a converted two-storey brick warehouse called the Dream Factory in the inner-city suburb of Collingwood. We were fortunate enough to have had a fifty-year lease to the building donated to us in 2002 by Flight Centre's founder, Geoff Harris, and his wife, Sue. Painted in large letters on the wall just inside the door is my view on what the organisation must always keep in its heart.

I truly believe that every person, especially young people, has unlimited potential, and that we all have a unique 'voice' which wants to be heard. Deep down, behind all the bullshit, we just want to be ourselves, and when young people are given the opportunity to express their real selves, they can achieve whatever they want, and they can have all the love, happiness and success they require. Very often this process starts simply by someone believing in them.

By 2009, part of the vision for Reach was to hand over more responsibility – particularly aspects of my role – to some of those younger leaders within the organisation. The arrival of cancer on my doorstep ensured that, really, I had no choice in the matter. This came against the backdrop of the organisation's first moves to establish a foothold in Sydney, with a view to setting up a northern base and running programs in New South Wales. Going national, though, was a long way removed from where it all began.

The truth is that Reach was born of blessed serendipity. Back in 1993, I was almost a decade into my football career with Melbourne. I had graduated from teachers' college with a Bachelor of Education and was wondering which direction my life would take.

After the usual Christmas break in Ireland, I spent ten days in the United States, during which time I was inspired by reading about the inventor and visionary Buckminster Fuller. By the time he died in July 1983, at age eighty-seven, 'Bucky' had been hailed as 'one of the greatest minds of our times'. He devoted his life to seeking solutions to some of humanity's great problems in areas such as energy, housing, education, the environment and poverty.

Rather than simply philosophising, Bucky had a practical approach to engineering change. He demonstrated his ideas through 'artefacts', which were prototypes or models that set out his designs and principles. With these, he believed, people were more likely to engage in the discussion. Essentially, he argued that it was up to all of us to act, to do something, to facilitate change. A legendary AFL coach, Hawthorn's John Kennedy, had famously expressed a similar sentiment during the 1975 Grand Final, when he demanded of his charges, 'Do something! Do! Don't think, don't hope! Do!' Had Bucky been a football coach, his half-time address might have included one of his famous quotes: 'Man knows so much and does so little.'

When I returned to Melbourne in early 1994, this had me thinking about how we educate young people. From what I had seen during my teaching rounds and school visits, I did not particularly agree with the approach of the education system. The balance seemed to be too heavily weighted towards academic pursuit rather than a personal journey. It was fine to encourage the gifted and motivated students. But in what ways were we challenging the average kids to aspire to anything beyond mediocrity? I began to wonder about ways to apply Bucky's approach. There was no point simply criticising the system, I realised – I had to produce an arte-fact. If people could see an alternative method, it would be a starting point from which we could effect change.

Buckminster Fuller had sowed the seed, but it took a young drama teacher called Paul Currie to help it take root. That year I joined forces with friends Pam Embry and Dale Richardson to establish Sportscamp, a seven-day residential program tak-ing in a variety of sports during the school holidays. The idea was to help improve kids' sporting skills, but also to harness their enthusiasm for sport and help apply it to life skills. The motto was 'Passion For Sport, Passion For Life'.

The first camp was at Campaspe Downs Country Resort, about an hour north-west of Melbourne, set around a lake, with cabins and a dining room. We had organised motiva-tional speakers, sporting heroes such as basketballer Andrew Gaze, former Test cricketer and Melbourne footballer Max Walker, swimmer Linley Frame and marathon runner Steve Moneghetti. Each delivered a stirring address, and was well received by the budding athletes.

What happened next was a lesson in keeping an open mind. My girlfriend at the time, Jackie Tarabay, knew Paul and was familiar with his theatre workshops, which employed group interaction and creative expression. We decided to invite Paul to run a workshop at the camp. We were nervous about how it would be received by a hundred-odd kids who might be expected to relate more to Ablett than Hamlet. We warned Paul to expect a restless group.

'Well, they do seem to be climbing the walls in there,' he replied. 'I think it's because they're bored with all that "rah, rah, rah" talk. But don't worry, I'm going to throw it over to the kids, give them their voice.'

After a fairly rowdy beginning to the session, Paul turned it around with a few simple exercises. He used role-playing. He used anger-displacement, where each kid had to visualise someone they were angry with and vent it. He discussed mythology and the American scholar Joseph Campbell.

To our surprise, dozens of teenagers dropped their guards and released their emotions in a safe, non-judgemental environment. All week we had been looking to connect with these kids through sporting analogies and metaphors. Now a drama teacher had shown them a level playing field, and it didn't matter whether they were show-offs or quiet kids, whether they had money or good grades or athletic ability. They all came away with a sense of worth, and there was a new, more cohesive dynamic among the group for the rest of the week.

At the end of the camp, when the teenagers filled in some

exit paperwork, nearly all of them nominated that session as being among their highlights. I felt like I had found the missing ingredient for my 'artefact'. I spoke with Paul about how all the kids had entered the spirit of the exercises. How he had given them their voice and they had all wanted it to be heard.

'It's great to hear you say that,' Paul said. 'It strikes me that a lot of high-profile guys would be more interested in themselves or their camp than the actual kids. We should do some more stuff like this together. Maybe some school talks.'

We agreed to catch up back in Melbourne, and when we did I wanted to know everything he could tell me about his drama school and how it could be applied to youth work.

'You should join one of my classes,' he said, laughing.

'Maybe I will.'

'Great, let's do it. But don't expect it to land you a role in *Neighbours*.'

A future in television or theatre was definitely not for me – as anyone who saw me in my subsequent TV commercials will attest – but I knew some of the ideas and techniques I was learning would be beneficial in relating to teenagers. The experience of mixing in a different circle, with budding actors and models, also dragged me outside my comfort zone, which helped me grow as a person.

In the meantime, Paul and I made contact with several schools, offering one-off workshops during school hours. The first of these was booked at De La Salle College in Malvern, and we eagerly arrived to find a hall filled with about 200 schoolboys.

We began our first workshop. There was some snickering and the odd eruption of laughter. We noticed that about half-way down the hall, one kid was making a few smart-alecky comments. I decided not to ignore him. I would single him out, but I'd make sure I did not put him down.

'Okay, mate, what's your name?'

'Rupert.' Another explosion of Year 9 guffawing.

'No, really, who are you?'

'Dunno.'

'Maybe that's the real answer. Now tell me, who are you?'

'My name is Jules.'

One of the teachers wanted to eject him from the hall, but I knew that would be counter-productive so I asked that Jules be allowed to stay. For the next ten minutes or so he remained on his feet, our conversation an exercise in thrust and parry.

Eventually, I asked him, 'Do you realise how much influence you have over this group? How much control? They'll keep silent, be reluctant to join in while you're taking this down a really negative path. You don't even realise it, but you've got a gift. You're a natural leader. Maybe you should explore that, tap into it.'

He was thrown by being given respect and the mood changed in the hall. The rest of the workshop progressed quite smoothly.

Jules Lund was a fifteen-year-old trying to find his way. Two weeks later he surprised us by being one of thirty or forty teens who elected to show up at our first after-school workshop, which was held at Presbyterian Ladies' College.

He eventually became one of Reach's first youth leaders and a man I am proud to call one of my best mates. Sixteen years on, I would be the one skylarking for the crowd as a grooms-man at his wedding.

We were up and running. But Paul and I had no idea *where* we were running. One workshop became two, which led to a six-week program – one evening a week – and then a couple of weekend camps. The whole thing was practically being run out of the backs of our cars, with a third key person, Amanda Freeman, sorting out the administrative tangle. We decided to set up the whole affair as a not-for-profit founda-tion, and settled on a name: Reach For The Stars. Next was determining a structure and a direction, the genesis of which was to be found in a most unlikely place. It originated back in Dublin, with my sitting a Grade 6 Irish exam at Ballyroan Boys' School.

In primary school, I was always more interested in any kind of sport than I was in study, particularly the two subjects that required sitting down and reading: Irish and English. My parents were beginning to worry that I might have to repeat a year before graduating to high school. Against that backdrop, I was less than thrilled to learn that we would be doing an Irish exam. I could count and manage the basic greetings in my native tongue, but when it came to the home-work, I could never remain still long enough to allow any Irish to seep through.

To my delight, though, a classmate had managed to get his hands on the exam paper, and I convinced him to let me run off a copy. That night, at home, I impressed my father by diligently devoting some quality time to my 'homework assignment', a paper that had to be translated into English. My plan was working perfectly when he offered to help. The problem was that, when I sat the exam later that week, I only managed a mark of thirty-one per cent.

Dad was dismayed. 'I can't believe it,' he cried. 'Especially after all that study you put in. You be sure and show me that exam paper so we can go over where you went wrong.'

As you can imagine, I found all manner of excuses not to show him the paper, but Dad kept insisting I produce it. When I eventually did, he twigged in an instant. 'Oh my Jesus, you can't even cheat properly.'

I was in massive trouble. However, my teacher, Mr Lynch, did a wondrous thing by sitting me down and saying he believed in me. It would have been easy to destroy the confidence of an eleven-year-old boy, but his simple show of faith helped me turn the corner.

My struggle with Irish as a subject remained, though, and needed to be addressed – students could not graduate from high school if they did not pass Irish. In desperation, at the end of that year Mam and Dad sent me to a *gaeltacht*, to a summer camp where kids are only allowed to communicate in Irish. I had a great time, primarily because that rule was never enforced and the camp proved little more than a holiday program with outdoor activities. You can imagine my embarrassment, though, when I could only cough out the odd sentence when I returned home a couple of weeks later.

In my first year at high school – which, coincidentally, was De La Salle College Churchtown in Dublin – I found myself considerably off the pace in my Irish studies. One evening, up at Ballyboden St Enda's football club, Mam was discussing the issue with a couple of teachers, mentioning her exasperation that not even the *gaeltacht* had managed to improve my Gaelic vocabulary.

'Which camp was he along to then?' asked one, and when she proffered the name, he replied, 'Oh, no, sure they're rubbish. Domhnall Ó Lubhlaí is your man.'

But who was this Domhnall Ó Lubhlaí (pronounced Donal O'Lovely in English)? Mam investigated further and discovered that he had founded Coláiste na bhFiann, an organisation that had been running camps for the past decade. She swung into action, and before long I found myself being dragged into the city for an interview, with Sharon brought along for good measure. To be considered for enrolment, we had been asked to prepare for the interview by learning words to the national anthem and the college song. With great trepidation, we entered an office and were greeted by a figure who looked every bit the headmaster: greying, erudite and intense. He had a presence – to my mind, it was almost an aura.

Domhnall began speaking to me in Irish, although he might as well have been reciting Chinese algebra for all I knew. I sat there anxiously wondering how I could possibly contribute anything. I was not even sure I would remember or properly pronounce the words to the songs. He switched to English and explained to Mam that the *coláiste*, or college, believed in total immersion. Formal lessons would be interspersed with activities such as music, sport, dance and art. There was more to the camps than learning the language.

'You need to understand where you come from, your heritage,' Domhnall said. 'You need to see that it's deeply rooted in you. If you don't understand that, you will drift aimlessly in life.'

The significance of those words may not have rocked my twelve-year-old world, but another of his statements certainly did: 'If any student speaks one complete sentence in English during the camp, no matter the reason, he or she must leave the course and return home. We will not offer any refund.'

To the family's surprise, we were accepted into the *coláiste* course. The prospect of not speaking English for three weeks did not make me nearly as nervous as the thought that I might be expelled and waste my parents' money. I could visualise Dad strangling me. Adding to my angst was the news that I had been accepted into the top-tier camp for advanced Irish speakers. Domhnall believed it would fast-track my development and had assured Mam he would take a particular interest in my case. I could only envy Sharon, who would be going to the beginners' course.

My camp was to be held at a 700-year-old Franciscan

monastery with a college attached in Multyfarnham, which is in the heart of Ireland, in Westmeath. The day before I left, Dad came up with a plan that did little to ease my sense of foreboding.

'Pretend you're dumb,' he said. 'If anyone speaks to you, just point to your mouth and shake your head. Don't speak at all, just listen and learn. That way you might pick a few words up.'

If that sounded like a hare-brained scheme, it was still better than the strategy I actually employed. On the first day of the camp I simply could not make head nor tail of proceedings; the first full sentence I spoke came when I turned to a boy next to me and whispered, 'What the hell's going?' If he had reported me, I would have been on my way home before I'd even unpacked my bags, but fortunately he simply whispered back, 'You're not allowed to speak English.'

The rest of the week passed without incident. The omnipresent Domhnall was floating around the periphery, keeping us all on edge, with a blast here or a disapproving look there. As promised, he often cast an eye in my direction, which I interpreted initially as picking on me, although over time I began to realise that he was actually taking an interest in my development.

Each day would begin and end with a military-style parade, which, I am sure, was a carry-over from Domhnall's time in the Irish-speaking First Battalion in Galway. The camp also had a hierarchy of *cinnirí* (student leaders), ranging from the head of the dormitory to principal leaders of the boys and girls. While the headmaster ruled the camp with strict and clearly defined standards, these leaders set the example and the tone of what we did. We could relate to them and we respected them too.

I took part in all the activities, made a few friends and, magically, began to find a few basic ways to communicate in Irish. As always, sport was my refuge, but it was almost my undoing as well. In the second week, I was playing a game of table tennis against a friend, Darragh, when we had to put down our paddles for mealtime. As we waited in the dining room, we began disagreeing about what the score had been. He insisted he was leading, I insisted he was not. He was adamant the score was 8–7, to which I shouted back, 'It isn't!' In English.

The room went silent and all eyes turned to me. Then all eyes turned to Funcai, the senior student leader in the room. She was a couple of years older than me, and someone I had come to really admire and follow. I could see that she was dreadfully upset. There were tears in her eyes, as she knew that what I had said before a roomful of people left her no option but to report me. I sat there, miserable and barely eating my food, waiting to be called before Domhnall.

I knew of several kids who had been sent home from the *gaeltachts*, including my brother Brian's best friend, for telling someone to 'eff off' – although that barely qualified as a sentence, surely. Back in Dublin, Mam later told me, she had endured a summer of hearing that 'so-and-so's son is on his way home', and she and Dad had spent the whole time dreading a phone call from Domhnall. So when I walked into his office that evening, I did so with my head bowed, convinced I had let everyone down.

I could not believe it when he announced, 'You haven't broken the full sentence rule, but you should consider yourself extremely lucky.'

I never did discover whether that was just a lenient interpretation or whether Domhnall had a higher motive, but I do know that it was a fateful moment which had a major bearing on my life. I threw myself into the remainder of the camp, and at the end of it negotiated to stay on for another three-week term. When my six weeks was up, I was among thirty students invited to go on a special seven-day outdoors camp, where we stayed in tents beside the lake and cooked on open-air fires.

What appealed to me about those seven weeks was that there were dozens of kids, of varying ages and backgrounds, who found themselves thrown together, but they were able to relate to each other on the same level. There was nobody judging you, or blocking you from aspiring. Where you had come from, there were people who had formed an opinion about you, and you might find it difficult to get out of that pigeonhole. At the *coláiste gaeltachts*, on the other hand, there were no limitations put on what you could be. You spent your days thinking about your potential, not your limitations.

When I returned home to Rathfarnham at the end of that

summer, I was invigorated. I was also so fluent that I found myself spontaneously responding in Irish when people spoke to me in English. I enthusiastically returned to Coláiste na bhFiann the following summer, and I would even attend a third *gaeltacht* as a leader. During the year, I would occasionally get along to a youth club that the organisation ran in the city, on the waterfront near Blackrock. There, former students could gather on Friday nights to talk, laugh, discuss life and play games. One of those former students, who became a great friend, was Funcai, and we would invariably laugh about who was actually leading that table tennis match in Multyfarnham and wonder how I had managed to avoid expulsion.

I can't help but believe it was because Domhnall knew the significance of that moment. How critical it was to my development. Over the years, he became a great mentor to me, someone whose counsel I would seek even after I moved to Australia. I was captured by his intensity and never-give-in attitude. He didn't care if people thought he was crazy. He had drive and passion, and I really responded to that. You never came away from him without feeling that you had learned something.

He was a man with a vision. He wanted to create young leaders who could help get the country going again, young men and women who could speak in their native tongue and who embraced the Irish culture. He realised there were teenagers from all corners of the island who had leadership potential but needed a way to express it. He implored us to make our lives extraordinary.

Without doubt, his sacred credo was to improvise. Domhnall always encouraged his students to find a way to move on, no matter what adversity confronted them. If you got stuck, look around and there would be another way. Don't be afraid to take a risk, take on a challenge, try something new. Improvise! Think independently! That is how his *gaeltachts* worked. You had to start at the hardest point and work back, whereas at school you started at the easiest point and worked forward.

All of those experiences were swirling around in my head in 1994 as Reach For The Stars began to gain momentum. Paul and I were challenging kids to aspire to greater heights, asking them to improvise. But that was because we were a couple of guys who loved life and were very passionate about sharing that message. We didn't know where the whole undertaking was going to end up, but the kids we worked with took it to where it needed to go. So we responded, and took the next step. Over time, my experience with Coláiste na bhFiann helped shape Reach's grander vision: the formal programs, the youth leaders, a drop-in centre, the resources. But the reason Reach worked from the outset was simply because it became a great environment, for both the kids and the leaders.

Rather than explaining to you how the programs evolved, I would like to share what the programs began to teach me.

I learned that asking kids to be vulnerable is a bit like

conducting an archaeological dig. You chip away, gradually removing one layer at a time, but you don't know how deep you will be able to go. For fourteen- and fifteen-year-olds, that can be quite scary. And you can't just expect them to take responsibility for themselves straight away, because, to begin with, they have all the excuses in the world: society, their parents, their school or their friends have stuffed up their lives.

So you can't begin by demanding that they not feel sorry for themselves. If you do, their response will be: 'Who the hell are you, and how would you know, anyway?' They can't relate to where you're coming from until they are given a chance to share their stories. Then they will relax and realise that this is an environment where it's actually quite heroic to share your story. Some will never have done this with anyone, and will fiercely guard that – but usually they're actually desperate for someone to listen to them.

And the more that kids listen to other people sharing their stories and getting positive feedback, the more they will think, *I might give this a crack*. Some will pour out their souls. Others will make up a great load of rubbish, but that's not always a problem. Maybe that's what they need to do to feel good about themselves. You still listen and start to build a rapport – then maybe you can get somewhere. If you don't, and you put them down, it just gives them another reason not to trust in someone.

There have been kids who have made a fool of me because I've trusted them or taken risks for them. I want to believe in people, and I make no excuses for that. I would never change that. However, you have to do it for the right reasons. Sure, you want to feel good about yourself for helping someone, but the motivation must be to help the young person. If the kid knows that, they will trust you. When you keep up a wall, people can sense it and will have trouble believing you are authentic. Then there is no vulnerability in the relationship.

Reach helped me understand all of this, and for that I am infinitely thankful. Not because I had to read books and study, but because of what happened in camps or in a group environment, where kids have let go of some terrible, terrible hurt. That is when trust is needed, to allow them to be vulnerable and begin to heal. In the early days, some kids wanted to come along but had been hurt so badly that it took a year, maybe two years, before they were prepared to open up to anyone.

I had a poor understanding of drugs and what they can do to you. People would ask how it was feasible to understand kids who had taken drugs when I had no experience of them myself – I had never used or even tried them. I found that it was more important to love the kids whose lives were being wrecked by drugs. I didn't need to have taken drugs to offer them that. You can accept people for who they are, with all their faults, their hurt, their shame. And that is the level at which you can meet.

I remember one incident at a camp in Lorne that really got to me. I was called to help a young girl who was lying on the floor of one of the cubicles in the toilet block. She was in a bad way, crying and emotional. She had swallowed some pills and couldn't make sense of her world. We had real concern for her. I lay down on the filthy concrete floor so that she could see part of my face sticking under the door. I lay there talking with her, just engaging. Waiting for that time to pass. It was horrific. She didn't know what she was crying about.

Afterwards, I realised that I'd been forced to meet the girl where she was at – I couldn't expect to meet her on my terms. I began to understand that the goal of Reach should not be to 'fix' kids – it was simply about accepting kids.

It is inspiring work. The leaders at Reach learn that they have to find ways to inspire kids with their own lives. It is a privileged position to be in. And, yes, it is selfish, because it makes you feel that you are a better person because you're helping others. You must sit in a room with 400 or 500 kids and ask them to open up, to share their secrets and to trust that whatever is said won't leave that room. They reach inside and pull up stuff that they have never told even their closest mates.

The amazing thing is that the other kids accept that vulnerability. They understand that they have been trusted with someone's insecurity, and they respect it, and commit to keeping the information to themselves. When kids are happy they don't need to escape, whether it be through alcohol, drugs or eating disorders. They learn that their past does not control their future. Kids want to know what's out there. Where are we going? What are we going to do? They want to be excited by life, but they also want a purpose.

We all have a purpose – we just need to find out what it is.

And you do that through your struggles. You do it through facing adversity.

Throwing myself into Reach may have helped wean me off playing for Melbourne but, as the club theme song goes, every heart beats true for the red and the blue. I had come to love Melbourne Football Club so dearly, and I found that it was so intrinsic to my experience of living in Australia that I wanted to remain involved and keep contributing when my playing days were finished.

In 2000, just twelve months into retirement, I returned to the Demons. I became an assistant coach for three seasons, and after that time I realised it was not a career path I wanted to follow seriously. By then, Reach was consuming more of my time, and it also coincided with Sam and I starting our family; Matisse was born in September 2001. I also had increasing business interests, notably an involvement with the Pacific Early Learning Group and its management of childcare centres.

In 2007, however, I found it incredibly disheartening to see Melbourne struggle so badly that it lost its first nine games of the season; ultimately, Neale Daniher was sacked as coach. Even more distressing was the fact that the club was in turmoil off the field. The focus in 2008 should have been on the celebrations for the Melbourne Football Club's 150th year; instead, it was apparent that the club was drifting, lacked spirit and enthusiasm and was in serious financial trouble. The club was headed for a loss of more than $1 million for the year, on top of which it was already more than $4 million in debt.

I talked about this with several of my former teammates – guys like Anthony McDonald, Garry Lyon, Anthony Ingerson, Paul Hopgood and Greg Healy – and we agreed that the club needed drastic change. The Demons had already set out in a fresh direction on-field, under newly appointed coach Dean Bailey and football manager Chris Connolly. But the club also had to be rebuilt. For that to happen, change had to come at board level. It was easy to criticise from afar, to be complacent and expect someone else to tackle the problems. What Melbourne needed was for people to get their hands dirty.

The president at the time, Paul Gardner, suggested I join the board, but I did not believe it was taking the club in the right direction so I declined. Granted, the board had put in place some vitally important plans, such as a new training and administration base in the Olympic Park precinct and a summer training base at Cranbourne. But its members seemed drained of energy, of passion. They struck me as a group who were looking for someone to hand the baton to.

After all, that's how football clubs work. You try to be the best servant you can to the club, and then when the time is right you hand on the baton to the next servant. I asked at reception for a list of Melbourne's directors and discovered that the information was unavailable. So I started asking around; most people knew a couple of board members who were providing great service, but that was about it.

It was obvious to me that Melbourne needed a new broom to sweep through the boardroom, and a leader to rally the club. It seemed like a moment in the club's history when substantial change was needed, change that would make a difference. It had to be new and vibrant and energetic. We had to get it right because we knew Melbourne might not get another chance.

Still, I wasn't sure where that change would come from. Several former players from my era were prepared to promote change but did not want to take on the role of front man. Garry Lyon said from the outset that he was prepared to help and support in any way he could, but that he did not want a formal involvement due to a perceived conflict of interest. I found myself being pushed towards the front of the queue.

I contemplated the prospect of heading up a group that might largely replace the existing board. Apart from doubts about whether my level of business expertise commanded enough respect, there was a voice in the back of my mind saying, *This is not smart; this not what you need in your life right now.*

I had a young family and had just taken on a major involvement in the childcare business. The level of commitment I would need to give to the football club would be selfish. Some of the people I sought out for counsel suggested that my personal and business life would suffer if I became president of an AFL club.

I raised my doubts with Sam one evening. 'I don't know if this is right for us,' I said. 'We're already under a lot of pressure. Maybe I should just back off.'

The conviction of her response surprised me.

'No, I think you should do it,' she said. 'You should do it because you can. I know you'd do it well, and that's what the club needs. It doesn't need somebody who doesn't really want to take the presidency on. And I know that if you don't do it, you'll regret it.'

Her words allowed me to push forward without feeling guilty. It was only later that I thought, *What else was she going to say?* Sam was always supportive whenever I was considering a challenge. But I was so caught up in my own world at the time, I was oblivious to that. I did not stop to contemplate that I was actually shifting the responsibility onto her, so that if she had doubts and I didn't take the role on, I would have someone to blame.

Once I had decided to head up the reform movement, the challenge was to bring in quality like-minded people around me. Fortunately, in those early days I had the outstanding support of Don McLardy, a successful businessman whom I knew through his involvement with Reach. I wanted to gather people who had a calling to Melbourne and who were prepared to use their talents in ways that would transform the football club. It was not about finding ten great barrackers, or ten great accountants, or ten solicitors. I was looking for ten people who, if I brought their skillsets together, could produce something powerful. I was also determined to find people who did not have any baggage from previous tumultuous times at Melbourne, such as the failed merger with Hawthorn in 1996. The right people might not be easy to unearth but I knew they were out there.

So I started talking to people – one of the most productive discussions was with a group of four or five advisors from a firm called Pitcher Partners. What became apparent was that I did not have to work out who the right people were – instead, I had to establish what the right roles were. So I sought advice on what expertise we needed in order to have an exceptional board. I learned that if I talked to people who were well regarded, they would recommend others whom they rated highly, and I'd work my way up to the cream of the crop.

As we identified these people – someone with expertise in finance, then a legal expert, a marketing person and so on – we began to build a credible nucleus. But I knew there'd be doubters who would want to cut me down – people who'd say, 'What would he know? He's just a footballer. He's just going to fill the board with his old teammates.'

Another potential obstacle was that I did not want the names on the new ticket to become public knowledge just yet. That meant that as I was assembling the group, I was unable to tell each person who the others were. When I went public, I wanted to present a bloc of candidates so that our group could not be easily dismissed. If one or two names got out into the media, it would be easy for critics to pick at them, and the whole challenge would lose momentum and unravel. This meant that my candidates did not know each other, and we were not a cohesive group to begin with, but I knew that all were committed to bringing their expertise to a common cause.

It also meant that we were creating a sustainable model for whomever became president; at that stage, I was intending to bring the group together and then find someone else better suited to the presidency. What became evident, though, was that the people coming on board had an expectation that I would fill the role.

I still had doubts – about running board meetings, about the processes involved. But the others said, 'Don't worry about that – we can do that with our eyes closed. What we need is someone to lead the group, to make everyone believe in it.'

I went to see the AFL's chief executive, Andrew Demetriou, who suggested the role would be more demanding than I expected. 'I think the club has lost its way, Jim,' he told me. 'It's damaged. It doesn't stand for anything. It's a monumental task to take on the presidency. You don't really understand the time required. Do you really want to do this? We'll help you, but it's not going to be without pain.'

In the end, we assembled a group that impressed the football community, including Demetriou. I had the support of Don, Guy Jalland, Stuart Grimshaw, Peter Szental, David Thurin and Russell Howcroft. In June 2008, Gardner and six other club directors stood aside for our group, together with incumbents Karen Hayes, Andrew Leoncelli and Peter Spargo.

Once we got in, we began to uncover the extent of the debt. Worse still, we found out that the debt was growing day by day. The accounts guys couldn't keep track of it. Melbourne had massively overspent. In a general sense too, the club was a mess. Nobody trusted anyone. There were leaks to the media. There was a divisive backdrop. Our recent history had included pro- and anti-merger groups, as well as some polarised views about Joseph Gutnick's presidency a decade earlier. The club seemed to have splintered, and had rifts and factions. Fortunately, our group did not carry that baggage. People knew I was a long-time player, motivated purely by the club's best interests.

My belief was that we had to work together and simply concentrate on the values that make football clubs strong at any level, whether it be bush or suburban footy, or Ballyboden St Enda's back in Dublin. We needed to be inclusive, and we had to ensure that anyone who came into contact with our club came away feeling positive about that experience. Whether players, coaches, sponsors, employees or fans, you had to feel Melbourne was doing it as well as, if not better than, anyone else.

That attitude had to permeate the entire club, which was one of the reasons we replaced chief executive Paul McNamee during the first few weeks of my tenure. I simply believed he was not the right fit. His idea was to position Melbourne as a prestige club – to have an elitist appeal at the top end of town. But I knew that part of Melbourne's problem was that it was viewed that way already.

I would look out across the MCG stands on game day and think, *I'm not seeing a team being supported by wealthy people, by prestige supporters*. I didn't buy that whole nonsense about Land Rovers and the ski season. I saw families, mums and dads and kids. Of course there were also those who lunched behind the glass of the private boxes, but that was no different to any other AFL club. We welcomed those supporters, catered for them and thanked them for their generosity. But I was firm that they should not *define* Melbourne. I have never believed that those supporters got involved because of Melbourne's supposed 'prestige'. That has never been what brings people to a football club, what makes them want to buy a membership, to sit under a plastic poncho in the rain in July.

That is why I have always felt so proud and emotional about the Melbourne presidency. Playing football was a challenge, but it was more about a personal adventure and my competitiveness. Starting Reach was a challenge, but it came about more by happenstance, and grew from goodwill and a desire to help young people. The Melbourne presidency was about picking up a great organisation that was down on its knees, massively in debt, and fighting for survival. An organisation that meant so such to so many. And it came despite many people doubting me. Despite my own self-doubt.

As a board, we created the Debt Demolition program, which eradicated more than $5 million in debt and allowed us to stand on level footing with other AFL clubs. That financial improvement was something of which I was immensely proud, but it wasn't the greatest achievement that took place during my watch.

To me, the greatest success was the creation of trust. There is often not a lot of trust in big organisations, but I believe that changed at Melbourne. People began to trust in the Demons again and wanted to be associated with the club.

We welcomed back disenchanted club stalwarts and renewed our alliance with the Melbourne Cricket Club. We tried to have trust and integrity in all of our dealings, and to forge an identity. To stand for something.

My first twelve months as Melbourne president was hectic and exhilarating and challenging. Most of all, though, it was rewarding. I could see how excited people were about regaining a club that had passion and energy.

One of the benefits of the role was that it gave me a public platform. AFL club presidents can deliver their views on football and society, point out inequities, suggest improvements, lobby for change. And because they speak on behalf of Melbourne or Collingwood or Hawthorn, their views gain exposure and, often, traction.

By the middle of 2009, I was gaining confidence in the role and looking forward to devoting more time and energy to the football club. It would take something extraordinary to slow me down.

5

'THERE MUST
BE SOME MISTAKE'

The days immediately after I was diagnosed with cancer were frantic, yet life seemed to be happening in slow motion. My mind was desperately trying to persuade the rest of my body to believe that the malignant growth had been excised, and that this would just become my biggest wake-up call. The whole episode would simply add another layer to the story of my life. It would become another tag attached to me: Irishman, Brownlow medallist, Reach co-founder, cancer survivor. That was when my ego was at the wheel.

In between times, my brain was entertaining all sorts of other scenarios, including some dark and morbid notions. Every time I kissed or cuddled Matisse and Tiernan, I wondered whether I would have many more opportunities to do so. I began to think about making a list of the activities we wanted to do as a family, places we wanted to visit, so that we could start ticking them off, just like in the film *The Bucket List*. I started to question everything I was doing in my life – whether certain aspects were necessary, whether there were irrelevant pursuits taking up precious time. What were the priorities that would make a difference to my life and those of my family?

I was staggered to realise that I had never really looked at life in the knowledge that we all must one day die. Now I could not help but feel that the stopwatch on my life had begun. While I could have no way of knowing when it would stop, I wanted to make better use of whatever time remained, whether that was to be months, years or decades.

That's what I was thinking. What I was doing, however, was throwing cancer into the mix of an already frenetic lifestyle. Nobody else was going to slow life down for me. At that stage, nobody even knew about my medical condition, partly because the details remained so vague. Dr Graeme Southwick had also offered some astute advice. 'You need some "me time",' he said. 'You need to absorb this before you start telling others in your life. They care about you and will want to ask a lot of questions. But you need to get your head around it yourself first.'

The problem with the 'me time' theory was that the week ahead already loomed as one of the busiest of my year. The following Monday, 8 June, Melbourne was scheduled to host its annual Queen's Birthday match at the MCG. The game has become an annual fixture on the AFL calendar. The Demons play against Collingwood, which has one of the largest supporter bases in Victoria, and so a crowd of at

least 60000 is the norm. The previous year, Andrew Demetriou had suggested that Melbourne's involvement on the day
could not be taken for granted; this was a real concern, given
how critical the match was for the club's balance sheet. As
club president, I was centrally involved.

The game would also have an extra dimension for Demons
fans, with widespread interest in the playing debut of Jack
Watts, a young forward who had been selected with the number-one pick in the previous year's national draft.

A few days later, on the Friday, the Reach Ball was being
held. It was an annual gala event that could be relied upon to
raise more than $100000 for the foundation. This year there
was to be a Motown theme, and although several meticulous
organisers, including my sister Sharon, were preparing for
the night, I would have an important role to play.

Meanwhile, I was working the internet overtime in my
quest to research cancer and its various treatments. Already
I had some ideas about overhauling my diet, even though it
had always been relatively disciplined. Pathologists were still
trying to determine what type of cancer we were dealing with,
and I needed to have a CAT scan and blood tests. Graeme
had managed to book me in for the scan on Thursday, and I
was to have a follow-up appointment the next afternoon.

'The twelfth of June?' I asked. 'That's Friday – the Reach
Ball is on that night.'

'Jim, listen to yourself,' Graeme replied, and I was suita-
bly chastised.

A CAT scan is an X-ray procedure. You can't eat for hours

beforehand, and then they inject you with 'contrast material' or dye. You lie on a narrow examination table – my feet stuck out over the end – and slide into a tunnel-like scanner. The computer uses the X-ray images to generate cross-sectional views of your body. One simple explanation that was offered to me is that it is like cutting a loaf of bread into thin slices, then using a computer to reassemble them and tell you what's inside the loaf. I was praying this scan would be the first step towards putting the whole cancer episode behind me.

As Sam and I drove to Graeme's rooms on Friday afternoon, I rang Sharon, knowing she would be overseeing the setup for the Reach Ball at Crown Palladium. I usually liked to swing by in the afternoon, tweak a seating arrangement here, push back a table there. They were usually finicky changes, but they helped ease my mind that everything was just so ahead of the big night.

'Sharon, I've got a meeting I can't get out of, so I won't be coming in. I'll see you tonight.'

She knew straight away that it had to be something important. 'Is everything all right?' she asked.

'Fine – I'll see you tonight.'

Just as Sam parked the car, it occurred to me that it was exactly one year since I had taken on the Melbourne presidency. They had been twelve tumultuous months, and I wondered what the next twelve had in store.

The results of the scan and blood tests were in a folder on Graeme's desk. He picked them up with great care.

'I'm afraid it's not the news we wanted,' he began. 'The cancer has spread from your primary tumour. Your scan shows a shadow the size of an orange on your lungs. Also some glands in your mediastinum, which is the middle of your chest cavity.' He patted the palm of his hand on his heart. 'The fact that it's spread there tells me you might have more issues elsewhere in your body.'

He mentioned lymph nodes and a couple of technical terms that I struggled to comprehend, and for the second time in as many visits to his office I was hit by a wave of shock. I was numb and my stomach was churning.

I thought, *How can this be? There must be some mistake. I'm supposed to beat this.* It just didn't make sense. How could my body be peppered with tumours when I felt so healthy, so strong? Sam had a stream of tears tumbling down her cheeks. I didn't want to ask Graeme the gravity of the situation because I wasn't sure how I would be able to cope mentally.

Frustratingly, there still remained no definitive answer about what type of cancer I had, but the options had been narrowed down to two: melanoma, which is one of the main types of skin cancer, or a much rarer form of cancer called reticulum cell sarcoma. The treatments would be different, but either way Graeme had begun to assemble a team of doctors to treat me. He explained that I would need a more thorough examination – a PET scan – to determine if the cancer had spread anywhere else in my body.

It was clear to me that I was in real trouble. I decided to broach the question that both Sam and I were thinking. 'Could this thing kill me?' I asked. 'What sort of life expectancy are we talking about?'

His response was that he'd 'never, never, ever' tell a patient that they will die of cancer in a certain timeframe. 'Tumours have amazing ways of behaving. You can never predict with any certainty where they will take you. All I will say, Jim, is that when cancer is in multiple centres, the chance of a cure goes down.'

I suggested that this sounded like a gentle way of telling me I was going to die.

He offered an eloquent response: 'In this life we all have one thing in common. We are all going to die. If you are lucky enough to get the heads-up that your time may be looming, you'll fight tooth-and-nail to hang around for as long as you can.'

Sam and I emerged from Graeme's practice in a daze, but were jolted back to reality by the peak-hour traffic and our wristwatches telling us we should already be somewhere else. But, following a suggestion from Graeme, we walked up the road to a little sandwich shop and sat down for a coffee.

We were in disbelief. Every time we mentioned the children, tears welled up in our eyes. We discussed how we would tell our family, our friends. Sam needed to talk to her mum. My parents had only recently returned to Ireland. Because my brothers and sisters had all, one by one, followed me and set up lives for themselves in Australia, Mam and Dad now lived in Melbourne and flew home every year for a few months during the northern summer. One thing I was determined to avoid just yet was making my situation public knowledge. I knew there'd be a media circus if word got out.

'What about my brothers and sisters?' I wondered aloud. 'They're going to be at the Reach Ball tonight. I don't think I could cope with that. I could organise a get-together tomorrow to tell them. Maybe breakfast.'

Sam looked up at me through red-rimmed eyes and said flatly, 'I can't go to the Reach Ball.'

I thought about the 1000 tickets that had been sold, the weeks of planning. What the night meant to so many of the kids at Reach.

'We have to,' I said. 'We're going to go home, get dressed and do what we have to do.'

'Well, I don't think I can do that.'

I understood why Sam had doubts about the wisdom of driving home, frocking up and heading out on a Friday night. Trying to act normal in a room with a thousand other people.

When we got home, she had an emotionally draining phone conversation with her mum, Mary Williamson, but nobody else knew. After that, we got ready and went to the ball. It felt surreal when we arrived at the venue and made our way through the Crown Atrium, with its black marble walls and crystal ceiling. It seemed absurd to be dealing with my inner turmoil while surrounded by trick lighting and spouting water.

At the escalators I saw the familiar smiling face of Don McLardy. A more likeable man with a greater zest for life you could not meet. He greeted me and said I looked distracted. I blurted out that I had been to see the doctor that afternoon, and that I was riddled with cancer.

He was stunned. 'What are you doing here?'

I was not thinking clearly and didn't know what to say. I was the MC and needed to be here. It was an important night for the Reach kids, and for the Crew, who planned to party for all hours. I told Don that I had not meant to tell anyone that evening, but here I was blabbing it out in my first conversation of the night. As always, Don was a rock of support. He and wife, Clare, guided Sam and me into the ballroom.

I find it hard to describe what that night was like. I was dazed but my senses were alert. It was emotionally tough but the function was a seamless success. Normally, I was a control freak at such fundraisers, but that night I just chilled and thought, *I don't need to worry about all of these little hassles – they're insignificant.* After completing some of the formalities on stage, I hung around my table and let things slide by and not bother me.

A handful of people noticed that Sam and I were unusually quiet. I had suggested to my sisters and brothers that it would be good to catch up for breakfast the next morning; they had sensed something was wrong but just put it to one side. Now that I thought about it, some of them were going to struggle to see breakfast after finishing up here.

Later in the evening, Sam's brother, Wayne Ludbey,

arrived after his late shift at the *Herald Sun* newspaper, where he worked as the pictorial editor. He walked in and gave her a big hug, and she just burst into tears. They shuffled over to a quiet corner near the kitchen to talk. Sam later told me that some of the waiters were carping, 'You can't stand here,' but before she or Wayne could reply, their boss, Rita, barked, 'You leave them alone.' She remembered Sam from previous functions and found a secluded spot for her and Wayne to be alone.

When the phone rang the next morning, it was a croaky Sharon on the line. 'Now, what's the story with this breakfast?' she asked. 'I have a throbbing head. Do we really need to do this?'

I told her that we did, and it was important.

Her voice became sombre. 'I'll be there.'

Unbeknown to me, she rang around our other siblings and made sure they got the picture. She could not raise my youngest brother, David, who had been shaping as some sort of chance to have his breakfast on the way home from the ball.

Sure enough, he was still absent without leave about an hour later as the family gathered at the Pelican café in Fitzroy Street, St Kilda. My sister Terri-Ann gave David's phone another try. 'Nope, through to voicemail.'

Sharon, who was there with her husband, Sean, piped up, 'All right, enough of the chitchat. Let's cut the crap, Jim. Why are we here?'

Ever since I'd woken up that morning, my mind had tumbled over endless ways to broach the subject with them, but Sharon's direct question drew out a candid response. 'It's really bad news,' I said. 'I've got cancer.'

There was a collective sharp intake of air. I pressed on, telling them about how the lump in my back had been a tumour, and the extent to which the cancer had spread.

Sharon spoke first. 'This is so unfair!' she said angrily, her head leaning back to try to stop the tears. I turned towards Terri-Ann, who looked dumbfounded, almost incapable of showing any emotion. My youngest sister, Dearbhla, was sobbing. There were tears and hugs, and I felt blessed to have so much unconditional love in my life.

I would need to track David down later. Then there was my other brother, Brian. Last night's Reach Ball had been just about the first he had missed since their inception a decade before. He was preparing for a business trip back to Ireland. I had already had one conversation with him about the lump before I went in for the exploratory surgery. I rang him with the update. 'Brian, you know that lump . . .'

He listened. Then he swore, and there was a long pause. 'I'm almost driving the car off the road. Hang on a minute, I'm just pulling over. I'm on the hands-free phone – I've just dropped the boys off at a kids' party.' He didn't know what to say.

'What are you going to do, Jim?'

'I'm not sure, but I'm not going to just roll over.'

As heart-wrenching as it had been to tell my siblings, what I most dreaded was the phone call to Mam and Dad in Ireland.

I summoned up the courage later that evening, settled myself in a quiet corner of the house and dialled their number. With all six of their children living in Australia, they had sold the family home in Dublin and bought a cottage down the coast in Wexford, on a hill overlooking mountains and the Irish Sea.

I held my breath, waiting to see if anyone would answer. It was my mother's cheerful voice.

'Hi, Mam – it's Jim,' I said. 'Is Dad with you?' I was asking because I wanted them to be together, but she presumed I needed to speak to him.

'He's out in the garden. I'll just fetch him.' Her voice trailed away. 'Brian! Brian! It's Jim.'

In the silence while my dad came to the phone I could hear my heart beating.

'Hello, son.'

'Dad, would you mind cutting your visit home short?'

'What do you mean? What's wrong?'

'Well, I have cancer.' He was speechless. What can you say when your child is on the phone talking about his terminal illness?

My parents are remarkably resilient people, but I felt for them, knowing they would feel isolated and helpless since they were 17000 kilometres away.

'Don't worry,' I told Dad. 'I've met every challenge in my life. I'll meet this one too.'

I could hear Mam stressing in the background and she came to the phone. 'Jim?'

I tried to explain as much as I could about the cancer, the outlook and the treatment. How it might be melanoma or a rare sarcoma. Mam, ever the optimist, declared that she hoped it was the sarcoma. If it was so rare, she reasoned, the doctors might not really know the extent of my illness, and therefore I might recover quicker than expected. She knew about the lump on my back. Before returning home, she had felt it and declared – you guessed it – that I should get it examined.

Before I got off the line, Mam made a vow. 'Jim . . . we'll be praying for you every day.' I knew she meant it.

6

GETTING MY HEAD AROUND IT

Knowing that cancer had spread through my body did not make me worried. Worrying is what you do when you have doubts about the circumstances you can control. It made me scared.

The medical team being assembled instilled me with confidence, however. Graeme was lining up the elite in their respective fields. I was also confident that I had the determination to take on the challenge. That was how I came to view this disease: as a challenge. It is easy to get caught up in the jargon of cancer and talk of being 'up for the fight'. But I did not see it as a fight.

Fortunately, I did not have the worries that burden some cancer patients – things like a lack of emotional support, financial woes, employment hassles, transport issues, physical fitness. All things considered, I had less to worry about than most people who found themselves confronting cancer.

But I was scared. There were circumstances that were beyond my control. It scared me to imagine how hard it would be for Sam and the kids if I died. And I was scared for selfish reasons too. That I might not make it to my forty-fourth birthday, might miss out on growing old with my wife, might not watch Tiernan and Matisse mature and experience great moments in their lives. These were the negative thoughts creeping in, the ones that had to be banished.

In that first week after learning the tumours had spread, Sam and I packed up the kids and headed down to Rye for three days, to clear our heads and consider a way forward. It was there that I realised just how scared I was, but also where I decided not to allow thoughts of dying to gain any traction. I had spent the past fifteen years telling teenagers that they needed to face their greatest fears, using the analogy 'slay your dragon'. I realised, however, that I had never been personally challenged to confront my own deepest fears. To slay my dragon. Regardless of how I'd got cancer, what I had to accept was the reality that it was now in my life.

There is a scene in the Academy Award-winning documentary *When We Were Kings* that, to me, expresses the essence of what it is to confront fear. The 1996 film examines boxing's historic 'Rumble in the Jungle', the world title fight held in Kinshasa, Zaire (now the Democratic Republic of the Congo), in 1974. The undefeated George Foreman, a brute of a man rated one of the most powerful punchers of all time, was the reigning heavyweight champion. Muhammad Ali, known for his supreme skill and confidence but considered a fading force at age thirty-two, was the challenger.

Ringside was the great American novelist and essayist

Norman Mailer, who describes in the film what he witnessed that day.

Mailer recounts studying Ali in his corner between rounds, contemplating going back out into the ring with a stronger man, one who looked unstoppable and determined to knock him out. Mailer describes seeing a look on Ali's face that he had never see before. There was fear in the great boxer's eyes. But then it was 'as if Ali looked into himself and said, "All right, this is the moment. This is what you have been waiting for. This is that hour. Do you have the guts?" And he kind of nodded to himself, like, "You gotta get it together, boy. You really gotta get it together. And you are going to get it together. You will get it together."'

Shortly after Mailer observed this, Ali began employing a tactic that would become known as 'rope-a-dope'. He spent three rounds leaning against the ropes, absorbing Foreman's most fearsome shots, to the point where the champion was exhausted. Ali then stunned the world by knocking Foreman out in the eighth round, validating his claim to be the greatest of all time. This was an object lesson that inspired me, and I had often cited it – I'd even reproduced it in Reach literature. Now I needed to follow its example.

Much as I tried not to feel sorry for myself, I could not help but feel heavy-hearted for Sam. She had been through the cancer mill before. Her parents had divorced when she was fifteen, and eventually had settled down with new partners.

Sam had divided her time between her father Don's vineyard in Mount Macedon and her mother Mary's house in St Kilda. When she was in her early twenties, her father had been diagnosed with prostate cancer. Told he would be lucky to live twelve months, Don eked out six years before passing at the age of sixty-one.

While we were at Rye, we spoke about her father's struggle. 'I don't think Wayne and I really understood what Dad was going through,' she said. 'I know there were times when he would be in bed the whole day, but if he knew one of us was coming to visit, he would spruce himself up and try to make the situation as normal as possible.'

There had always been the stress of wondering whether Don would make it to the next birthday or the next Christmas, and when he did make it, the running joke was always that he was just putting on this whole cancer act for the attention. The morbid humour had helped dissipate the underlying sadness. 'We need to remember to laugh,' Sam said. Hearing this reinforced my belief that staying mentally strong and positive was going to be crucial, no matter what lay ahead.

Despite the obvious cloud, our time together over those couple of days yielded some very simple but beautiful moments. I asked Sam how she was coping. She told me how she hated being alone at the moment, how it gave her time to become miserable. She needed to stay busy. Somehow I knew that wouldn't be hard to manage in the coming weeks.

We returned to Melbourne in a better headspace. I had an appointment for the PET scan, which would be used to pick up any active tumour tissue. Having a PET scan is similar to having a CAT scan. The difference for the doctors is that it is a specialised imaging technique that uses short-lived radioactive substances to produce three-dimensional coloured images.

It did not take long to get the results back, and they showed that – apart from the one in my lung – there was one tumour in a lymph gland on the side of my lung, plus a spot in my neck and a lump the size of a grape at the back of my right thigh.

I needed Graeme to again explain lymph nodes to me – what they were and why I kept hearing the phrase in discussions about my condition. He explained that the lymphatic system was part of the immune system, which collected and carried tissue fluid (called lymph) through the body; it ultimately drains back into the bloodstream. Lymph nodes are small rounded organs found all around the body; as the fluid drains through them, they act as filters. The cancer was using the lymphatic system to spread throughout my body. What remained a mystery, though, was the site of origin: where had the cancer come from? Was it melanoma or sarcoma? Graeme explained that the biopsy tissue was being examined by specialists in Australia and the United States.

The next step for me, he said, was to meet with my oncologist, a physician who specialised in cancer and tumours. He had organised for me to see Max Schwarz, head of medical oncology at the Alfred Hospital. 'I have the utmost respect for the man,' Graeme said. 'You will be in the hands of one of the leading oncologists in the country.'

I went to see Dr Schwarz, who clearly knew his stuff but had a very scientific approach. He mentioned the possibility that we were dealing with a rare form of lymphoma and recommended that I begin chemotherapy as soon as possible. He spoke about how the cancer had spread and what the statistics told us. He seemed to believe that I needed to begin treatment immediately, otherwise I might not live beyond nine to twelve months.

I guess that is a common challenge physicians face: everyone wants to know 'how long have I got, doc?' But I wondered whether patients were best served by knowing what percentage chance they have of surviving, or how long they have until they can expect to die. I did not want to dwell on the negatives – I was looking for positive reinforcement.

Some people, when they are diagnosed, don't want to know much about cancer. I was like that at first. I tried to stay away from any literature that had a gloomy outlook. I was more interested in material that offered constructive and affirmative messages. That offered hope. Most of those messages seemed to be found in non-traditional medicine, in natural therapies. I asked Dr Schwarz his views about alternative treatments.

He laughed and told me to be careful. Those alternative cancer therapies were a load of hocus-pocus, he said. They made $3 billion every year by cashing in on the hope of sufferers.

'They may well do,' I said, 'but how much do you think traditional cancer medicine makes?' I was angry. Dr Schwarz might have been one of the best in the business, but the fact that he had a closed mind to alternative approaches suggested to me that we were poles apart in our approaches to my treatment.

Nine months. I thought about it. That worked out to be about 275 days. It couldn't be right. I even had appointments in my diary that were beyond then.

Having an actual number hanging over my head gave the challenge a different dimension. The temptation was to repeat the number to my family, to reinforce it, perpetuate it. I had to resist doing so and shift my mindset, to deny the dark side.

I rationalised the information. Nine months was the worst-case scenario, I told myself, but the best-case scenario was living to a ripe old age if I got to the cause of the disease. Then there was somewhere in between if, as Dr Schwarz suggested, the cancer responded to conventional medicine. My view was that I needed to rely on modern medicine to treat the symptoms, but I needed natural medicine if I was to get to the cause of the cancer and live out my life.

I began by overhauling my diet. There would be no meat, dairy, sugar or wheat. No preservatives and no processed food. This meant that the bulk of my diet now involved raw or semi-cooked veggies, a little fruit and plenty of nuts. Some of Sam's friends – in particular, her good mate Amanda – were unbelievable in their enthusiasm to track down the finest organic food in town.

Then the modifications began. I was intrigued by the book *Cancer-Free: Your Guide to Gentle, Non-Toxic Healing*, written by Bill Henderson. An American great-grandfather, Bill became devoted to the study of alternative cancer treatments after his wife, Marjorie, died of ovarian cancer in 1994. He had found it difficult to endure her four-year struggle with conventional treatment, and determined that there must be a better way.

After identifying with some of the principles in Henderson's book, I took his suggestion and added a morning dose of flaxseed oil and cottage cheese to my regimen. Furthermore, a whole raft of supplements was added to the equation after I consulted Dr Peter Eng, a local GP who practises natural medicine. I also began to explore the healthy lifestyle approach advocated by the Gawler Foundation, run by a well-known Victorian, the long-time cancer survivor Ian Gawler.

Part of the difficulty in forming a comprehensive approach to the future was that I still did not know what type of cancer I had. Very few people knew I had cancer. I was still not ready to tell the world, although I looked forward to the day when I did not have to carry the secret around anymore.

What intrigued me, though, was how often I was now hearing about other people who had cancer. While doing my research, I read that half of all Australians would be diagnosed with some form of cancer in their lifetime, although clearly the vast majority would not be anywhere near as serious as my own situation. I began to realise that, up until now, I had had very little understanding of the disease.

It is hard to explain how realising this felt. The best analogy I can think of is having kids. After you've had a child of your own, you begin to look at other people's children through different eyes. You really notice them. Of course, they've always been there, it is just that now you have a better appreciation of them.

I now had a sense that everywhere I went felt different, like I was seeing it through different eyes. Interacting with people who didn't know I had cancer felt weird. I decided that it would be a good idea to talk to someone who had been in a similar situation.

The one name in football circles that came to my mind was Adam Ramanauskas, the Essendon player who had retired in 2008 after a decade and 134 games; he had been the youngest member of the Bombers' 2000 Premiership team. In 2003, an unusual lump on his neck had been diagnosed as fibromatosis, a rare but low-grade cancer.

As fate would have it, Melbourne was due to play Essendon at Etihad Stadium that weekend. Adam was now involved in a development coaching role with the Bombers, and was one of the two runners who ran out the senior coach's messages on match day.

Before the game I went onto the stadium's surface and

sought Adam out, mentioning that I was keen to catch up with him for a chat. He was obliging, although I'm sure he was thinking it would be a football discussion, and gave me his mobile phone number.

Later that week I rang him and explained the situation. We spoke for about half an hour. I knew part of Adam's story: after surgery to remove the lump, he had bounced back to play a handful of games towards the end of 2003, only for the cancer to recur. But he filled me in on the rest of his remarkable tale: radiotherapy treatment, a return to football only to injure a knee at training, which required a full reconstruction. Then, on the eve of the 2006 season, the cancer reappeared, requiring more invasive surgery as well as chemotherapy treatment.

We spoke about surgeons, radiation, chemotherapy and its side-effects, diet, rest – the full gamut. 'You're probably already thinking this way, Jim,' he said, 'but I genuinely believe half of the battle is keeping a really positive frame of mind. Get plenty of opinions before you decide which direction to take. Decide on who you are going to take advice from and stick with them, but try to be well informed before you make any decisions along the way.'

It was a really beneficial and reassuring conversation. Given that Adam had been through his cancer treatment while inside the bubble that is AFL football in Melbourne, I was especially interested in his advice about dealing with the media. 'Just be open and honest with them,' he said. 'Give them as much information as you can, and then ask them to respect your privacy. Tell them you'll give them updates along the way when you can.'

It struck me that this was the time to strip everything back. To remove some of the hindrances and get the external stresses out of my life. Then, once I'd simplified things, I would be in a better place to learn, a better place to make decisions. In the AFL, Melbourne was headed on a road trip to Queensland that weekend for an away match against the Brisbane Lions. It was an ideal opportunity to take a break from football and Reach and my business interests.

One suggestion was to go to a health farm, but that was not what I needed. I felt the need to connect spiritually. So I headed to an ashram, a spiritual hermitage, about an hour and a half out of Melbourne. It was about as removed from the blokey world of football as you could get.

There is a degree of cynicism among some people about places like the one I went to; they see them as the domain of soy-latte-sipping greenies. But for me it was perfect. Five days of total seclusion. Basic living and food, even though I was probably staying in the equivalent of the five-star quarters.

It was as liberating and relaxing a time as I had experienced in my life, and it allowed me to get my thoughts together. Clear out the clutter. Cut off contact with the outside world, with no mobile phone, no email. It just made sense.

The ashram was in a tranquil setting in the bush, with plenty of silence and time for reflection. Peculiarly, though, the most powerful moment came via the loudest, most impulsive person in the whole place. She was one of the residents, a woman probably in her early twenties. She had what I'd describe as a raw sense of humour and could be quite blunt. One morning I was out walking through the bush – the Wombat Forest – and she asked, 'Do you mind if I walk with you?' I said, 'Sure, let's walk.'

Of all the people there, she was someone you would notice but not necessarily someone you would choose to join you on a contemplative stroll. If I wanted advice, I'd have looked for a 'wise old man on the mountain' type, someone whose sparing use of language suggested a profound wisdom. Not someone who laughed at inappropriate moments; at times she seemed completely incongruous in that environment. I was thinking, *Who is this?*

We wandered along for some time and eventually she started talking. 'You seem very troubled,' she said. 'What's wrong?' Nobody there knew about my illness, but it didn't strike as a place where the news would go viral. I held off for a while, then eventually I thought, *Bugger it – I'll tell her.*

She listened, then said something profound: 'You have to thank this cancer for coming into your life right now, because you have been so distracted. This cancer has got your attention back on what's most important to you.'

It was as simple as that, and it was so true. Here was this young woman, who I had underestimated, and she had nailed me. She didn't know who I was or what I did, and yet she had summed up exactly where I was at. Up to that point, I had not seen cancer in that way. But it made sense: here was a blessing that was going to teach me something and become a really important phase of my life. It was precisely what I needed to hear.

I've tried all my life to not discount people, to believe that every person has something to offer if you're prepared to listen to them. You can learn from anyone if you're prepared to have an open mind.

It was as though this woman knew that she needed to talk to me. There was something wrong, and she was the person to listen when I opened up about it. And I felt that something would flow from this. I had a strong feeling that she'd been sent to give me this message. It was really powerful. Until then, I had been stuck, lost. I hadn't known what I was doing.

To this day, I don't know the woman's name – I don't know anything about her. As we wandered along and kept chatting, I explained my situation and told her I had to consider how to release the information to the public.

She had more unaffected advice to offer. 'Just tell people you're ill and will need to step back for a while until you get better,' she said. 'Say that you would appreciate family privacy.'

It was true. I needed to take my ego out of it. To stop thinking that this was such a big deal and just get on with life. There was a new clarity to my thinking.

That afternoon, I had a yoga class. The focus was 'I will be cancer-free'.

My time at the ashram had helped me, and I thought, *Right, it's time to let people in.* For anyone who discovers they have cancer, I think the right approach is to break the news to others when you feel ready. Experts will tell you there are some other guiding principles: expect questions, consider asking family and friends to help spread the word, and establish boundaries about how much information you wish to share.

The timing was also right because I had been booked in for surgery at the end of the week. Graeme explained, 'Regardless of whether it's melanoma or sarcoma, it's better to get as much malignant tissue out as you can.'

I called a meeting of the Melbourne Football Club board for the Tuesday to explain the situation and discuss a media strategy. Don McLardy, one of our vice-presidents, was among the few people I had already confided in. He is a wholly trustworthy man, a man of great integrity who is not only competent but always full of optimism and energy. He's the sort of man I like to say is good at life. Given the calibre of the other people on the Melbourne board, I was confident of their understanding and assistance. But I underestimated just how personally supportive they would be.

They also had some astute advice for me, suggesting that I should let the public know that it was more than just a simple illness; to do otherwise would prolong the media spotlight. Don would take over my day-to-day duties as acting president, and I would stand aside indefinitely while I recuperated.

'I think we're all agreed, though, aren't we, that Jim should remain the Melbourne president?' Don said.

'Whether you want to stay in the role or not, Jim. Whether you can attend meetings or not, have any input or not. You remain the Melbourne Football Club president.' The sentiment was unanimous.

Yet doubts remained in my mind. There was a certain amount of prestige in being the Melbourne president but the role did not define me. It involved an enormous amount of work for an honorary position. The aspect of the job that I loved, though, was that it allowed me to influence decisions, to shape what I believed were the best interests of the club. That would be hard to give up. But where did it sit in my priorities right now?

That same day, a group of my closest friends received either a text message or a phone call from a third party, inviting them to come over to our house in St Kilda the next evening. There was no reason given, just an emphasis that 'I would really like you to get there if you can'. For the next twenty-four hours my phone lit up with texts and calls back, but I wasn't answering. No questions, no calls, no rumours.

When Wednesday evening came, there was current of excitement in the air. After all, I was going to host a gathering of my most cherished friends. We left the front door open so that people could just walk down the hall and into the open living area, where my family were standing around, chatting. That way I didn't have to individually greet every arrival and answer the inevitable 'What's going on?'

Instead, I wandered into a soiree that was already underway, as a caterer passed around finger food. Of course, most
people sought me out anyway and asked, 'What's this about?
Is everything all right with you guys?' I even had one friend say,
'What – don't tell me you're moving back to Ireland?' Everyone looked at me inquisitively but I just smiled and handed
them drinks, saying they'd find out in a moment. Soon everyone was laughing and chatting, catching up with old friends.
Eventually, I stood up to speak and they all fell silent.

'Guys, thanks for getting along tonight,' I began. 'It's great
to see you all, and to catch up with some old mates, including some who I haven't seen for too long. The reason I asked
you to be here is because I have cancer. I had a lump in my
back, which was taken out, and it was malignant. The doctors hoped that might be the end of it, but it has spread to my
chest and I am going in for surgery in a couple of days to have
it cut out. You guys know me better than anyone and know
I will be up for the challenge that's ahead of me now. I feel
confident, and it's great that I have got people like you to give
me strength. But I'm the same person, so don't treat me any
differently. Sam and the kids are going to need your support,
and the best thing you can do to help me is to help them.'

The room was completely still, apart from the odd sniffle
and some restless shuffling of feet. I looked out over a sea of
stunned faces.

Then a couple of friends spoke up, stating their belief that
if anyone could beat cancer, I could. One of the questions
was about the public finding out; I explained that I would be

doing a press conference at the MCG the next day.

One mate made the point that my friends wouldn't want to be constantly pestering us for updates on my health; he suggested that those in this room could try to keep each other informed. He made me promise that Sam and I would never hold back in asking for assistance, no matter how great or small.

I was feeling emotional about the warmth and positivity surging through the group, and, as people often do in those kinds of situations, I attempted to defuse the tension with some lame humour. As I ended my speech, I said, 'Anyway, I'm not dying, so let's have a good night.'

I have never had as many people embrace and squeeze me as I did that night – even from some of the guys who would usually defer to machismo before ever allowing themselves to bear-hug a man. Garry Lyon grabbed me and told me he loved me. I had shared a house with Garry when we were bachelors, and considered him a great mate. He now worked in the media, and he told me that several reporters were already on the trail of the story. In my pocket, my phone was bleeping madly but I had no intention of answering it.

Later in the evening, someone mentioned that the nine o'clock news had run a bulletin stating it was believed the Melbourne president would step down for illness reasons. The feeding frenzy had begun.

The next morning, I woke up to see page-one headlines about me in each of the Victorian newspapers. The whole front page of the *Herald Sun* was devoted to the story, under the headline 'Shock for Demons legend: Jim's health fight'.

Before the media conference, which was set for 1 pm, I had planned to have a quick chat with the Reach staff at the Dream Factory, followed by another with the Melbourne players and staff.

The situation at Reach was different from that at the footy club. Was I stepping aside until I could resume my role when I recovered? That was not what it felt like it. Rather, it seemed like an opportunity, and I realised that it could be the making of Reach. While I felt incredibly proud to have helped create an outstanding organisation, I hoped Reach would evolve into something truly special. I was doing something like 200 talks a year with Reach, but I had begun to see that this level of involvement was not sustainable in the long term – especially since, by their nature, a lot of those talks covered the same ground. I wondered if I was going to start boring myself, let alone others. And then one day I might wake up and have nothing left to talk about.

There was more to it than that, though. I didn't want the kids to become Reach clones. The whole idea of the place was to learn about yourself, then go out into the world, take risks, make mistakes and develop even further as a person. To come back and give something to Reach, but then to go back out and gain more information and be inspired by your own life. To come up with ideas but never to get stale or comfortable. To get something out of life.

For Reach to thrive, it had to be about young people

inspiring young people. That was the vision, and it was happening, but I knew I needed to hand over even more control to the leaders coming through.

In the back of my mind was Coláiste na bhFiann. In recent visits back to Ireland, I had sensed that the group had shifted its philosophy. The *gaeltachts* and the focus on the Irish language remained central to the organisation's operation, but what about some of the broader principles? Was there the same value placed on making your life special, on improvising? Coláiste seemed a more polished outfit, but now that the raw edge was gone, had it lost some of its bite? I was reminded of Domhnall's grand vision, and of what, deep down, was at the core of Reach: it was about believing in kids, giving them a voice, encouraging them to aspire.

These thoughts helped me clarify what was important when I spoke to Reach's staff that morning. I told them that this day could be a real positive for Reach, that others would get the chance to step up, and that they should never lose sight of the grand vision. I also told them how thankful I was that Reach had helped me prepare for life with cancer. I was already thinking more deeply about life, about people, and about what we can endure. Reach had armed me to slay my dragon.

The MCG had become like a second home to me since I had arrived in Melbourne at the end of 1984. In those early days, I had spent hours of my spare time at the Melbourne Football Club's offices in Jolimont Terrace. I had practised kicking a Sherrin across the road in Yarra Park. In pre-season training we used to run up and down the steps of the Northern Stand to improve our fitness. I had been there for AFL matches, concerts, functions and announcements about coaches being sacked. I was there in the front row, thirty metres away, when Collingwood and Essendon officials had started brawling in the 1990 Grand Final. I had come to expect it all. But I had never imagined walking into the great stadium to announce to the world that I had cancer.

On 2 July 2009, my first port of call was the club's changing rooms, where I spoke to the players and staff. I explained the situation and made it clear that Don McLardy was stepping up to take on the day-to-day responsibilities for the foreseeable future.

Among those who came up to me afterwards to offer support was a solemn Chris Connolly, our football manager. I had been mates with 'Connolls' for more than twenty years, dating back to when we were teammates; his career had been prematurely ended by knee injuries. A few days earlier, I had run into him at the club, by which time the effect of my changed diet meant I had shed about five kilograms. Connolls had looked me up and down before declaring, 'Jeez, mate, you're fading away to a ghost. Don't go and die on us – we can't afford that!' We could both see the black humour in that conversation now.

The media conference was to be held upstairs in the Harrison Room, overlooking the ground. Earlier that week, while writing some notes about what to say, I had shut myself in the study at home. Actually, 'study' is probably the wrong description. It is our spare room, part study, part storage space, part dusty vault. The walls are lined with bookshelves, while on the floor are cardboard boxes that are constantly moved around like one of those sliding tile puzzles. In that room can be found all manner of relics that don't have a home anywhere else: a bottle of Melbourne Demons port, old videotapes of long-forgotten games with the labels peeling off, piles of the kids' kindergarten paintings, plaques to express appreciation for delivering a talk.

In rifling through some of my football remnants, I'd found some old football jumpers, including one with the number thirty-seven on the back, which I had worn in my debut season before assuming the number eleven. It had dawned on me that this was the jumper I'd been wearing when I ran across the mark in that notorious 1987 Preliminary Final. I showed it to Sam. 'Maybe it's an omen,' she had said. 'You overcame that challenge, now you're going to overcome this one.' It had seemed too apt an analogy to ignore, and so I had brought the old guernsey with me.

The Harrison Room was crammed with close to 200 media people. Sam and Don sat on my right, and the club's chief executive officer, Cameron Schwab, settled beside me to the left. The players stood at the back of the room. At first I couldn't look up, for fear of becoming overly emotional, and when I did about twenty cameras started clicking furiously. Instinctively, I rubbed Sam's back, took a few deep breaths, then began. 'Okay . . . now, I'm going to try to get through this in one piece.' Apart from some prolonged pauses when I fought back tears, that is what I managed to do.

I explained about the lump on my back. 'I found out that it was cancerous . . . I thought it might just be located in that one area but it's not; it's spread quite a bit and I have a journey to go on.

'I need to understand it and work with it. I've got some of the best people in the country working with me. My body has something in it that it needs to release, and I've got to find a way of doing that.

'I'm not stepping down from Melbourne, I'm not walking away. But I will be taking a break and I'll need to take the rest of the season off so I can focus on this and focus on my family.'

The most difficult moment came when I mentioned Matisse and Tiernan. 'I have two young kids,' I began, 'and . . .' I had to pause for what felt like minutes to get my emotions under control. Camera shutters began clicking away, first the odd one here and there, then they filled the silence, like when it begins to hail on a tin roof. 'And particularly for them I need you to respect our privacy,' I finally managed to say. 'They're going to school and they've got friends. One of them understands what's going on, she's aware, she's an amazing young girl . . . but she doesn't need to be reading about this.'

At that point I had to change the subject, because I knew that if I thought too long about the kids I would lose it. I told the media that I would be heading to hospital in the next few days to begin therapy, and that I then intended to gradually return to Melbourne and Reach, albeit in a reduced capacity.

'The other thing that I'd ask is for people not to treat me any differently . . . Don't look at me in a weird way. I'm still the same guy and I'm going to get on with my life.

'Wear your jumper to the game; wear it with pride.'

I urged Melbourne fans to choose a jumper that had special significance for them, then I reached under the table and held up my number thirty-seven. 'I came across this one. It's not the number that most people would be familiar with, it's the number that the club gave me in my first year of senior footy. As it turned out, that was the number I wore when I ran across the mark. It was a challenge at the time . . . and now I face another challenge.

'But I've always said, football and sporting challenges are nothing compared to what some people have to go through. I've worked with a lot of kids and they've been through far worse than what I'm about to embark on, but I'm just looking forward, being very positive about it.'

With relief, I realised there was nothing more to say, so I handed over to Don, who made a quick statement. 'Jim is not stepping down,' he said. 'He's just taking some time off to get himself right. And we'll be ready for him when he comes back.'

Naturally, there were a few questions from the assembled media. In answering one, I mentioned the young woman at the ashram and, for a second time, had to pause to gather my emotions. 'She said to me, "This could be the greatest blessing that you've ever had. Because your soul needed to communicate something to you."'

Sam was asked how she was holding up. She spoke with incredible poise. 'I'm okay, thank you. In light of the fact that we have two young children, we need to stay strong and move forward as best we can.'

That made me declare aloud what I was thinking to myself. 'Sam is an amazing human being,' I said. 'Very blessed.' And then, hardly loud enough for anyone to hear, I said again, 'Very blessed.'

As the media conference ended, I stood up, took a few deep breaths and then put an arm around Sam, before giving her a kiss. One of the journalists shouted out, 'Good luck, Jimmy,' and the room broke into a round of applause. Sam and I headed outside into the sunshine, to the concourse overlooking the MCG's famous turf.

I remembered taking Sam to the centre of the MCG very early in our relationship and kissing her in the quiet darkness after playing a match, on our way to the car. I suspect it meant more to me than her at the time but it was a very fond memory for me.

I didn't know when I would be back there again.

7

UNDER THE KNIFE

I didn't have a hell of a lot of experience with surgery. A couple of ankle operations after my football career were about all I had to go on. Now they were going to cut me open like a Christmas turkey.

Regardless of the type of cancer, Graeme Southwick believed surgery was the best way forward. The theory was what he described as 'cell reduction therapy', whereby you keep the number of cancer cells in the body as low as possible, so that the body can combat whatever cells might remain. 'But it's no small operation,' he warned. 'We will have to open up your ribs. It will take several hours.'

Graeme had to find a thoracic surgeon – a specialist in chest/lung surgery – who was prepared to take on the operation. Several candidates were reluctant, given how far the secondary cancer had spread in my body. Their response was, 'What's the point? Just use medication or radiation to keep the cells in check.' But eventually Graeme found a willing young cardiothoracic surgeon, Randall Moshinsky.

For the past few days I had lost myself in planning how to

make the news public. Now that the hullabaloo of the media conference was over, the only thing on the horizon was the next day's surgery.

We sat down to dinner as a family that night. The kids were so gentle and restrained, knowing I was heading into hospital the next morning. At times I would find myself not eating, just watching them and grinning.

Wayne and Jules were with me for the short drive to Cabrini Hospital, so that Sam could remain at home and look after the kids. I was nervous as we pulled into the car park, but I also felt wired, like I was about to enter the changing rooms ahead of a huge game of football. Except with significantly more at stake.

I grabbed my phone. 'Have a look at this,' I said. 'I've got 264 messages.'

Wayne has the capacity to cut through the nonsense and make some thoroughly logical observations. 'Why aren't you opening any of them?' he asked. 'You realise they're all going to be from people offering their support, don't you?'

I told him I would read them while I was lying in my hospital room after the operation.

'Just open one,' he said. 'Random.'

To humour him, I scrolled down and opened a message. It was from one of the Melbourne players, Jack Watts. 'He's wishing me all the best and thanking me. Says that when I'm around people, they leave feeling better about themselves.'

'There you go,' Wayne smiled, chuffed to have proved his point.

'Pretty mature effort from an eighteen-year-old,' I said. 'I don't know that I would have been thinking like that at his age. I have a feeling this kid will captain Melbourne one day.'

After being admitted to hospital, I had a few hours to wait until surgery. Wayne and Jules were the perfect people to keep my mind off the scalpel. The fifteen-year-old smart-aleck Jules had now grown into a more socially acceptable thirty-year-old smart-aleck. Like many of the Reach Crew from the early days, Jules held a special place in my heart. He had become a facilitator of some of our programs and had also forged a career in radio and television. Despite his celebrity status, I loved that he knew how to stay grounded but still have fun.

Jules brought a camcorder along, recording footage that would later be used to make the documentary *Every Heart Beats True*. Mucking around and laughing was the perfect way to take my mind off the operation. We arrived in the hospital room like three naughty schoolboys who had managed to sneak out of assembly.

There were all sorts of menial tasks that had to be done before I was ready for surgery, and for some reason we found them all hilarious. One source of mirth was the bed, which was standard-issue size. When I lay on it I ran out of bed at my ankles. There was much laughter and a king-size bed was sought.

I had to supply a urine sample, and I remember offering the other two a drink, because it was better than anything they could buy on the black market. Then I had to take off my shirt so that a nurse could hook up half a dozen electrodes between my chest and a monitor.

'Look at him,' Jules chirped. 'He's so vain! He's still trying to flex his muscles. You know, you've got a Bondi body. That's a Bondi chest – because it's far from Manly.'

After she had finished, the nurse handed me an electric razor so I could shave my chest to prepare for the surgery. While I removed the small clump of hair on my chest, Jules appeared in the bathroom with his camcorder. I told him I had never shaved my chest before, prompting him to counter, 'Yeah, well, you'll never go back now – you'll be doing this for the rest of your life.' The other subject of great mirth for the boys was the ridiculous fishnet underpants that I had to wear during surgery; it felt like putting your groceries into a string bag.

I was ready for the operation. In the back of my mind were Graeme's reassuring words about people who were best placed to cope with substantial operations such as this. They were mentally strong, had a fierce desire to live, had good support around them and were physically fit. He had told me to remember that I ticked all of those boxes.

When he had visited me before surgery, Graeme had urged me to think about something that made me smile. 'Think of Ireland,' he suggested.

As I reclined on the trolley, ready to be wheeled towards the theatre, I was summoning happy thoughts.

'You should see the crap I'm going to write on your head

when you pass out,' Jules laughed.

I smiled. 'Hey, Jules – this is the same theatre where they operated on Kylie Minogue.'

Within moments I was fast asleep, without even a moment to think about the surgery ahead.

If I had died on the operating table, then this must be heaven, because I could hear delightful laughter drifting down to greet me. But no, after more than six hours of surgery – which included removing the upper lobe of my right lung, as well as cutting into my back and my right thigh – I groggily peered up from my bed to see Sam, smiling and talking to a nurse. It was great to open my eyes to see that beautiful face.

'I think he's awake.' Sam clasped my hand. As my eyes began to focus on my surrounds, it became clear that hers was not the only familiar face in the room. Over there was Mam. To her side, my sisters. Friends. The Reach Crew. Old football teammates. Even a few of the lunatic fringe from the old neighbourhood in Ireland. All in photographs, printed in colour and plastered on the wall of my hospital room.

'What's this?' I managed in a raspy voice.

Sam nodded towards my laptop. 'Jules.'

Apparently, Jules had been fiddling around with my laptop computer while I was under. The idea had come to him to get some of the photographs printed out and mounted on boards. It was an incredibly generous gesture. How special I felt, waking up surrounded by love.

Then it dawned on me: the operation was over. The tumours had been cut out. Easy. There wasn't even any pain; the epidural had done its job.

I looked down at my body and got a shock at how many tubes and wires were hanging out of me. Some of them were going places where no man wants to have things hanging out of him. One clear tube – a surgical drain – wouldn't have looked out of place hosing plants in the garden. My skin had a weird yellowish hue, which I found out was tincture of iodine, a disinfectant. I was a mess.

But I didn't care. I was thinking about being cancer-free.

That lasted until the following morning, when my surgeon visited to see how I was recovering. The operation had gone as well as could be expected, but there was an issue with a couple of suspect cells that he wanted to remove. He needed to go back in, although it would be a relatively brief procedure. He would get me back into the operating theatre the next day, which was Sunday. It was more frustrating than anything else. The pain was quite manageable.

That afternoon, Wayne dropped in and we watched the broadcast of Melbourne taking on West Coast at the MCG. We had only managed to win one of our thirteen games for the season, but the Eagles were a mid-table team and the commentators were talking up the chances of a Melbourne win. There was considerable discussion about the emotion of the past week and how it would motivate the players. There was a nice touch before the game from the cheer squad, who had 'Get well Jimmy' written on their massive crepe-paper banner.

When the match got underway the Melbourne players seemed to play with a real intensity, and we ended up kicking our highest score of the season. It also made me smile that Mark Jamar, a ruckman coming back from injury, put in a strong game. After Melbourne's twenty-point win, our captain, James McDonald, and teammate Aaron Davey held up my old woollen number thirty-seven jumper like a banner and carried it from the field in a show of support. I was delighted, not least because I thought the team had shown real spirit after some recent insipid losses. It was the sort of win that could give a season momentum, and it would certainly keep the media off the players' backs for a while.

Once my football diversion was over, though, it was back to contemplating more surgery. Perhaps because I had hours to lie there and think about it this time, I was more nervous. Next to my bed was one of those monitors that beeps and needs to be checked every hour, and I struggled to sleep through the night.

The next day, a few cases of emergency surgery pushed my operation back by five hours. After they did get me in and completed the second operation, I woke up with my shoulder and arm in agony. It felt like there was something pinching a nerve; every time I tried to straighten my arm, it was as though there was an electric shock to my wrist. What's more, the garden hose sticking out of me was beginning to feel like a red-hot poker. I was constantly wincing and reaching for

Dublin

I had a blessed childhood. I was happy, healthy, resilient and surrounded by a large, loving family.

Apart from role models like my parents and Uncle Joe, the biggest influence on my life was sport. Not only was it an outlet for my excess energy, it was tremendous for my self-esteem.

Melbourne

I arrived in Melbourne
in November 1984 and
played senior footy in 1987.

September 1987

This was the lowest I had ever felt in my life, after costing Melbourne a place in the Grand Final. Coach John Northey bellowed, 'Don't you ever effing do that again!'

1988 I made a commitment to myself not to be remembered as the man who ran across the mark. Whether I was on the track or playing, I gave it my all.

1997

Sam accompanied me to the 1997 Brownlow Medal night – back then, she was my girlfriend.

1998   I played in eight International Rules matches (five for Australia and three for Ireland) in 1987, 1990 and 1998.

Family

Sam and I got married in 2000. My brother Brian and my great friends Warwick Green and John 'Chippy' Kernan, who I grew up with, were the groomsmen. Matisse was born in 2001 and Tiernan in 2005.

the button on the morphine drip.

By Monday, the pain had eased, although I nearly passed out when the nurses tried to help me get out of the bed. On Tuesday my challenge was to use a bedpan in a meaningful way for the first time. Sam stood up to leave the room. 'Honey, I love you and you can rely on me to help you whenever, but I think you're on your own with this one.'

I also began to realise that because I was struggling to swallow any food, I was dropping weight – and I didn't have a lot lying around in the first place.

Wednesday began much the same way, but by the end of it I was describing it as the worst day of my life. As the morning wore on, the pain around my shoulder blade started to drive me insane; it reminded me of the agony of a bulging disc. My suffering was so intense that, at times, I had to just lie there with my face twisted, unable to open my eyes. My brother Brian, Jules and a few other friends visited that day. Through gritted teeth I asked them to lean me forward and hold me there. It was only position that seemed to help the pain. The fantastic Cabrini nurses were trying everything they could to assist, but to no avail.

'Can we please give him a higher dose?' Sam pleaded. But they were worried about 'respiratory distress'. It was not a term familiar to me, but to be honest I didn't care if there was going to be respiratory distress or a damsel in distress – I could not go on for much longer. 'You're going to have to knock me out or I'll pass out,' I groaned.

After four hours in which the nurses did their absolute best, an anaesthetist arrived and agreed to inject some local anaesthetic into my back. There was almost instant relief. 'It's like that scene in *Pulp Fiction*, where John Travolta stabs a shot of adrenaline into Uma Thurman's heart,' Jules chuckled.

Sam was concerned enough by the incident to organise a schedule of friends to conduct twenty-four-hour surveillance. My old Melbourne teammate Anthony Ingerson got the graveyard shift. We ended up having a deep and meaningful discussion, well into the night. I felt sorry for him the next morning when, after only four hours of broken sleep, he had to head off to a busy day at work in the building trade.

At least he didn't disgrace himself like some, though. Another mate, Hugh Ellis, passed out on the stretcher bed and snored so loudly that he woke me up.

During his shift, Wayne decided to entertain me with a few impersonations. One of the night nurses came in twice to suggest that he was being a touch rowdy. After the third time he was kicked out. Even in my drug-induced state I had a little chortle. There's a cliché about laughter being the best medicine. Sometimes, if you ignore the fact that they get over-used, clichés make a lot of sense.

Don't underestimate how liberating it is for a patient to be able to get out of bed again, even if it is just to totter across the room. I began to start walking as much as I could, shuffling around in my hospital gown. Six days after that second operation, it felt like a triumph when I made it to the hospital café with a friend one morning, even if they had to bring me back in a wheelchair.

On the seventh day I made it to the hospital chapel, where I rested . . . and nodded off to sleep. When I woke up, there was someone sitting next to me. I was a bit vague because of the medication, but after about thirty seconds I realised that it was one of the Reach graduates, Harley Webster. He had forged a career as a hiphop artist, known as Phrase, and his music was a long way removed from what was being played during that small service in the chapel.

I smiled at him, pleased to see his face for the first time in a while. I leaned across and mischievously whispered, 'So, how long since you've been in church?'

He suppressed a laugh, then whispered back, 'I can't remember – I don't even know if I have been to church before.'

It made me smile for the rest of the day.

When I returned home after ten days in hospital, there were three large boxes of letters and parcels in the front room. Over the next few days I began to sift through them. There were get-well cards, letters of support, inspirational quotes. It was so uplifting. Drawings from kids who had obviously sat down and thought about how they could cheer up a sick person. The vast majority of this mail was from people I had never met, and I was profoundly touched that so many cared enough to go to that effort.

There were parcels with self-addressed envelopes from people who wanted signatures on football cards, photos and jumpers. I signed many of them, trusting that they were from people with genuine, not mercenary, motives. There was a great deal of religious material, some of which made its way to a mantelpiece in our bedroom, which Sam jokingly referred to as 'the shrine'. There was holy water that had been blessed by the Pope.

One item that intrigued me – and moved me deeply – was a bottle of Aboriginal bush medicine, sent in from Yuendumu, a remote community in central Australia. One of Melbourne's footballers, Liam Jurrah, was an initiated member of the Warlpiri people, whose largest community is at Yuendumu. Many of the parcels included books or DVDs, potions and products, with suggestions about the best way to tackle cancer. Increasingly, I found that many people I spoke to had advice on the issue – such as a story about how an uncle or a sister had been diagnosed and followed a certain group's advice to make a dramatic recovery. I found them all fascinating, but really I was becoming more and more confused.

No doubt this is one of the most difficult stages for anyone diagnosed with cancer. You start to get your head around the fact that you've got it, and then you hear so much conflicting advice about how to deal with it. I recalled Adam Ramanauskas's counsel about becoming well informed, and then deciding who you are going to take advice from and sticking with them. It made sense, and he had lived it. Logically, I realised, listening to others who had first-hand experience also would be beneficial.

One name that kept coming up was Ian Gawler, the Melbourne man who had founded a cancer group in 1981. Ian's story was remarkable. He was a veterinary surgeon and decathlete who developed bone cancer (osteogenic sarcoma), which had forced doctors to amputate his leg at the hip in 1975. But the cancer had returned later that year, spreading to lymph nodes in his pelvis and chest. Ian had adopted an intense program of personal development, including meditation and a strict diet.

By the early part of 1976 Ian was expected to live for only a few weeks, but he recovered to be cancer-free by 1978. He now lived with his wife, Ruth, in Yarra Junction and was therapeutic director of the Gawler Foundation, which offered various forms of support to people with cancer and other serious illnesses.

I contacted Ian and he was gracious enough to visit me at home. We sat together and chatted for nearly three hours, discussing a broad sweep of issues. Ian had a simple approach and it made a lot of sense. He was not too 'out there' or fanatical, he was simply a true believer in meditation and a diet based around raw food, grains, vegetables and fruit. He also was a big advocate for getting plenty of sleep.

He didn't push me in a certain direction but just explained what had worked in his experience. Like Adam, he encouraged me to find an approach I was comfortable with, and to then believe in it to the hilt. 'When you embrace what you do,' he said, 'you release all the positive potential of your mind, emotions and spirit.'

In the month or so that I had been living with cancer, there had been two times when I had managed to find some clarity in my thinking: while down at Rye with the family, and while away at the ashram. The obvious conclusion was that escaping the clamour and the distractions of daily life was conducive to clarity of mind.

It was not just a matter of easing back my workload. Life in the Stynes family was like any busy household – appointments to keep, running around after young kids, endless phone calls, shopping, bills. I also could not detach myself from checking what was going on at my various workplaces: the Melbourne Football Club, Reach and the Pelican and Penguin childcare centres. Now I also had doctors and specialists to visit, treatments to undertake, and an overhauled diet to follow, which required more planning and cleaning up (albeit often by Sam) than I had expected. In that environment, it was not easy finding time to relax and to think.

Sam and I discussed getting away, to give us all some mental and emotional space, and so that I could start to heal. It felt like a new dawn. I was daring to believe that if I made all the necessary changes, the cancer would not come back. Maybe the past month would become life's tap on my shoulder, the one that told me worse times were ahead unless I listened to my body and spirit. I was convinced that I would one day look back and see this experience as the greatest thing that had ever happened to me.

Physically, my body was recovering well from the surgery. It felt like I had a chest full of broken ribs but the pain was manageable. Naturally, though, I began to push it, and I paid the price. Part of my rehabilitation program was to lift some light weights. I overdid it one day and ended up with referred pain in my right pectoral muscle. That night I could barely sleep; it felt like someone was torching me every time I tried to move.

A fresh round of tissue samples from my tumours had been sent to leading pathologists for a variety of tests, in the hope that we might understand more accurately the nature of the cancer, and which chemotherapy drugs, if required, and other therapies might suit my diagnosis. But there were no definitive answers by the time the family boarded a plane for Thailand in late July.

It only took a few days in Phuket for the tension to drain out of me. The kids were loving going for a swim every day. If you make a list of the things that give you an instant surge of pure happiness, it is hard to go past hearing your children laugh freely. I thought about the busy world I had constructed back in Melbourne. Was it as important as hearing these children laugh more often?

When you have time to think, cancer is an accommodating subject. It is a vast universe of questions and theories. I had time for many of these to bounce around in my head while I recovered, but for all the confusion, there was one mantra that resonated: 'Healthy people have many goals, the sick only have one.' What did I need to do to heal, and to help stop any more tumours from appearing?

I knew that I wanted to keep the changes to my diet, and I knew that I wanted to meditate more often. Those were easy decisions to make; it was simply a matter of executing them. But what about the rest of my lifestyle? Should I just walk away from it and lead a quiet life? I wondered how much of what I did was being driven by a need to fuel my ego.

Many AFL footballers miss the adrenaline rush and the adulation after they retire. I had been fortunate to have Reach as a way of weaning myself off football. It had been a place where I could redirect my energy and still feel relevant. But I knew that my main motivation behind Reach was altruistic: to make a difference to young people's lives. If it had been about ego, there were high-profile jobs in business or the media that would have met that need.

But now there was also the Melbourne presidency. I had not sought the job in the first place, and I had total confidence that the board would carry the transformation through. Together we had achieved so much in just over a year. Nobody would have an issue with my standing down. But did I have an issue with that prospect? Being away from the bustle of the AFL environment was the perfect chance to think about this and make a decision, especially since I had so much time to reflect while the rest of the family was at the beach or out shopping.

One morning, after returning from a meditation class, I lay on the bed and flicked on a movie. There is a saying that sometimes you don't pick a book, a book picks you, and the same may have been true about this film. It was called *The Express* and was based on the life of Ernie Davis, who in 1961 became the first African-American player to win the Heisman Trophy, awarded to the best player in American college football. Davis was a running back who overcame overt discrimination in the American south to become a star player with Syracuse University.

At the end of the 1961 season Davis was taken as the National Football League's number-one draft pick, by Washington. Yet the Redskins, who had never before had a black player on their roster, immediately traded him to the Cleveland Browns. Before he was able to play a professional game, however, he was diagnosed with leukaemia. Soon afterwards there was an emotional scene in which the Browns introduced Davis to an ovation from the fans at Cleveland Stadium during a 1962 pre-season game. Within twelve months he had died, at age twenty-three. The powerful moments of the film centred on how Davis influenced attitudes towards racism not only in football but in American society more broadly.

As you can imagine, I was quite emotional while watching the film. Rather than dwelling on Davis's illness, though, I found myself wondering how I could take something from the film that would make Melbourne a better football club. I was thinking about the fantastic Indigenous players we had on our list – there were six at the time – and the difference they could make in their own communities, let alone in the wider context. Melbourne had something special with those footballers; there had to be a way to nurture their leadership skills and create some kind of pioneering program, something special.

As the days passed and my ribs and wounds healed, my mind was drifting back to the football club more often. I knew that a crucial fundraiser, the Foundation Heroes dinner, was approaching. It had been a function I really wanted to attend, and in any correspondence back home I kept sniffing around for clues about how preparations were progressing. When I learned that the evening had raised more than $700000, I embarked on a whole new flurry of phone and email exchanges. All the reports were that Garry Lyon had delivered an inspirational speech; I began to feel miffed that I'd missed the function. I was becoming restless.

There were only a handful of games left in the season. Melbourne was on the bottom of the ladder, and the major discussion point was whether we would receive a 'priority pick', an extra selection in the end-of-season national player draft. These were used to assist teams that had performed poorly over consecutive seasons. To qualify, Melbourne could win no more than four matches.

At that stage we had won three, which made for a peculiar situation. I was sitting in Thailand hoping to have my spirits boosted by the team performing well, but at the same time hoping we would hang on to that extra draft pick.

There is incessant controversy in the football world about teams that find themselves in this situation, and whether they deliberately try to stay under the threshold of four-and-a-half wins. Some claim that teams conspire to lose, which is known in AFL circles as 'tanking'.

Melbourne never sat down our coach, Dean Bailey, and instructed him not to win games. But he, I and everybody at the club knew what an important bearing on the club's future that extra draft pick might have. People at the club found themselves shrouded in that reality. It went against the grain to find solace in failure, but that was the system in place.

I do not agree with the AFL's priority pick rules; I see them as being fundamentally flawed. The system was intended to even out the competition, but the process does not always work and effectively questions people's integrity. Teams that are genuinely in trouble are faced with a disincentive to win. I do not believe clubs should get extra draft picks based purely on how many wins – or, more to point, losses – they get in a season.

In my view, a whole range of factors should be taken into consideration, such as the number of wins over three to five seasons, how much revenue the club is generating, and membership and sponsorship levels. If a club is in trouble, based on that holistic evidence, the AFL could then use its judgement or a broader set of guidelines to award a priority pick. But it certainly shouldn't set a target before the season and give a club a disincentive to win.

As it was, the system in place had an AFL club president, who should have been twitchy with the anticipation of an upset win, messaging friends at the ground, wondering if his club was going to lose that day. The Demons were facing North Melbourne at the MCG. My phone would beep: 'Martin goal. Demons 4pts down qr tm.' I'd wait a few minutes and then text someone else, asking for a score. Another beep: '10pts down 2nd q.' Soon I had more beeps coming in than I could keep up with, and it was becoming clear that Melbourne would not win.

The ten-goal margin was deflating, but later that evening there was good news: second-bottom team Fremantle had won, making it ineligible for a priority pick. It was now possible that we might end up with the first two selections in the national draft.

My mind was finding something other than cancer to keep it occupied. The better I felt, the more restless I became, and the more I wanted to get back to work. But on what terms? Could I be busy and not get stressed? Should I get involved gradually or should I take on specific roles, such as running Reach's Crew training, doing selected talks, trying to generate a bit of enthusiasm around the new set of written values we'd introduced in our childcare centres. Then there was the timing: should I begin when I returned to Australia or wait until next year?

I had set out on this healing time in Thailand fairly certain that I would significantly scale back all of my roles, and relinquish the Melbourne presidency. I had been pretty sure that doing so would allow me to channel all of my energy into staying alive. But what I had come to realise was how important it was for me to have a purpose in life.

I wanted to spend more time with my family, I wanted less stress in my days, but I could not simply stop having a purpose. With the unqualified support of Don McLardy and the rest of the football club's board, I decided to stay involved at Melbourne and, at the same time, keep a balance that allowed me to concentrate on my health. The Melbourne presidency was giving me a purpose and genuine enjoyment. I began to believe that I needed the role to help keep me alive.

8

WHITE COATS

'Definitely melanoma,' Graeme Southwick declared. Some tissue that was excised during my surgery had been sent to the Harvard Cancer Center in Boston. There, Professor Christopher Fletcher, an expert pathologist and the world's leading authority on spindle cell tumours, had determined, beyond doubt, that we were dealing with melanoma.

So it was skin cancer. Bloody hell. I immediately remembered all those times when, as a young man, I'd stripped off my top at footy training or the beach, thinking I was invincible. The stinging skin. All for a tan. Nothing more. Vanity. And what did that tan mean in my life now? How was it going to help me? There were still people who thought sunbathing was worth the risk. You would see them down at St Kilda beach. If they understood what I was feeling now, they would pick up their towels and head home.

'So you're telling me this cancer was caused by being out in the sun,' I said flatly.

Graeme explained that they still could not say definitively whether the primary cancer had originated from a skin lesion or whether the cancer had first appeared in the lungs and then metastasised – or spread – from there. He said there had only been fifty-two cases of the latter type recorded worldwide, so it seemed unlikely.

'The bottom line,' he continued, 'is that you're an Irishman with a fair complexion, a large number of moles and pale eyes, and you've been exposed to the sun. I think any theory about it being caused by the sun would be the safe bet.'

This news took a while to sink in. As it did, I began to think about ways to turn it into a positive. At least we now knew precisely what we were up against, and which treatments would be most effective, which specialists to seek out. Graeme explained that treatments such as targeted radiation, chemotherapy or immune-system therapy might come into the frame later. But he maintained that surgery had been the appropriate starting point: cutting out as many malignant cells as possible would give my body every chance to combat what, if any, problem cells were left. In the meantime, it was a matter of waiting and concentrating on my diet, meditation, exercise and relaxation to get my body as healthy as possible.

There was a gardening analogy: you picked all the weeds you could, making sure you got their roots so that they wouldn't grow back. If any other weeds appeared, you pulled them out too. But I also had to treat the soil, feed it organically. I had to hope that the healthy plants would crowd out the weeds.

My chest had recovered well from the surgery, and I had started to regain weight. There were times when I felt unusually lethargic during the day, but I rarely felt down in the dumps. Overall, my attitude was very upbeat; it seemed to me that I had turned the corner.

There was more to it than my own outlook, though. Now, when I was out in public, most people knew I had cancer. Some brought it up in conversation and showed genuine concern, and that did not bother me. Sometimes it was quite touching to know how much people cared. Yet, inescapably, it felt different, sometimes awkward, being around people.

Having cancer is never far from your thoughts, and I guess I became a little paranoid that it was never far from anybody else's thoughts when they were around me. If two people were standing over to one side talking discreetly, I might get it in my head that they were talking about me. At times, I found my mind was not as sharp as it had been, which was frustrating and undermined my confidence. There were times when I struggled with migraines – mostly, I noticed, during and after exercise.

But of my new insecurities, by far the most acute was the fear that the cancer would reappear. The tumours had been cut out and I was convinced that I would be cancer-free. But any little niggle, any little ache, bump or blemish on my skin, now preyed on that insecurity, creating doubt that the cause might be something more sinister.

So it was incredibly deflating when, while having a swim in the ocean one morning in early September, I noticed that a lump had appeared in the hollow next to my collarbone. Shortly afterwards, another became obvious on my neck – tellingly, it was in a spot where doctors had suspected there might be a tumour in the original scans but could not be sure. I refused to let these new concerns get me down, though. I needed to stay positive. These might end up being short-term setbacks, but my belief that, in the long term, I would be fine remained.

I was not surprised that Graeme insisted the two lumps had to come out. Armed with the knowledge that my cancer was definitely melanoma, he also took the opportunity to closely examine every centimetre of my skin, even checking my eyes. He was looking for pigmented lesions – discoloured or suspect moles or skin blemishes – that might provide a clue about the primary source of my cancer. 'There is an unusual mole on your calf,' he said. 'When you come in to have these lymph glands out, we'll cut that out too and have a look at it.'

My plan to stay tumour-free had lasted just two months, then. By mid-September I was back in Cabrini Hospital again, recovering from an operation and with tubes hanging out of me. Graeme had removed the two lumps, as well as another thirteen lymph glands from my neck. A few hours after the surgery, I remembered that they had also taken the mole off my calf. Ultimately, the tests came back negative, meaning the primary source of my cancer remained unknown.

Sam asked Max Schwarz what the chances were that I would get more tumours. 'I would say ninety per cent,' he replied, 'but when and where, we will never know.'

The fact that I had come out of this latest round of surgery relatively pain-free, however, boosted my morale and strengthened my belief that I was getting on top of cancer. It would not break my spirit.

Two episodes that weekend reinforced for me that there was no value in feeling sorry for myself. Also in the hospital was a five-year-old, Sam, who was having brain tumours removed. If it was tough taking on cancer at age forty-three, it was simply unfair to have to go through it at five. Anyone looking for some perspective will find it by the truckload if they meet children with cancer and watch what their parents go through, and how they find a remarkable courage deep within themselves.

Another reminder of what the human spirit can endure came the day after I was discharged from hospital. The AFL rang and wondered if I was up to escorting Prime Minister Kevin Rudd to the Yarra Valley Mountain District League's Grand Final, which was to be held at Woori Yallock, about fifty-five kilometres east of Melbourne. The match, between the Kinglake and the Olinda–Ferny Creek football clubs, was to be played in the long shadow cast by the Black Saturday bushfires seven months earlier. The tragedy had claimed the lives of forty-two Kinglake townspeople and had destroyed more than 500 homes. Just nine days after the bushfires, about 150 Kinglake locals had gathered on the scorched oval and determined that the town's football and netball teams would not become further victims of the flames. The wider football community had rallied around the Lakers. The

Melbourne Football Club had donated training jumpers, boots and balls, and had established a relationship with King-lake. Now here they were in a Grand Final, which meant so much to the community, and to the whole state. I decided to attend, and I was glad I did.

The club president, Cameron Caine, was a no-nonsense local policeman who had helped people escape from the flames during Black Saturday, only to face even darker days in the aftermath. He had the gruesome task of discovering many of the deceased, and having to break the news to family and friends.

At the Grand Final, he told journalists, 'The footy club kept us going. Living in amongst it all day, every day, you need something else to think about and talk about. The footy club has given us something to grasp on to . . . Now we can move on.'

He told the story of a local woman, Carole, who had lost her husband, Garry, a Lakers life member, to cancer twelve months before Black Saturday. The money she had been saving in a jar for Garry's headstone had been destroyed in the fires.

At the Grand Final, I met people who had lost daughters, husbands and brothers. They had every reason to wallow in grief but the day was marked by a fierce optimism, even the odd hint of humour. In the end, the Lakers conceded a couple of late goals to lose the match by six points. But it was one of the most uplifting experiences of my life, an incredibly powerful day.

Many of these people had experienced more suffering

than I could comprehend. But I could relate to what they showed me that day: never let your spirit be crushed.

Being in such a positive frame of mind would be incredibly important in the weeks ahead. In fact, the next few weeks would totally revolve around what was going on inside my head.

I began to be troubled by some ferocious headaches. I'd had relatively mild dizzy spells before, but nothing like this. These were debilitating. One afternoon, while on the phone, I began to struggle badly with blurred vision. As I was talking on the phone, I became unable to find the words I was searching for, and when I did, they came out all jumbled. I was incoherent, like a diabetic whose blood-sugar levels are desperately low. I excused myself, hung up and went to lie down. Sam was distraught, especially because for the next five minutes I continued to struggle to speak. It felt like I was having some kind of stroke; my brain just would not function properly, as though its wires were all crossed.

When things settled down I rang my doctors, who expressed concern and advised me to take it easy until my next series of scans. Looking back on it now, I suspect they must have had fears about more tumours but were reluctant to present a pessimistic forecast. Despite their advice to scale things back, though, I continued to take on more. After all, it was still just a fraction of what I'd done before cancer came into my life.

I found that when I stewed on something for days, it had a tendency to drag me down. If I could get the concern, whatever it might be, out into the open, I moved on quicker. In some instances, that might mean talking to Sam, or a friend, or a work colleague. I enjoyed going out on bike rides, not just for the exercise but also because they gave me opportunities to talk with whoever was along for the ride. Often it was my old housemate Michael Scott, who is a great listener.

At other times I dumped all my feelings down in a diary entry on my laptop. I also opened a Twitter account; not only did it seem to work as another outlet, but it was also a good way to keep people informed about what was going on in my life, as I had promised I would.

The problem was that I was increasingly struggling with words. Reading the simplest text was impossible; it was such a weird experience. I found myself repeating things I had already said. At one point I spent an hour trying to write one line on Twitter. I couldn't remember facts, and when I talked to doctors I couldn't comprehend parts of what they were telling me. When I spoke, I felt like I had a fraction of my vocabulary to draw upon, which was incredibly frustrating. It also could be embarrassing.

I attended the Brownlow Medal, and although the condition was not too debilitating that night, I did feel like there were times when I struggled to speak properly. I suppose footballers do struggle to speak as Brownlow night wears on, as Carlton full-forward Brendan Fevola proved very publicly that year. In any case, whenever possible I sought to stay away from group conversations because they tended to befuddle me.

I noticed my mental struggle most when I agreed to speak at a Melbourne past players' function. When I got up to speak I could barely remember basic details about teammates, seasons, even the names of the other teams in the AFL. I forgot to mention my old mate Anthony McDonald, who had done a brilliant job re-energising the past players' association in his role as president. Apparently, a couple of people there wondered whether it was meant as a snub.

Basic life skills were becoming increasingly difficult. It got to the point where I struggled to use my mobile phone; it felt too intense for my brain to cope with all the buttons, the letters, the functions. I stopped using it unless I had to, which was not a bad thing anyway. But clearly this could not go on.

I was due to go in for fresh scans a few days after the 2009 AFL Grand Final, which was played between Geelong and St Kilda on the last Saturday in September. I hoped the tests would provide an answer about what was going on with my head, but I was also praying that no more dark spots would show up on any of the images.

That Tuesday was intense. It began with a PET scan at 7 am that went for nearly three hours. After that came another hour spent having an MRI scan (in which radio waves are used to produce images of the internal organs). Next was an intravenous dose of vitamin C. By 12.30 pm I was lying on a treatment table while Graeme Southwick removed stitches from my leg.

While I was there, Graeme was handed the results from the scans, which came through much faster than I had expected. He had good news: the PET showed no new tumours in my body. Awesome. Then the bad news: there was a suspicious dark area showing up on the scan of my head. A brain tumour. That would explain why I was struggling with my speech and reading. I would most likely need some targeted radiation treatment, in which high-powered rays are aimed at the tumour. But it would be a couple of days before we could work out the best way to proceed. First, I had to consult the brain specialists.

Given the difficulties I had been experiencing, this latest development did not come as a huge shock, but it was certainly a setback to know that the cancer had spread to a new area of my body, especially one so fragile and vital as the brain. The hope was that the brain tumour could be treated without surgery, at least to reduce it in order to make it easier to cut out.

For the first time, the challenge began to engulf me, but I was determined not to let myself be overwhelmed. If I could not control what was happening inside my body, I had to try to control what was going on inside my mind. I had to be impossibly optimistic, push these thoughts somewhere out of the way and get on with healing. I was reluctant to discuss any dark thoughts with others, in case they created a new reality: one in which my health was doomed to deteriorate.

Ever since I revealed I had cancer, my mate Michael Scott had been sending me daily phone texts with affirmative messages. One of Scottie's recent texts had been a quote from the nineteenth-century English writer Edward Bulwer-Lytton, the man who had coined the phrases 'pursuit of the almighty dollar' and 'the pen is mightier than the sword', among others. This particular quote resonated with me: 'Refuse to be ill. Never tell people you are ill; never own it to yourself. Illness is one of those things which a man should resist on principle at the onset.'

Perhaps that attitude goes some way to explaining why, when the family headed down to Rye the next day, I decided to organise a bike ride with Scottie. No brain tumour was going to dictate terms to me. I grabbed my bicycle from the shed and went inside to change clothes. With the changes in my diet making an impact, I had dropped several kilograms in bodyweight and my lycra shorts looked miserably saggy. I looked down at my legs. I had never really had much in the way of calves, but now I realised there was hardly any muscle, just two long, bony limbs. Embarrassed, I slipped out of the lycra and rummaged about in the cupboard for a pair of cargo shorts.

I pedalled down to the Point Nepean Road to wait for Scottie, who had come across on the ferry from Queenscliff, and we set out along the coast. A few kilometres up the road, at Dromana, we decided to take on the steep little climb up to Arthurs Seat. Although you only ascend about 300 metres above sea level, it is a challenge for recreational cyclists.

About three-quarters of the way up, Scottie and I stopped for a breather and had a long chat while we took in the sweeping views. 'Come on,' I urged him after a spell, 'we have to make it to the top.' We scaled the peak and rolled the twenty kilometres – mostly downhill – back home.

That evening, as I sat there in my imaginary red-polka-dot jersey, revelling in my achievement, my body began to punish me for overreaching. My skull felt like it was in a vice, and gradually my vision and speech began to desert me. After a couple of phone calls seeking medical advice, Sam was told to call an ambulance.

By midnight, Sam and a bleary-eyed, pyjama-clad Tiernan (Matisse was at a sleepover) were sitting in the emergency department at Rosebud Hospital, waiting for an ambulance to transport me back to Melbourne. Apparently there was swelling on the brain – its way of telling me that I could not just ignore cancer and pretend it was not there. To combat the swelling, the doctors placed me on a steroid called dexamethasone. Worse news followed: closer examination of my scans suggested there were three tumours in my brain, not one. That made for a grand total of ten since I had been diagnosed.

Over the next twelve months, doctors would treat me with almost every known cancer treatment available to conventional medicine: radiation, surgery, chemotherapy, immunology. It began with a visit to the radiologist.

You would think someone who had lived with cancer for a few months would have a bit of an understanding of radiation therapy, but I didn't really know what to expect. Fortunately, Gail Ryan, a radiation oncologist from the state-of-the-art facility at Epworth Hospital, gave me a comprehensive explanation. Because we were now dealing with multiple brain tumours, she told me, as well as the possibility of more hidden spots, they wanted to begin with radiation treatment for the whole brain, followed by specific spot-beam therapy later on. For that, I would need to wear a specially made immobilisation mask, which would keep my head perfectly still.

The side-effects, which I was told might develop a couple of weeks after treatment began, could include hair loss, itchy skin and general fatigue. Also, there was likely to be more swelling of the brain.

I listened carefully to Gail, who also debunked several of the common misconceptions about radiotherapy. One was the nonsensical myth that you should not share food with your family straight after treatment because you were temporarily radioactive.

'Do you have any questions?' she asked eventually. As much as it embarrassed me to raise it, the one query that came to mind was about losing my hair. Gail was not fazed, and with a gentle smile observed that it was probably the most commonly asked question. Hair loss might begin about two weeks after the first session, usually in the area being treated. Hair might fall out in clumps, but it was usually temporary and would begin to grow back within weeks of the last session. Curiously, the new growth might not be the same texture or colour as my original hair. 'I've always wanted to shave my head for a charity,' I said, 'but I've never had the guts to do it. Probably too vain. Well, it looks like I won't have any choice now.'

Everyone has some sort of insecurity when they look in the bathroom mirror of a morning: maybe you pull in your gut, wish your nose were not so crooked, curse those wrinkles under your eyes. For cancer patients, who are already feeling particularly vulnerable, losing your hair feels like a cruel flashing neon sign telling the world about your insecurities. You feel like cancer is taunting you: *Now that I've punched you to the ground, I'm going to give you the odd kick to the ribs as well.* But the more I thought about it, the more I welcomed the idea of a side-effect that could be fixed with something as simple as an electric razor.

What was concerning me more was the way my moods were being affected by the steroid medication. The dexamethasone was disrupting my sleep; worse than that, though, it was also making me angry – an irrational anger that I did not feel I could control.

'What's going on?' Sam had demanded one morning. 'Lately you're looking for a fight all the time.'

This was never more obvious than when Sam drove me to my first radiation session in the first week of October. She knew how to get to the hospital, yet I kept barking directions from the passenger's seat. The more agitated I became, the harder I found it to explain myself properly. In the end, I had to get out of the car en route and take a few deep breaths to calm down.

The doctors had ordered me not to drive for a month in case I had a seizure, and I was finding it very hard to accept that, for the first time in my life, not only had I lost control of my world, but also it would not be a simple matter to regain it. As if to force home that point, when I arrived for the radiation treatment, Sam was advised that there was a possibility the treatment might make me depressed. I found it curious that they did not bother to mention this to me.

My first experience of the radiation therapy itself, though, went relatively smoothly. Nevertheless, it was a slightly unnerving experience. You are asked to lie back on a treatment table, and then technicians place a mesh mask over your face. This is clamped tightly to the table, leaving you feeling like you're a magician's assistant, and he's about to explain to the audience how you could not possibly escape from this securely fastened position. That's how I remained for about twenty-five minutes. Initially, I was so relaxed that I began to doze off, but then the machine started to make a bit of noise. Whether real or imaginary, I thought could smell burning and started getting nervous. I focused on my breathing and visualised pure energy. It was a relief when they unclamped the mask, but I got up from the table thinking I could manage having that sort of treatment. One down, ten to go.

Almost every day over the next fortnight I returned for another radiotherapy session. There was even room for some humour. Of course, as I was unable to move, some of my friends used the opportunity to have a few laughs at my expense. Wayne was captured in an iPhone photograph wiggling his fingers above my head like a mad scientist. I ended up posting the photograph on Twitter, complete with a caption that contained an unfortunate typographical error: 'Wayne providing some come relief', rather than 'comic relief'. He copped some ribbing over that one – then plenty more when a newspaper asked if the photo could be reproduced. He agreed, as long as his silly antics were cropped out of the picture. They weren't, and the photograph appeared full size on page three.

With mates keeping me company, I found those radiation sessions quite bearable. If anything, it just felt like a hassle knowing I would have to be back doing it again the next day. After a little while, the side-effects started to kick in. I felt flat, often nauseated, with a constant terrible metallic taste in my mouth. I generally lacked enthusiasm and still found it hard to talk to people, especially on the phone.

My emotions seemed to be extreme. One morning, while listening to some of my favourite music, tears began streaming down my cheeks as I thought of beautiful moments from the past and the future. It was actually a really cleansing experience. But if I could make sense of that, I wasn't so certain a couple of nights later when I found myself bawling like a baby towards the end of the film *Mao's Last Dancer*. Admittedly it is a beautiful film, and quite touching when the main character's parents turn up to watch him dance at the ballet – the first time they had seen him since he was eleven. But I was crying so much that I was absolutely heaving. I was just thankful there was nobody else sitting in the same row at the cinema.

To help me get through some of my low moments, I picked up the book *It's Not About the Bike*, written by champion cyclist and cancer survivor Lance Armstrong. I had devoured the book years earlier, but now I read it with a renewed fascination. Occasionally, I found it troubling that the challenges surrounding cancer seemed never-ending, even though I had only been confronting them for about four months.

The radiology course concluded and I felt energised by the knowledge I'd gained, although I knew I would need to return for a handful of more specifically targeted radiation sessions in five or six weeks. To celebrate, I was looking forward to making a public appearance for the first time in weeks, along with about 800 supporters, at the Melbourne best-and-fairest count. The morning before the function I woke up with a normal head of hair. By that night, it had started to fall out in clumps, so off it all came.

I surveyed my shaven dome. *Hmm, not too bad*, I thought. *A few battle scars, but otherwise passable*. I wondered whether I should have done it years before – a number-two cut during the searing heat of pre-season training would have been good. I remembered the summer I had worn a cap to beat the heat during pre-season matches, which had created a flurry of discussion and debate. Now, of all those scores of AFL players who had chased a football that summer, I was the one shaving my head because I was being treated for skin cancer.

I soon came to realise that a bald head becomes a very conspicuous and, in some ways, confronting reminder to people that you have cancer. Some people who already knew I had the disease now seemed slightly unnerved about the fact that there was no hair on my head. Where before they had been relatively relaxed, now they were slightly edgy. People seemed unsure of where to look, like a middle-aged man not wanting to let his eyes drop down to glance at a woman's cleavage.

I felt for those who struggled with their awkwardness, and often I attempted to puncture the tension with humour. I got lots of comments about how much the cleanskin look suited me, and a few comparisons to my brother Brian, who had been sporting a shaven head for years. I began to wonder whether people would be as complimentary about my hair-cut if I didn't have cancer. It was a relief when one of my close mates, Peter Day, laid eyes on my nude nut for the first time and declared, 'Whoa! That looks deadset shithouse! I don't reckon it's the look for you, big fella. You'll scare the kids.' For what seemed like the first time in weeks, I had a decent belly laugh. The idea of having no hair did not bother me as much after that.

When I walked into the Melbourne best-and-fairest count the next night, with cameramen rushing to capture film or photographs, I just smiled. I knew how the media worked and could understand the fascination. The only issue I had was when the media published stories or aired news items and decided that the accompanying photo should show me looking grim or miserable. It was as if they had decided I could not possibly have cancer and smile at the same time.

Eventually, I not only stopped being inhibited about being bald, I actually embraced it. One day, while visiting Challenge – a playgroup in North Melbourne specifically for children with cancer – I met a young boy who had recently been treated for a brain tumour. He drew himself up to his full height, glanced at my smooth head, and a look of satisfaction flashed across his eyes. 'You're like me,' he said.

It dawned on me that he had probably been ultra-sensitive about his lack of hair but would draw some comfort from being around other kids, even grown-ups, who were going through similar experiences. He was not so different after all. I hope that playgroup experience helped him, because it certainly helped strengthen my resolve. The more I met people who had cancer – and their families – the more I marvelled at their resilience. Because of my public profile I had been blessed with an abundance of help, support and good wishes. But there was a whole community of people facing similar struggles, all going about in a very silent, very humble way. They just got on with it and did not make a fuss.

I thought about all the times footballers visited hospitals or supported charities. Most welcomed the opportunity, while a few grumbled. Almost invariably, though, they found it humbling and gratifying. It reminded them what a gift it is to live a happy and healthy life.

The first thing that struck me about Dr Grant McArthur was his energy. It was as though he had caffeine in his veins. He bounced over to shake my hand, and spoke crisply and enthusiastically. His smile was never far away.

After it had been confirmed that my cancer was melanoma, I had been referred to Grant, an oncologist with melanoma expertise who was heavily involved in several clinical trials being conducted to treat the disease. We met on a Monday evening in late October at the Peter MacCallum Cancer Centre, the only public hospital in Australia solely devoted to cancer treatment and research.

We began with a general discussion about who was in the medical team treating me, and my personal support group of family and friends. Then we moved on to a broader discussion about melanoma. How Australia, along with New Zealand, had the world's highest incidence rate for melanoma: one in eighteen Australians gets some form of melanoma in their lifetime. But of those people, most simply had a blemish or a mole removed, and in nine out of ten cases that was the end of the matter.

I asked Grant about the fact that nobody had managed to find the primary source in my case. How had there been no tell-tale blemish or mole?

'It's not as uncommon as you might think,' he replied. 'About ten per cent of people who have secondary melanoma tumours never find out the site of origin.'

When melanoma did spread to other parts of the body, though, it became incredibly dangerous. In such cases, only about one in every ten patients was still alive three years later.

'It's a dismal statistic,' Grant said. 'But the one thing I would say about melanoma is that it's an unpredictable cancer – sometimes that's good unpredictable, and sometimes that's bad unpredictable.'

He said there had been occasional instances where melanoma patients had experienced spontaneous regression, even before treatment began. My concern, though, was that Grant was now the second oncologist who had painted a bleak picture of my prospects.

'The difficulty,' Grant said, 'is that with melanoma, once it's spread like this, we're never prepared to say you're cured. You can get to a point where you're in remission, meaning there's no evidence of it in your body, but the word "cure" is tough to use with melanoma.'

He explained that, by spreading to distant sites around my body, the melanoma was at stage four. The fact there were tumours showing up in the brain added significantly to the challenge.

'That ups the ante,' Grant said. 'Cancer is harder to control in the brain than elsewhere in the body. So that treatment needs to be a priority.'

I suggested that it sounded like I needed a miracle to survive. Was there anything working in my favour?

'Well, sometimes melanoma can be very aggressive. There can be lumps turning up everywhere. The positive thing is that this is not happening with you – and that's good because it gives you time to try other treatments. As far as the melanoma that's spread, it's in the less aggressive bracket. You're not in the no-hope category. You've still got something to work with.'

Over that initial ninety-minute consultation, Grant ran through my various treatment options. He explained that about fifty per cent of melanoma patients had a mutation in one gene – BRAF – which created a protein that made the cancer cells grow and stay alive. In such cases, doctors could use a drug to turn off the mutant protein, causing tumours to regress.

'It's been a big step in treating the disease,' he said. 'But, unfortunately, your tests show that your tumours do not have that mutation.'

He agreed with Graeme's cell-reduction philosophy, whereby you used surgery to remove as many dangerous cells as possible. 'But it might not be possible to just keep cutting them out. For example, if you were to get a tumour in the liver, or bone, or another one in the lung, the operating theatre might not really be the best option.'

Grant essentially bracketed the treatment options into three classes: radiotherapy, chemotherapy and immunology. I had already begun with radiation treatment, and I expressed an aversion to chemotherapy. To me, chemo was a way of chemically blasting your body, hoping you destroyed more bad cells than good. But the prospect of collateral damage concerned me.

Grant suggested that chemotherapy was a much-maligned therapy. The term covered a broad range of drugs, and in some cases it was the most effective treatment for particular types of cancer. 'For melanoma, there is good news and bad news with chemotherapy. The good news is that there are not many side-effects from the melanoma chemo. The bad news is that only ten to twenty per cent of melanoma patients get substantial tumour shrinkage through chemotherapy.'

The other option worth considering was treatment that stimulated my immune system. There were several types, and the one Grant believed might be most suitable was ipilimumab, a potent antibody that helped the body recognise and destroy the cancer cells. Treatment involved a series of injections, probably starting at once every three weeks and then increasing in frequency over several months. The side-effects could vary greatly, because each person's immune system varies greatly. They could be severe – in rare cases, even fatal – but most commonly were limited to problems such as diarrhoea or skin rashes.

'With this treatment there's a subset, a small percentage of people, where the melanoma goes away,' Grant said. 'This hospital has two patients who have used the treatment and who are now in remission: one with cancer in the liver, one who had quite nasty lumps in the bones.'

With each of the treatments – radiation, chemo and immunology – Grant had spoken more about the hope that they might shrink tumours. Remission seemed to be about as likely as being handed a winning lotto ticket. I suggested to him that this was the reason I was looking into some of the unconventional therapies, hoping they would help to change the makeup of my body and prevent tumours from coming back.

'It's a really tough one,' Grant said. 'There is nobody who is an expert in the field of conventional medicine and at the same time an expert in the area of alternative or complementary treatment. That person simply doesn't exist. I always try to keep an open mind. All I will say is that the evidence that we've seen about a lot of alternative therapies has never been solid enough for us to feel we can give you good advice about whether they are worthwhile. But the bottom line is that if you want to run the two streams parallel, it's up to you. It won't change the fact that I will always do the best I can, as will any other doctor who treats you.'

I appreciated Grant's candour but also the fact that he was not simply dismissive of non-traditional therapies, as the doctor who was his mentor, Max Schwarz, had been. This was important to me because for my whole life – in particular, during my football career – I had used such therapies to treat injuries and physical complaints.

I realised how important it was for me to have an oncologist who was on the same page as I was. As long as Grant was convinced that the alternative treatment didn't interfere with the effectiveness of my other treatment, he was supportive of whatever I chose to try. People make a point of finding a builder they can relate to when they're doing a home renovation, or an accountant they can relate to when they need tax advice. But your health, your very life, is far more important than a house or a bank balance. To deal with cancer, I needed to have an oncologist who had my complete faith. Over the coming months and years, Grant, together with Graeme Southwick, would act like the conductor of an orchestra of specialists treating me.

All that remained was to determine the immediate course of action after this meeting.

'I often say, to keep it simple, what I would do if it was me in your position,' Grant said. 'Certainly I would keep going with the planned radiation treatment for the brain. That's a priority, given the problems you've had with speech and whatnot. After that, when you get off the dexamethasone – which slows down the immune system – I would be looking at another treatment. We'll have to run more scans first to check your body. The strategy I'd recommend would either be chemo – if any more lumps come up – or one of the treatments that boosts the immune system. As a general principle, it's good to tackle treatments when there's not much tumour activity present.

'The thing about treating cancer, though, is that you need to be flexible. We want to be ahead of the game but we still need to adapt to what the cancer tells us.'

With melanoma you don't get cured. I just could not seem to put that idea to one side. It kept occupying my thoughts. It made for a challenging few days – perhaps the most challenging week, mentally, of my cancer journey to that point. I knew it was simply a matter of getting my mind to reframe Grant's words; I had to set my compass to 'remission' instead of 'cure'. The problem was that my mind was struggling.

I was hampered by bouts of tiredness and my short-term memory was appalling. A few times people phoned me and I told them I would ring back in an hour, only to completely forget. There was occasionally a nagging pain at the rear of my head, and at times I felt dizzy as I got up off a chair. My eyes hurt when I looked up, down or to one side.

I was not filled with enthusiasm, then, about the prospect of returning to the Epworth for my last couple of radiation sessions. It had been almost six weeks since the previous course had finished, but this time I would be having stereo-tactic radiation, a highly precise treatment in which narrow beams of radiation would be directed from different angles at my brain tumours.

The most daunting part of the process was the device they used to keep my head completely still and protect the healthy brain tissue.

The radiologists secure your head in place with a medi-eval-looking metal brace, including a mouthpiece. Above that is a transparent plastic dome, with holes through which the beams will penetrate. You end up looking like a cross between Hannibal Lecter and an astronaut; I jokingly used to refer to the equipment as 'the frame of horror'. But the truth was that those sessions looked a lot worse than they felt. There was no pain. I was only uncomfortable because

I knew I couldn't move – which, of course, made me all the more desperate to move.

There was a time when the same could be said about my life: unless I was moving, unless I was doing something, I was restless and discontented. But over the past six months I had been forced to slow down. Surgery and scans and hospitals were hardly the mainstays of an idyllic lifestyle, but neither were the manic pace and stress that they had replaced. The spotlight, the responsibilities and the need to be busy – they had been an addiction, and I knew it would be easy for them to creep back in.

As the most extraordinary year of my life drew towards a close, it seemed remarkable to think that I was enjoying life more than I ever had. There were times when I forgot I was sick at all. Scans after those final two radiation sessions showed that the three tumours in my brain had shrunk slightly, and that there were no new ones elsewhere in my body. It was the closest we had come to receiving good news in the six months since the cancer diagnosis.

Our family celebrated that festive season in a spirit of optimism and hope. On Christmas Day about twenty-five members of the extended family came over to our house, and it was just one of those days when everything unfolds perfectly. Kids running around gleefully, laughing adults in ridiculous crepe-paper crowns chipping in to help Sam lay on a delicious spread. Afterwards we all played a rambling game of soccer in the fading afternoon sun down at the park. It was bliss.

To start the new year, Sam and I had organised to take the kids away for a ten-day boat cruise from Mexico to California, taking in visits to Disneyland and San Diego Zoo. The kids thrived on the experience – not just at the ports we visited but also the activities on board the ship. Sam was in her element, captivated by the stunning views and the chance to explore the local art and culture.

Initially, it seemed the ideal getaway for me too. No distractions, and I was sleeping more than twelve hours a day. One morning I awoke from a dream in which doctors told me the tumours had disappeared. As the days wore on, though, my health deteriorated; it got to the stage where I could not swallow my pills.

Towards the end of that trip I was riddled with guilt. The kids were incredibly excited about going to San Diego Zoo but I felt like someone battling the hangover from hell. I had a throbbing head, was aching all over and felt nauseated. I hated the fact that the sole obstacle preventing the rest of the family from enjoying a perfect holiday was this damned disease.

By the end of that trip, the swelling in my brain had become so severe that Sam needed to phone Australia to seek counsel from Grant McArthur. 'I'm not even sure about putting him on a plane,' she said. Grant prescribed four times the normal dose of steroids to reduce the swelling, which allowed me to safely negotiate the return flight home.

Once in Melbourne, I was booked in for another round of scans, which revealed three more small tumours: another in the brain, one behind the shoulder and one in the duodenum – which is the start of the small intestine, immediately beyond the stomach. Worse still, the doctors were concerned that surgery might not be viable with the brain and duodenum tumours; they felt chemotherapy would be the most appropriate treatment in the short term.

The doctors knew of my aversion to chemo, my concerns about the side-effects and my fear that it might weaken my immune system. Yet I realised I had to accept that the experts to whose care I had entrusted my life now agreed that this treatment was the best way forward. It would be counterproductive to harbour doubts about chemo, I decided. Better to fully embrace it, and to ask my mind and body to be its allies.

Chemotherapy can vary widely from cancer to cancer, from patient to patient. Generally speaking, it is the use of chemicals to destroy or slow down the fast-growing cells in the body – and therefore cancer. Because adults have essentially stopped growing, the healthy cells that can be affected are bone marrow (where the blood cells are produced), hair and nails, and the digestive tract. People generally associate chemotherapy with a patient sitting in an armchair while an intravenous drip empties into his or her arm, but chemo can be given in other ways, including orally, through injections or via a skin cream. In my case, it involved taking capsules of a drug called temozolomide.

Within a few days of starting the treatment, I found that the side-effects had begun. I struggled with fatigue, presumably because my red-blood cell count was down slightly. But the worst was to come after about a week when constipation started to kick in – to such a degree that I thought my bowel was going to explode. The pain became unbearable. It's not an experience I would wish upon anyone. It got to the point where I could not put another morsel of food in my mouth, and it took about three different medicines to burst the dam.

Over the next few weeks, I would come to realise that, in my case, the side-effects of the chemo course were not too debilitating. I had good days, better days and days when I simply needed to sleep for hours. By the time I was ready to turn in each night, at about 10.30 pm, my whole body would start to shut down. My legs would go weak. They'd feel like jelly and I could hardly stand up.

My gravest concern remained my brain. The migraines returned whenever I overexerted myself; frustratingly, therefore, I had to abandon any sort of strenuous physical exercise. Two disconcerting episodes convinced me that the wiring in my brain was not right.

In early February, I made my first public appearance of 2010 at the Melbourne Football Club's annual general meeting. Midway through my speech, while talking about how much Melbourne had reduced its debt, I came to the names of the three auditors working with the club. My brain froze and I simply could not get their names out.

After a prolonged pause, I looked across to Don McLardy, who was standing beside me on stage. He asked if I was all right, but all I could do was nod and point to the names in my notes. There was a heavy, unsettling silence in the room, and I'm sure the television cameras were capturing what they thought would be a juicy story for their next news bulletin. Fortunately, Don defused the awkward moment with a joke about how 'the very thought of mentioning auditors scares Jim'. After a few more words from him, I knew I could continue my speech.

I chose to ignore that glitch but I could not do so a few weeks later when the most mundane of tasks gave me a scare. After returning home from a weekend in Rye, we parked the car in front of the house and began to unpack. After taking one load inside, I came back out to the nature strip. The car was nowhere to be seen. My heart sank. Surely not . . . I'd only been in the house for about ninety seconds – was that enough time to steal a car?

Up and down the street, I looked, but the car was nowhere to be seen. Just as I was contemplating calling the police, I realised that I was standing right next to the car. It was before my very eyes, but some blurred vision meant I hadn't even seen it. Not once, but several times.

I desperately wanted to believe I was healing, but the rest of my brain was telling me otherwise. Another long discussion with Graeme and Grant was on the agenda since it seemed that chemo was not working. As it turned out, an appointment was not required. A few days later I was rushed to hospital in an ambulance, with such a crippling migraine that I thought my head was going to implode. There, scans revealed another lump in my brain and a second small growth in my duodenum.

There was no way of avoiding it any longer. It was time for more surgery, this time on my brain.

9

INSIDE THE BRAIN

I knew it was ridiculous but I couldn't help it. Every time I saw my brain surgeon, Professor Jeffrey Rosenfeld, I thought of the Australian stand-up comedian Elliot Goblet. Never mind that Jeffrey had studied for at least a dozen years to become a neurosurgeon; indeed, he was a leader in the field. Whenever we met I just kept expecting him to ask, with deadpan delivery, something like: 'Did you ever wonder where bridge toll collectors go for a toilet break?'

In truth, Jeffrey had a quiet authority that filled me with confidence whenever he spoke. He was very measured and tended to offer straightforward and simple explanations. To help me understand what to expect from brain surgery, he sat me down at one of the Alfred Hospital's computers to show me precisely where the tumours were in my skull. There was a nasty shock: the scans had revealed another tumour deep on the left side of my head. It was in a part of the brain connected to eyesight. There was a possibility that the vision in my right eye would be impaired.

I felt cheated. It was onerous enough dealing with cancer

itself; I was not supposed to be getting disabilities along the way as well.

The morning of the surgery flew by – too quickly – until an orderly came and wheeled me to the operating room holding area. I lay there for about fifteen minutes, just wanting the surgery to be over and done with. Each minute seemed to take an eternity. I was thankful that a nurse and the anaesthetist engaged me in small talk. Yes, Melbourne had been unlucky on the weekend to lose its Round 2 match to Collingwood by a point. True, true, the young players had looked impressive. I kept wondering how long it would be until the surgery began.

And then it was all over.

During five-and-a-half hours in the operating theatre, Jeffrey had removed five tumours. He had entered my skull through a 'bone flap', an incision resembling an upside-down horseshoe. To close it, he had inserted forty staples in my head.

Not that I knew much about any of this for the first forty-eight hours after the operation, as I swam between intense pain and a drug-fuelled semi-consciousness in the post-brain-surgery ward. I would look up at the ceiling, convinced that four days had passed, only to discover that it was later the same day. There were usually three or four patients in the ward, each at various levels of comprehension, each of us amenable to having a conversation with whichever patient was prepared to listen, even if it was just a faceless voice behind a curtain.

Every half-hour a nurse would check on me, peering into my eyes with a torch and asking a series of basic questions: 'What's your name? What's the date? What hospital are you in? How many fingers am I holding up?'

Occasionally, I'd wake up to find that I could barely see anything, and I feared for my eyesight. At times everything was a blur, and it seemed as though I had less peripheral vision on my right-hand side. Questions about permanent damage were deflected; it was too soon after surgery to tell. The swelling had to go down and tests be undertaken before we'd know.

Sam had been by my side when I came out of surgery, and then organised family and friends to come and sit with me at various intervals. By about the third day, as I returned to health, Sam was able to start laughing about some of our experiences in the ward, or the Mad Hatter's Tea Party, as she began to call it. 'You should have seen yourself,' she said. 'They wheeled you in, and this prim and proper Englishman was in the next bed along from you. Well, you were both completely out of it, but that didn't stop you striking up a conversation. He was like, "Oh, you're Irish. Well, you must have read James Joyce's *Ulysses*. Absolutely fabulous." And there you were, taking the mickey out of his posh accent. "Yes, it's simply fantastic, old boy." The two of you were chatting away. It was hilarious.'

Well, that's an encouraging sign, I thought. *My brain must be*

functioning reasonably well if it still recognised a chance to take an
Englishman down a peg.

'Oh, that's right, there was something else,' Sam laughed.
'Do you know what your first words were when you woke
up after surgery? You said, "The next time we play Collingwood, we're going to kick their arses."'

A nurse entered the room and began her regular check of
the patients. I could hear her beginning the routine: name,
rank and serial number. 'Quick, Sammy, you've got to hide
me,' I said. 'I can't do the questions thing again.'

The nurse wandered over and examined the electronic
monitor next to my bed.

'Three,' I volunteered.

'Three what?' she asked, puzzled.

'Fingers you're going to hold up.'

She chuckled. 'Cheeky. You're clearly feeling a lot better.'

Having been so apprehensive before brain surgery, it was
good to laugh again, perhaps because of the relief of having come through the operation reasonably well. Jeffrey
confirmed as much when he dropped in to check on my progress later that afternoon. 'As far as I can see,' he said, 'we've
removed all signs of tumours from your brain.' But he warned
me not to assume that my brain was now cancer-free. Dealing
with metastasised melanoma was not as simple as that; it was
like blowing a dandelion head into the breeze and then trying
to round up all of the seeds.

'One of the things I've been wondering,' Sam said, 'is what
it actually looks like when you go to cut it out. The cancer,

I mean. What does it look like? Little dumplings? Nuggets? You always visualise it as being somehow sort of round.'

'It's not as clearly defined as that,' Jeffrey replied. 'It's like a grey jelly substance.' I had never given it any thought before that. No wonder cancer was so difficult to remove surgically. Like serving jelly with a knife.

I asked about the possibility of going home. 'It's only been a few days, Jim. There's still quite a bit of swelling. I think you need more time to recuperate.'

How about the prospect of going to watch Melbourne play at the MCG the next day?

'I don't think so. It won't hurt you to miss one game.'

I smiled. He was not the first doctor to have said those words to me over the years.

So, as Melbourne went in search of its first win of the 2010 season, against Adelaide on 11 April, I was propped up in bed at the Alfred Hospital, moping despite the best efforts of several close friends who had joined me for company: Hugh Ellis, Anthony Ingerson and Trisha Silvers, one of the early Reach Crew members.

'This is ridiculous,' I complained, a few minutes into the broadcast. 'My eyesight is so stuffed, and this TV is so small, that I can't even see what's going on.'

Whether they agreed or whether they simply didn't want to endure an afternoon of whingeing, I'm not sure, but they devised a plan on the spot. 'Right, come on,' declared Hugh.

'Put your clothes on – we're busting out of here.' After telling the nurses' station that they were taking me downstairs for coffee in the hospital cafeteria, they spirited me away and we drove the couple of kilometres back home – much to Sam's surprise – to watch the game in our living room. It was a scrappy match but I was delighted by the tenacious manner in which the Melbourne players drew away in the last quarter to win by sixteen points. I was less delighted, though, by the fact that, if not for the widescreen television, I would have struggled to see what was going on.

When I returned to hospital I learned that the doctors were keen to transfer me to the Epworth for 'a couple of days of rehabilitation'. As it turned out, a couple of days actually meant a couple of weeks, although I was allowed to return home on the weekend. While I was in rehab, a priority was to determine what was going on with my vision. It had improved, notably the focus and depth perception, but my reduced peripheral vision concerned me. When people approached from my right-hand side, I often did not notice them until they were directly in front of me. Wherever possible, I preferred people to walk alongside me on my left. One of the most annoying consequences of my impaired eyesight was that, because of my height, I was always bumping my head – not an ideal way to recover from brain surgery. So you can imagine how disheartening it was when the hospital's ophthalmologist – an eye specialist – ran a series of tests and advised me that the condition was most likely permanent.

To compound matters, I found that my concentration was

not what it had been. Occasionally, I had to get people to repeat sentences or instructions because I didn't always comprehend what they were saying the first time. I needed time to let the words sink in, and my memory was awful. Over the next fortnight, with the masterly support of the team at Epworth, I undertook a program of cognitive and physical rehabilitation. There were exercises to help improve my vision – even simple things like catching a tennis ball one-handed – as well as physical exercises, such as using a rowing machine and bike-riding in the gym.

A month after brain surgery, I had made significant progress. I finally had some weight back on my frame. When I'd been diagnosed with cancer back in June 2009, I had tipped the scales at 101 kilograms; by February 2010, that figure had dropped to eighty-four kilograms. Now, in mid-May, it was back up to around ninety kilograms. As the doctors had predicted, some of my mind's initial fuzziness had disappeared: my word retention just after surgery had been as low as twenty per cent, but now it was up to ninety per cent. I was also very encouraged that an eye test showed my vision had improved by twenty per cent.

I was beginning to feel strong in mind and body again. There was just the small matter of two tumours in my duodenum.

Sometimes I would stop and try to remember what it was like before I had cancer. Cancer constantly tries to remind you that it is in your life. It wants to dominate, and you have to refuse to allow that to happen. It tries to give you continual reminders. They can be simple things, such as having to take pills each day, or looking in the mirror at your face all puffed up by steroids, or realising that you need to make a new notch on your belt. Or they might be jolting slaps in the face: sorry, but you're not allowed to drive a car. Let's see how you go without your hair, your short-term memory, your peripheral vision.

Whatever cancer tries to take away from you, the one thing you can deny it is your surrender. You have to guard that dearly. Often, the time when that is toughest is during treatment. It can be gruelling to front up for your next dose of radiation, chemotherapy or surgery. It can be relentless. It feels like cancer is grinding away at you, trying to get you to give up. You need to find a way, mentally, to "maintain your surrender".

I used to recall the Hell Fire runs I used to go on when I was in my twenties. They came during the Christmas holidays, when I would leave Melbourne behind and head home to Dublin. During those breaks I used to like to challenge myself by going running. The aim was always to run further and harder than I had the previous year. Our home was in Rathfarnham, near the foot of the Wicklow Mountains, where winter would deliver bone-chilling temperatures and buffeting icy winds. I would pull on a couple of football jumpers, gloves and a beanie, maybe a hoodie, and before leaving I would set an alarm clock in the kitchen, a signal for

Mam to come and collect me in the car. Then I would take off, through the suburbs and into the hills.

During those runs, I used a technique to prevent my body from complaining deep into the journey. This was before the days when joggers began distracting themselves by piping songs through tiny white earphones. Instead, I would pick out something like a telegraph pole on the road ahead, and my mind would then convince my legs and lungs to go their hardest until that pole had been reached. Then another target on the horizon would be identified. And so it went, one telegraph pole at a time.

Five kilometres from our front door was the first crest, the 383-metre Montpelier Hill, a place known to the teenagers of south Dublin as the Hell Fire Club. On the hill were the ruins of a stone hunting lodge built in 1725 by William Conolly, the speaker of the Irish House of Commons. Folklore has it that after he died, high-society rascals commandeered the lodge as a meeting place for outrageous behaviour and depravity. A version of the tale had the devil turning up one night for a game of cards.

To me, it was simply the point where the Kilakee Road, which ran past the estate, began to change complexion. Beyond Hell Fire was where I began to be genuinely challenged. This was where I had to start digging deep. The road gradually wound higher, with only the odd stretch flattening out to give some respite. The landscape started to become less forgiving. I was no longer flanked by lush trees, stone walls and gates. Further along the road, the trees disappeared altogether. I would find myself totally exposed to the world. In a Dublin winter, that might mean an icy headwind, driving rain or snow.

My goal was always to push into that exposed terrain, as far as I could towards Sally Gap, which I estimated to be at about the twenty-kilometre mark. There were very few telegraph poles up there, just the road ahead, surrounded by coarse beds of heather and wiry sedge, with the odd glimpse of limestone. My goal was no longer a telegraph pole or a signpost on the horizon; it was a gorse shrub twenty metres ahead. Then, realising again that my body was hurting, I would focus my mind on the next little target, the next small shrub or rock by the roadside. Tricking the mind, maintaining the surrender. When you're confronted with any overwhelming challenge, it can be broken down into small triumphs like that.

After winning the Brownlow Medal in 1991, the idea that I should push myself to my limit was sown. The former Hawthorn champion Don Scott, who was the Melbourne ruck coach at the time, had challenged me to improve the next season. 'You're now looked upon as the best footballer in the AFL,' he said, 'but why can't you get better? How do you know what your limit is? When you push yourself too far, when you go over the edge, then you will know what your limit is. It won't happen in a game. It's not even some-thing that will happen at training, because players don't train to their limit.'

That Christmas, I resolved to try to find my limit. It was

a personal challenge, me against me. How much further could I run? My body might be exhausted but my mind could tell me to keep going.

I pushed on towards Sally Gap, despite the rain stinging my face and the road becoming slippery with ice. As the rain turned to sleet and I started to feel the cold through my sodden clothes, I was reduced to barely shuffling. My mind was perilously close to the edge. Finally, I conceded. *This is my limit.*

The only problem was that there was no sign of Mam. I guessed that her car must have broken down, but back in Rathfarnham she had been distracted and not heard the kitchen alarm. As I stumbled forward, I decided there was no point pushing on until I stopped and froze to death. I had to keep moving, however, so I turned my back to the wind and began shambling back down the mountain.

Visibility was dreadful, but I managed to flag down a rare car, telling the startled driver, 'I'm sorry, but I'm stranded and I desperately need a lift.' He gave me a spare coat and a blanket, and bundled me into the back seat. Eventually, we met up with Mam's car coming towards us and I managed to get home, certain that I had hypothermia.

I spent afternoon in the living room, rugged up, struggling to move and lying against the radiator. But after that I knew I would never again have to worry about pushing myself to the limit, whether it was in a game of football or a training run or anything else. I knew that I would never have to physically endure what I did on the Wicklow Mountains that Christmas.

Finding inner strength is vitally important when you have cancer. I found it in the knowledge that physical challenges would not bow me. The mind was strong enough to deal with issues that might weaken the body, but was I strong enough to deal with the doubts that lurked below the surface? I knew that deviating from a positive attitude would make the challenge seem insurmountable. But there were times when I needed to reach deep within myself to rediscover that positive frame of mind.

I understood that there would be more testing times ahead, but I was thankful that nobody had ever come to me and said, 'I'm sorry, but there's nothing more we can do; you only have a matter of weeks.' While there remained hope, I remained confident about persisting, about meeting the challenge. Of course, part of the challenge was reminding myself that I was not the only one entwined in this cancer struggle.

10

THE OTHER HALF

It wasn't just that I got cancer. We both did – Sam and I. It might have been in my body, but it was in each of our lives.

It is one thing to get your head around having a tumour and all of the medical consequences. A doctor can try to explain what you should expect. But for the partner of a cancer patient, it is different. Sam was initially so consumed with being emotionally supportive and helping to organise the practicalities around scans and treatments that she had very little time to consider how cancer was reverberating through her own life.

Of course, we would share some fears and anxieties about my health. But many of our other emotions and frustrations had to be negotiated as they arose. Sam was exasperated at realising that her life – and that of our family – frequently felt like it was stuck in a holding pattern. There was the extra stress and the strain on her own health when she did not eat or sleep properly. Then there was the raft of emotions she did not anticipate, such as anger, resentment, guilt and helplessness.

One of the things I love most about Sam was that I knew

she would purposefully work through these issues in her open and honest manner. She would do so because she cared. It is a special quality, the ability to care so deeply about others, and it is a quality that comes naturally to my wife. Her sweet, kind-hearted nature was one of the reasons I fell in love with her.

As for Sam, she had once told me that one of the characteristics that had made me an appealing life partner was that I was prepared to be in it for the long haul. But this was not the long haul that either of us had expected.

How Sam and I met still makes her laugh. It was at a pub on the end of a pier in Cairns. I was sitting at the bar with a handful of mates on the last day of an end-of-season football trip. Looking over my beer, beyond the barman and underneath the hanging wine glasses on the other side of the bar, I noticed a gorgeous young woman. Just at that moment, she turned towards me, caught me looking and smiled. She swivelled back to talk to her friend Jody, who was sitting beside her, but in that moment I was smitten.

What I didn't know was that Sam, then twenty, was in Cairns to visit her grandmother; she was in the bar to meet a family friend she had not seen since they were thirteen. She smiled at me because, although she knew very little about football, she somehow recognised my face and for an instant thought I might be her childhood friend, whom she remembered as being quite tall and with hair a similar colour to mine.

She walked around to where we were sitting and the smile faded from her face. 'Oh, sorry,' she said. 'You're not Stephen Pollard.'

Which, predictably, prompted my mates to declare, 'Yes he is – he is. He's Stephen Pollard.'

I apologised and offered to buy Sam and Jody a drink – an offer willingly accepted by a broke university student – and we started chatting. Sam later told me that she had been unimpressed by the company ('Ugh, footballers') but had warmed to my genuine smile; she thought I was 'just a big dag, but in an endearing way'. I established that she lived in Melbourne and had a win when she mentioned her surname. 'Ludbey?' I asked. 'Any relation to Wayne, the newspaper photographer? He's taken some awesome football shots.' Of course, he was her brother, and she relaxed slightly, thinking to herself, *He must be all right if he knows Wayne*. We had a few laughs, and when we parted, Sam took my phone number but would not hand over her own.

It would be weeks before I saw her again. A gilt-edged invitation arrived in the mail for 'Jim Stynes and guest' to attend a state dinner at Victoria's Government House with Ireland's president, Mary Robinson. I thought of Sam – but how was I going to track her down? Fortunately, one afternoon at football training, I noticed Wayne positioned on the boundary with an enormous camera, taking photos. After completing a few warm-up run-throughs, I peeled off and approached him. He was somewhat mystified when I told him I needed his sister's phone number.

My first date with Sam was unconventional. After can-apés, we were ushered to a cavernous Government House dining room, where I was seated at one end of the most enormous table I had ever seen. On either side of me were Joan Kirner and Jeff Kennett, the leaders of Victoria's two political parties. To my consternation, Sam was shown to her seat at the extreme other end of the table; she was seated next to the fashion designer Charlie Brown and the governor's secretary, who had clearly done his homework and knew all about what she was studying at Melbourne University.

Sam and I didn't get the chance to talk all evening; we just managed to pull a few faces at each other from about twenty paces. But in a way, the unorthodox date acted as an ice-breaker. Afterwards we laughed about the absurdity of it all, and Sam's only worry was that she had overdressed. She was wearing a black evening dress designed by a girlfriend who was studying fashion at RMIT. 'When I looked around I thought, *Oh my god*,' she said. 'It looked like I was wearing the same dress as the women in the string quartet.'

Sam and I dated for a few months, broke up for a few years, and then got together again when she came to my thirtieth birthday party. I still didn't know if she was the one, but I liked her plucky attitude. The first time she came to watch me play a game with Melbourne, she had waited outside the changing rooms along with the other wives and girlfriends, as was the custom at the time. After about fifteen or twenty minutes she had thought, *I'm not going to stand here and wait for this guy at a changing room door; it's so belittling* – and so she had simply turned on her heel and gone home. She was studying post-structural feminism and was not prepared to have her paradigm dictated by the accepted wisdom in AFL football.

But I nearly blew it with Sam towards the end of 1998. I didn't know whether I wanted to retire, play on, or perhaps go back home to Dublin and have one last fling at Gaelic football before it was too late. We discussed the issue one night. 'Dublin?' she exclaimed hotly – which was not surprising, given that it was the first time the possibility had been raised. 'How long for?'

'Oh, only two or three years,' I said.

'Right. And what happens with us?'

So consumed had I been with the direction of my football career that I had not given any consideration to what it meant for the relationship. Pressed, I replied, 'I'm not sure that "us" is going to work.' She was not impressed.

We left the situation unresolved, but at least I did reach one conclusion: that I should retire from AFL football altogether, a decision I planned to announce at Melbourne's best-and-fairest count. Sam agreed to accompany me, although she would have been within her rights not to. Afterwards, when we pulled up in the car at her mum's house in St Kilda, we just sat there and talked.

'This is ridiculous,' she said. 'What are we doing? If I genuinely felt you didn't want to be with me, then fine, let's break up. But I'm not getting that from you. We've put too much work into this to end it now. You've made your footy decision. Now get over yourself.'

I had been in a few long-term relationships, but whenever they had become serious and I had expressed doubts, the women had opted to walk away. This was the first woman who had not only refused to accept my dithering but had thrown it back in my face. It had a powerful effect on me, and I agreed. Why not have a proper crack?

That night, Sam basically told me, 'You're not going to treat me like this. You have no idea who I am, and it's about time you put some effort into finding out.' And because I was retiring, it was the first time in my life when I actually had space for a relationship. Before that I'd been too selfish – too caught up in training, managing injuries, preparing for and playing football. I'd been too consumed by myself. Everything else had always been secondary.

Essentially, 1999 was the first year of my life in which I did not play sport. There was room for our relationship to grow stronger, and it did.

Yet, as ludicrous as it must sound, I had never managed to tell Sam that I loved her. I could not trust myself to say so unless I was utterly convinced that I meant it. I had said those three words to a couple of past girlfriends, so I was holding back, making sure that it meant something rather than being empty words.

That year we did a lot of travelling, because we could. Back in Ireland for Christmas, we found ourselves in a pub at the lovely little village of Westport in county Mayo on New Year's Eve. The place was jam-packed, Irish fiddles and *bodhráns* (drums) – the atmosphere was electric. We had a great night, tipped in a few pints, and it ended with Sam singing to the crowd in the pub. As we tottered back to our digs, she stopped me, grabbed me by the shoulders and stared me in the face, frowning playfully.

'Jim Stynes, we've been together for three years now, and not once have you told me that you love me.'

'Well, I'm not going to say it now that you're telling me to,' I chortled, and she stomped off in mock rage. But that's how stubborn and immature I was: I would not utter that sentence while I felt under any sort of pressure to do so. It wasn't only that; now I had to feel like Sam would not be expecting it.

It took three more weeks for me to believe the moment had arrived. It was on a brilliantly sunny day in Rome and we were visiting the Vatican. As we made our way inside St Peter's Basilica, the stirring harmony of the choir's singing surrounded us. The sun beamed in through the stained glass windows. We climbed the steps up to the cupola – the famous dome designed by Michelangelo – and stepped out into the daylight to an exquisite view. A ray of light was glistening off the roof below, and beyond the metal rail, one of the world's great cities lay sprawling before us. I leaned across, quietly spoke into Sam's ear and then leaned back, certain it was the perfect moment.

'Aarggh!' she cried, prompting a few tourists to snap their

heads around in concern. 'I could throw you off this roof. After all this time, after all these chances, and you tell me on the roof of the Vatican!' But her tears told me that she wasn't really annoyed.

From the moment we were back in St Peter's Square, Sam had decided in her delightfully enthusiastic manner that marriage was now on the agenda. Again, this brought out a renewed stubborn insistence that I would not be pressured. Over the next few months, there were moments when I was planning to ask her, but each time that she dropped a hint I'd think, *Well, let's just wait a bit longer, then*. It was ridiculous.

One weekend we stayed in Olinda at the house of our friends Mike and Bernie Dolby. Their beautiful old home, 'Candlewood', featured a viewing room perched near the top of a hundred-year-old tree. In the evening, Bernie asked Sam if she would mind ducking out to the room, because she needed to discuss something. 'But it's freezing up there,' Sam protested. 'What's this all about? Can't you just tell me here?'

Bernie handed her a beanie, scarf and ugg boots and they made their way up to the lookout, where there was an aerial view of hundreds of candles. They formed a heart and the words 'Will you marry me?' I proposed to Sam that night with a Claddagh ring, a traditional Irish design with two hands clasping a crowned heart. She had to agree this time that it was a romantic masterstroke. We drank champagne into the night and were married in the summer of 2000.

By the time cancer came along, in the winter of 2009, there was very little room in our lives for romance. I was going 100 kilometres an hour with my foot pressing down even harder on the accelerator; Sam was doing fifty kilometres an hour in a residential zone. And there was every chance we might have pulled too far apart, had it not been for the roadblock that cancer created.

I was carried away with what I wanted to do in my life, even though there remained some uncertainty about the long-term direction. It is very easy when you are involved in a passion to get totally immersed in it and to lose perspective. Between Reach and the Melbourne Football Club, there were times when that happened with me. I would have workdays that began at 6 am and ended at midnight, or I might be away all weekend on a camp, and I would justify it by thinking about how it was helping the kids in the programs. Somehow I set aside the fact that I had kids of my own, and refused to consider what impact it might have on them.

As I was devoting so much time to work and football, I never stopped to consider Sam's perspective. My attitude would just be 'That's what I'm doing, this is what my life is, deal with it'. After an eighteen-hour day, she would sometimes ask, 'Did you miss me, honey?' I would reply, 'No, because I didn't have time to think about you.' I would actually say that. For me at that time, it was acceptable to be so intensely focused on whatever was ahead of me that I was too busy to spare a thought for my family. I now understand that I was showing no respect for what was going on in Sam's life, just as she had forewarned me all those years ago.

I had been fairly slow on the uptake when Sam had tried to send me signals over the years, which had resulted in some tumultuous times. We always seemed to find a way to make life difficult for each other. We would have an argument and then later wonder why. In reality, most of the problems were caused by my selfishness. Looking back, I see that I was constantly the one having to say sorry. At the time, I resented it. I would think, *I'm always the one admitting to being wrong*. But there was a good reason for that.

One time, during an argument, I shouted at her, 'Do you know how hard it is being married to you? You don't see yourself as a wife!' What I was implying was that she would not do things my way. I did not appreciate that we were supposed to be a team, not just one person living life on his terms and expecting the other person to follow.

Something had to give, and that something was me. But here was the catch: to learn that lesson, it took a few months living with cancer, during which time I was taking even more from Sam and giving even less in return. After the diagnosis, understandably, it was about what I needed to do to deal with the disease: *my* scans, *my* diet, *my* surgery, *my* schedule, *my* wellbeing.

Sam had little option but to place her own needs to one side and support me in that. Often, she had to be present not just for emotional support but also as another set of ears, to make sure the doctor's messages were getting through.

There were the constant visits to hospitals and waiting rooms, with endless forms to fill in. Whether I was at the Alfred, the Epworth, Peter MacCallum or Cabrini, Sam had to negotiate their car parks, cafeteria opening times, which kitchens served food I could eat, which menus needed supplementing. She began to know the names of nurses, the faces of other carers and patients. She knew to make sure the orderlies had bed extensions for when I came out of surgery. At the snap of a finger she could be relied upon to produce a list of the medications I was taking. She learned the names of the drugs, their functions and the relevant doses. She learned how to give me injections. Sometimes she almost seemed to be a step ahead of the doctors, which meant I didn't have to focus on the detail.

At home, there were weeks when she must have felt like she was a single mother, not only trying to keep some sense of normalcy in the kids' lives but also ensuring that they did not miss out on the activities that make childhood special, such as playdates, parties and sport. The phone never stopped ringing and the media never stopped enquiring; our daily mail arrived in bundles.

Changes to my diet meant changes to the shopping list. 'I can't just load it all into a trolley at Coles, you know,' she had sharply reminded me one day. 'I have to get the organic fruit and vegetables, then your special bread from the bakery. Find some bee pollen, quinoa and agave syrup, and whatever new foreign ingredient you decide you want. And when

I get home, do you ever say thanks? No, you just pick on me because I've bought a packet of chocolate biscuits for the kids.'

She was spot-on. I definitely had not appreciated her efforts. On top of everything else, she'd had to learn the details of my complex business involvements. Recently, she had tidied up the fireplace in the study, which was full of various business cards I had collected over the years. They usually lay there in a great messy heap, but Sam had arranged them in neat little bundles with elastic bands – yet rather than thanking her, I had complained that now I would not know where to find anything.

By late August of 2009, about three months after my cancer diagnosis, it was all wearing her down. We agreed that she needed some 'Sam time', a way of devoting time and energy to something she *wanted* to do, rather than the things she had to do for her husband and family. I was thinking of a weekend away with the girls, or a massage and spa retreat. But Sam has a bolder personality than that, and she suggested ocean sailing.

Hugh had mentioned vacancies on a cruising yacht that was heading out of Melbourne and up to Sydney, and Sam was captivated by the idea. The first thought that entered my mind, though – whether it was from insecurity about my health or just old-fashioned jealousy – was that my wife would be at sea with a crew of healthy, rum-drinking sailors.

Sam scoffed. Hadn't I been away alone numerous times, including several times with healthy, beer-drinking footballers? It was all about trust, she said, and she was right. But it was also about not always feeling in control, and I needed to experience that.

While those few days away were great therapy for Sam, I was back in Melbourne continuing my own therapy. It was during this time that I began to realise how severely my moods were affected by the steroid I was taking to prevent my brain from swelling. Whenever I was on high doses I would find myself screaming at other cars in traffic, and having no patience with family and friends, let alone doctors and nurses.

One such time came in October of 2009, and Sam and I would endure what proved to be the nadir, but also the turning point, in our relationship. We went to a surprise birthday dinner at Rockpool on a Friday night, for Sam's good friend Chrissie. It was a wonderful meal with charming company, but it deteriorated when I kept harping at Sam about how we needed to leave, given that we had planned to take the family down to Rye later that night. I was unable to get behind the wheel at the time, and Sam knew that meant we had to go home and get the kids and packing organised, and then she had to face the one-hour drive down the highway.

Perhaps it'd be better just to enjoy the moment and head off the next morning, she suggested. But I was adamant, and I badgered her in front of her friends Kirsty and Chris in the car. When we walked in the front door later that night a huge argument erupted, startling my parents, who were babysitting the kids. Sam threw the car keys at me and then delivered a withering spray at my father, blaming him for being such a male chauvinist role model. She then burst into tears. Mam shooed Dad and me away and packed Sam off to bed with a cup of tea.

My sister Terri-Ann drove the kids and me to Rye the next morning, but when we returned on the Sunday evening Sam remained extremely hurt. The result of medication or not, my behaviour had been intolerable, particularly in front of friends who had been so generous in their support of Sam and me over recent months. She decided that I should spend a week living with my parents in their house, fifteen minutes down the road in Hampton.

My desperate need to be in control had left me with no control whatsoever. Here I was at age forty-three, off work, unable to drive, living in the spare bedroom at my parents' house and undergoing radiation therapy.

That week gave me time to reflect. One thing I knew was that I loved Sam and wanted to make our relationship work. The thought of life without her horrified me. Yet I could not understand why I was so bothered by her carefree and breezy spirit. Why did it cause me so much stress and make me determined to pick at her? Perhaps I was envious.

Whatever the reason, it disturbed me that I was prepared to damage her spirit and erode her confidence. I had devoted my life to nurturing and encouraging self-belief in others, yet I was ignoring and hurting the person I loved most. I needed to stop smothering her and had to allow her to be her own person. I needed to accept that Sam had to seek out her own path – through cancer and through life. At the very least, I resolved to take one practical step: whenever Sam offered a suggestion or some advice, I should identify a positive aspect and discuss that, rather than beginning with a negative reaction.

That week out of home was like lifting the lid off a pressure-cooker. Sam and I kept in contact throughout, and by the end of the week I think we were both pretty relieved to be reunited. That night we spoke frankly.

I explained how I was ashamed of my behaviour towards her – of the fact that I tried to be open and accepting of anyone I met, and yet I could be so hostile towards and critical of the most important person in my life. I did not want to use cancer as an excuse, but I was finding it exhausting to maintain a positive mindset towards overcoming the disease. I needed an outlet, and I guessed that I tended to channel my negative energy towards Sam – all the more so when I was taking the dexamethasone.

Sam accepted that, but she found it particularly hurtful that the times I chose to denigrate her were often in front of her friends. 'And this is stuff that existed before you got cancer,' she said. 'You've been the one going out there and living the life you have always wanted, whereas I've been left to support your dreams. That's not a partnership.'

Sam has a master's degree in education from Melbourne University and had been teaching at Carlton Primary School before she became pregnant with Matisse in 2001. Then, in between raising the children, she had designed a range of women's apparel, set up several successful programs with Reach and written some freelance newspaper articles. There was no question that she had the intelligence and creativity to succeed in any number of careers.

'I don't know,' she said. 'I guess I've carried some resentment. Before you got sick I was left on my own to do so much of what happened at home and with the family, and I was looking for a connection, some support from my husband. But you were so busy. Gradually, I was getting myself into a good place. Tiernan was at kindergarten and I could see myself having the time to gain more independence. There was going to be scope for me to find my own way again. So when the cancer came, I guess I thought, *Are you kidding me? I have to give that chance up?*

'Now if feels like the roles have switched; I'm running around like a maniac while you ease off and concentrate on healing. I guess I begrudged the fact that I was still expected to give you that unconditional support and connection – the very thing I struggled to get from you.

'I know it sounds crazy, and I feel guilty even mentioning it, but I think there's something to it. I had a good talk about it with a friend the other day, who said to me, "Sam, it's actually worrying that part of you still resists accepting that carer role with Jim, and you need to think carefully about it. About whether you can step it up." Not in a condescending way, like I need to become the good little wifey. More that I needed to find it within myself. To dig really deep.'

She inhaled, puffed out her cheeks and let out a long breath that made her lips flutter. 'Of course, we also spoke about you,' Sam said, with a laugh, 'and how you needed to pull your head in. But that if we're going to ask for miracles, we should start with something easier, like a cure for cancer.'

I cradled her cheek. I was dumbfounded that Sam had doubts about her devotion, her support. I was thinking to myself that, had I been in her situation and cast in the role of carer, I would have struggled to handle it anywhere near as well as she had.

We both came away from that talk with renewed belief that we could get through this testing time in our lives, and that we'd be closer than ever. Inseparable. But the crazy part about that conversation was this: I resolved to stop presuming that Sam should run around after me, while Sam resolved to spend more time running around after me.

It was all about balance. I had to stop trying to control, and she had to feel she wasn't being suffocated.

It had taken six months, but by the end of 2009 I felt we genuinely shared our approach towards living with cancer. There was a real understanding between us, a better dynamic, and we seemed to be viewing the challenge from the same perspective.

One of the realisations that dawned on us was that we both found it difficult to allow others to help us. My determination to always be in control meant that even when

I was really sore and sorry after surgery, or feeling dreadfully sick, I still wanted to do things for myself. Sometimes Sam would say, 'Jim, just lie down. Rest.' But I could not stand feeling like I was a burden – I hated it – and I had to learn not only to accept help but also to appreciate it.

Sam had a similar instinct. If people offered assistance, no sooner had the words left their lips than she would be dismissing the offer. 'Thanks, but I'll be all right,' she'd instantly say. She found it even more difficult to ask for help.

Her friends, particularly Kirsty and Mel, could be relied upon to provide the emotional support to keep her centred and sane; even when Sam was too busy to be contacted, they would call her mother to make sure she was coping. They were understanding and patient. But when Sam realised that it was time to let them in to help with the practicalities of being married to a cancer patient, they jumped at the chance. There were times when I would be sitting in my hospital bed and one or another of Sam's friends would arrive with a basket of organic food, fresh pyjamas and forms that needed signing. Sometimes it would be delivered by one of their husbands.

Sam's mum, Mary, and her wonderfully supportive stepfather, Frank, sold their farm in Daylesford and moved back to a house just around the corner in St Kilda to help us. They frequently offered to drive me or the kids around town if Sam was unavailable. We also looked into paying someone to come into our home as a 'house manager', to help with cooking, cleaning, driving and looking after the kids.

Learning to be more vulnerable with family and friends – and trying to be more vulnerable with one another – did mean adjusting our thinking in other areas. Sam was used to my being stoic when confronted with adversity, and she found that reassuring. If I was vulnerable then she was more inclined to feel scared. When she allowed dark thoughts to creep in, there were times when she couldn't sleep. There were times when she lost weight through worry. Once, she asked, 'Is this what we're reduced to? Hoping for tumours that are in places where they can operate!'

I struggled too. Not having control made me feel insecure. One night, as we lay in bed cuddling, Sam became upset by how bony I had become. My legs and arms had so little meat on them. It was an irrational fear, but I had to get over the notion that I was a lesser man and she would leave me. In reality, we were closer, and we were supporting each other more.

During the first half of 2010 I became better at offering Sam more respect and trust, and I stopped trying to get her to live her life the way I expected. I resisted the temptation to always want to be the decision-maker in our relationship, and that room to move allowed her develop into an even more mature and confident woman. It allowed us to have some important and, at times, confronting conversations.

We discussed a funeral plan and my will; we went through our financial affairs, which had predominantly been my realm. We mapped out a plan for her to be self-sufficient in the event that I was no longer around.

Sam was still scared about my health, but she was strong. It helped that I was feeling robust in mind and body. The brain tumours had been removed and I had recovered well from the surgery. I was almost off the dexamethasone, and there was a plan to use an immune-therapy drug to tackle the two remaining tumours, the ones in my duodenum. Sam even had a dream in which my hair was back to its pre-cancer appearance; she saw that as a great omen.

I was beginning to feel like I had my wife back. Now we were daring to dream that I might get my life back.

11

FATHERHOOD

Cancer had put me through all manner of pain. Stomach pain so strong that I thought I would pass out. Forty staples in my scalp where the surgeon had sawn open the back of my skull. Ribs cut through during chest surgery. But this was just physical pain, and I knew it would subside. None of it compared to the pain of contemplating my kids without a father. It was like being stabbed in the heart with rusty steak knife. And I could never predict when that next jolt of pain would ambush me.

The first, most fearsome jolt had come within seconds of Graeme Southwick telling me I had cancer, but the anguish of what it might mean for the kids was so devastating that I had to try to bundle it up and store it somewhere in the recesses of my mind. It did not take much, however, for it to resurface. Whenever Matisse or Tiernan did something that reminded me how much I loved them, or how fast they were growing up, those beautiful moments would be followed by a pang of torment about the future. It could be something as simple as a painting of the family brought home from kindergarten, a throwaway line from Matisse about what she would do when she grew up, or watching the pair of them laughing with their mother. I found it almost unbearable to take a good look at a photograph of them.

The cancer diagnosis had given me reason to stop and reassess my life and my values, and pretty much the first change I wanted to make was to become a better dad. Instantly I had realised how important the kids were to me, and that, up until then, I had been prepared to put my time and energy into any number of other aspects of my life ahead of fatherhood. I realised it was easy to see yourself as a devoted father, even though deep down you knew you could be giving so much more.

When Sam and I had married in 2000, we wanted to have children straight away. Having grown up surrounded by big Catholic families, I was pushing for loads of children. Yet, upon reflection, I was not ready for the commitment parenthood demanded. In 2001, when Matisse was born, I was not only pouring long hours into Reach but also doing countless motivational talks, many of them in the evenings. In what I had perceived to be a magnanimous gesture – a sign of my commitment to fatherhood – I had cleared all non-essential appointments from my diary for the two weeks after the date Sam was due to give birth. That was fine in theory, but Matisse was two weeks overdue. No sooner was she born than I was back to work, leaving Sam to come to grips with parenting essentially on her own.

She wasn't ready for that adjustment, yet I expected her to

absorb all the responsibilities and sacrifices while I continued on as if nothing had changed. I had not expected life to be much different but it had shifted momentously. It was mayhem. Matisse was a difficult baby to settle and did not sleep well. Sam was up all hours. If she stopped rocking Matisse in her arms, she would be crying again.

I distinctly remember the day they came home from the maternity ward. That night we were sitting in the living room and I was rocking Matisse, watching the television. An image appeared on the screen from Manhattan in New York City: a plane plunged into the World Trade Center, then one of the twin towers collapsed before my disbelieving eyes.

The world felt like a different place; we had a week-old daughter, who would grow up in a world where, it seemed, any sort of atrocity was possible. I remember looking down at that face, the very essence of innocence, and holding her a little closer. I thought about how glad I was that we lived in Australia, so far away from all the violence. That she would be safe and I would always be there to protect her and watch over her. That nothing could possibly prevent me from being there to guide her through life.

If I had my time again, I would choose to handle the way we told the kids that their father had cancer differently. I don't think we did anything wrong, but I feel we could have done it better. We did not sit the children down and have a frank discussion, which might have given them an opportunity to ask questions or express their feelings and fears. All we did was tell them that their dad had cancer, but not to worry because he was going to get better. Looking back, I think they probably understood it as if we were telling them I had the measles or the mumps – I would be sick for a little while, then I'd get over it and life would go on as normal.

Now I think that it would have helped them to have a greater grasp of the disease from the outset, because without some information about what might lie ahead, children's trusting minds can be susceptible to doubts that adults dismiss as far-fetched. They needed to understand that cancer was not anyone's fault, that it was not contagious and that it did not change the fact that they were still loved just as much as ever.

It was not that we were trying to keep anything from the kids. I guess we were just waiting for them to pick up on it, and want to ask us about it on their own terms, in their own time. Whenever they did raise the subject we were very open and honest in the way we spoke about cancer.

Tiernan, being so young, was largely oblivious to the situation, at least initially. But Matisse would overhear snippets of conversations or phone calls, and then take that information away and form her own understanding of what was going on.

Our circumstances were complicated by the fact that my condition was public knowledge, meaning the kids were more likely to stumble upon the topic outside the home environment. One of boys at Tiernan's kindergarten told him, intending no particular malice, 'Your dad has cancer – that means he's going to die.' Tiernan carried that burden around with him for more than a week, before eventually breaking down in tears. It turned out that the other child's mum had breast cancer.

Matisse had kids at school telling her that their dad or uncle had said I would be dead by the end of the year. Some kids had overheard their parents saying, 'Isn't it terribly sad about Jim Stynes?' They'd understood that to mean that I was about to die. Then, naturally, they would bring it up with Matisse, who was not necessarily equipped with a way of coping. Young children rely on their parents to help them make sense of the world.

When Matisse and Tiernan began to raise some of these problems with us, Sam and I realised the need to give them more detail. We understood that we hadn't explained this massive new issue in their lives well enough for them, and we tried to clarify things. We always ended these chats with the fact that we couldn't really be sure what was going to happen.

I distinctly remember two conversations with the children, both in March 2010, about nine months after my diagnosis. One evening, Tiernan began crying because we'd told him it was too late for him to stay up and watch a film. He was tired and irrational, and after carrying him upstairs I lay on his bed with him and tried to soothe him. We were chatting about why 10.30 pm was too late for a five-year-old, when suddenly he asked, 'Why have you got cancer?'

After telling him that I did not really understand why, he came back with, 'How did you get it?' Again I said I did not really know, but the doctors thought it might be from not looking after myself in the sun. I explained that quite a lot of people got the disease, but that some healed faster than others. I asked him if he thought I was healing faster or slower, and he sort of shrugged and told me that he loved me. Then he drifted off to sleep.

A few days later, I was tucking the kids into their beds when Matisse stumped me with another poser: 'Why do you die when you get cancer?' I explained that having cancer did not necessarily mean the person would die, and that in many cases people survived. She let it sink in, and then had a little cry. Over in his bed, Tiernan piped up with, 'Well, if you die I'm not going to cry.'

It struck me as such a beautiful thing for your child to say. 'It's okay,' I said, 'you can cry if you want to – it's fine.' But he just said, 'No, Daddy, I won't cry.' And that was final, as though it was his job not to cry. As though it had occurred to him that it would be a way he could help.

The tears and the tough questions were not the only difficult fatherhood moments during those first twelve months, though. I still faced the everyday challenges of being a parent, although now I experienced them through the prism of my abnormal circumstances. And, like any parent, I made mistakes.

Whether it was because of stress, exhaustion, medication or my brain tumours I could not be sure, but there were times when I was terribly short-tempered with the kids. It felt like there were days when I was seeking confrontation with them. I would find myself shouting, sometimes in such a ferocious way that it scared them. Afterwards, I would feel ashamed. It was something I'd always said I would never do as a parent, and here I was making my own kids cry. Sam would say, 'You can't be like that, Jim.' And I was thinking to myself, *What's wrong with me?*

The kids were reacting badly to my bad reactions, and I had to get my head around it and work out a way to not let it happen. When I was coaching Matisse's basketball team, I realised I was being ultra-competitive, barking instructions, especially when the games were close. I had to remind myself that she was an eight-year-old girl, and that the games needed to be about learning and enjoyment, not stress and worry. It was a philosophy that I had to start applying with Matisse and Tiernan more often. I wanted to ensure that my time with them was quality time.

There seems to be an expectation that people with a critical or terminal illness should switch into a mode where they try to 'enjoy every moment', particularly with their loved ones. But that was not my experience. It might seem like only a slight distinction, but rather than trying to enjoy every moment, I tried to live *in* the moment with the kids.

Nevertheless, in that first year, we did try to ensure we had special outings and holidays as a family. There was the trip to Disneyland, and we made concerted efforts on both the kids' birthdays: shopping in trendy Chapel Street with Matisse, a day at the Australian Grand Prix with Tiernan. I also made an effort not to let petty issues around money become stress-ful. When we went to the Royal Melbourne Show, I did not squabble about another $20 to go on the rides.

The other effort I made was to ensure that I had one-on-one time with each child. I took Tiernan to the skate park and the cinema, we swam at the beach, played at the park, read books and played with his toy cars together. With Matisse I would shoot some hoops, go for a bike ride, share milkshakes at a café or go to the bookshop. Each of these activities allowed us to connect and talk about what else was going on in their lives.

As well as attempting to become more involved in their lives, I endeavoured to include the kids more in mine. For football-obsessed Tiernan, there was the chance to go onto the MCG before the opening match of the 2010 season, the Youth Round game between Melbourne and Hawthorn. He was enjoying himself so much that I had to chase him to get the ball back for the umpires to start the match. Another time, he got to run through the banner as Melbourne's team mascot. He joined in when the players did their run-throughs and warm-ups; when they stopped he did not know what to do, so he just began running rings around them. Had I not convinced him that he needed to come to the boundary line, he probably would have trotted to the centre square for the opening bounce.

I also learned to include the kids more when it came to my illness, believing that this would help destigmatise cancer for them. The first time I shaved my head, after my initial round of radiation treatment, I had gone to pick Matisse up from school, forgetting she had not seen her father with a bald head before. Upon seeing me, she had let out a sort of combined shriek-laugh, before I had managed to explain what was going on.

Tiernan had thought it was a cool look and immediately wanted to have his hair cut as short as possible. So the next time I needed to shave off my hair, I made certain that both kids were involved. The family assembled in the bathroom and Matisse took control of the clippers, at first leaving a little mohawk, which they all found hilarious. Tiernan then promptly demanded that his head be shaved too. It became a fun memory, not an awkward one.

It was all about balance. I was acutely conscious that there was a risk of trying to force life, trying to manufacture special moments because I was really sick and might die. I had to appreciate that if things did not work out as cheerfully as I anticipated, so be it. I could not expect every moment with the kids to be all happiness and light; rather, I had to bask in the happy times when they came along, and trust that the kids would look back on them fondly.

It was important for me to allow the kids to move on and not have too many hang-ups about their dad being sick. They did not really understand that because I had cancer, we might have fewer special moments together in the years ahead. Meanwhile, I did understand this, which was why I loved any time I could spend with them – good, bad or indifferent. Every minute meant something. Every hug meant something. It was not that I was hugging them or tucking them into bed like it was the last time, it was just that I really appreciated each moment.

It didn't need to have bells and whistles and Disneyland for the moments to be special. Things I had previously considered chores – feeding them, bathing them, helping them with homework – now felt like blessings. Just doing things together was wonderful, particularly because sometimes I was not even well enough to do that. Sometimes I felt too ill, or was too tired and could not stay awake. There were times when I was dealing with medical treatment, when Sam might need my help and I could not give it. Those times made me feel really inept as a father. There were times when I cried, thinking that the only memories the children might be left with woud be of a sick man, a dying father. Those debilitating times helped me appreciate that when I was there, I wanted to be really present. When I was with the kids, they had my full attention. I tried to really watch and listen. I concentrated on being in the moment.

My other firm conviction was that I did not want to deny the kids their childhood and their own experiences by compelling them to focus on me. Our family had already been forced to give up considerable time to accommodate my healing, so I needed to make sure the children had ample opportunities to do their own thing.

I had never before fully appreciated how fortunate I was to

have these kids, and I was beginning to appreciate them and know them better than I ever had. I learned to appreciate that Matisse was a strong-willed and determined young woman who seemed to know where she wanted to go and who she wanted to be. That she could put up a front but was very trusting and prepared to let in genuine people very quickly. That she was a beautiful, caring soul who really watched out to make sure her dad did not hurt himself or overdo it. I learned to appreciate that Tiernan was full of energy, excitement and enthusiasm, and that he had a rare and wonderful imagination. It was special that he had a gentle and emotional side that he was not afraid to show. I came to appreciate how affectionate the two kids were towards each other, and how fiercely protective of one another they were. It made me proud and emotional to think of that bond between them.

I came to appreciate that one of life's joys is getting to know your kids better and watching them grow up. It made me wonder how I could have let slip chances to spend time doing so in the past. I often watched other parents now. There were some who did not have a lot but who knew there was one thing they could offer their children that did not cost anything, other than their time and effort. And that thing was their love. Then there were some parents who had plenty of money but were running all over the place, busily making a success of their lives but forgetting to put time and effort into their family.

I wanted my kids to understand that cancer had reminded me of a most important truth. When it had forced me to start stripping back all the things in my life that were peripheral and to concentrate on what was most important, the most important thing of all was my family. I hoped the kids would always know that I loved so many aspects of life, but none more so than being their father.

I know that every parent, if they stopped to think about it, would feel exactly the same way. And I pray that those parents will never need cancer to remind them of it.

12

NATURE VS SCIENCE

So many thoughts occupied my mind as I neared the end of my first year of living with cancer, but foremost was the knowledge that I had defied the prognosis of some experts simply by still being alive. That was a tribute to the outstanding medical team around me, as well as the love and support of my family and friends. But there was also no question in my mind that the treatment from outside the realms of conventional medicine had contributed significantly. I had always believed in seeking medical treatment beyond what is considered orthodox, and my approach to cancer was never going to be any different.

It was a mindset ingrained in me from childhood. My parents were always open to the idea of home remedies and concoctions to treat ailments. In some cases, they simply had different ideas about diet.

When I was about eighteen months old, they discovered that I had problems tolerating milk, so Mam would trek across town to buy products such as goat's milk and Bulgarian yoghurt. They used to buy organic wheat and then mill their own flour. They believed in giving the children a spoonful of cod-liver oil every morning.

Then there were the home remedies, many of which Mam would file in a big book on a kitchen shelf. If anyone had eczema she would fetch a cabbage leaf from the garden, cut the leaf's veins and then apply it to the forehead, fastening it with a stocking. If we had a cold she would reach for garlic or ginger. For some allergies or skin irritations she had a more drastic cure, although none of the children realised it until many years later. Some mornings she would ask the relevant child to pee into a cup. Then, unbeknown to the patient, she would put a few drops of the urine into a glass of water for him or her to drink with breakfast.

Dad had his own way of getting in on the act. During football season, he would develop all sorts of concoctions, mostly using olive oil and *poitín* (Irish moonshine), and he'd offer them as a rub to warm up your muscles or as a spray when you received a knock during a game.

My parents' enthusiasm for home-spun treatments fostered in me a willingness to remain open to natural therapies during my football career. Undoubtedly, this was one of the reasons I managed to recover so well from injuries and play those 244 consecutive AFL matches over a twelve-year stretch. Put simply, I believed that natural remedies had given me an advantage as a footballer, and that they'd do so again now that I was a cancer patient.

If I'd been prepared to look outside conventional medicine to overcome a sore knee, why wouldn't I do so to overcome a life-threatening disease? I was determined to keep an open mind to healing of all forms.

There is so much confusion in this area of cancer treatment, and the term 'natural therapy' can be applied to everything from peppermint tea to some forms of outright quackery and fraud. My first Google search on 'cancer treatment' had turned up endless sites with treatments, therapies and cures. It can be absolutely bewildering trying to sift through all of the options, working out which treatment is best for you. I am reluctant to steer people in any direction because every person's cancer is different; each individual needs to find out what works for them. But in general terms, a solid starting point is finding out which treatments have worked for other people with the same type of cancer.

It is also vitally important to find somebody in the medical field whom you can trust, and then to give a lot of weight to their advice. Graeme Southwick and Grant McArthur were those advisers for me. The complication, however, was that none of my doctors was talking in terms of a cure; they approached my cancer as something they were trying to control, thereby giving me the best chance of surviving for as long as possible. In contrast, advocates of many alternative therapies believed that they could help reprogram my body and assist it to rid itself of malignant cells. I kept reading testimonies from cancer survivors who had turned to non-traditional treatment only after doctors had told them that there was nothing more that could be done. I knew these survivors would be in a minority, and that many other patients would have done likewise and still failed to overcome cancer. But I did not want to leave it until it was too late to consider non-traditional treatment.

For someone like me, who was used to being in control of most situations in my life, non-traditional methods were a way of regaining some control of my treatment. My life had been turned on its head and I had to accept that my doctors were the best people to advise me about things such as surgery, drugs and radiotherapy. But I could still use other treatments to listen to my body, get my internal balance right and form an intuitive understanding of where my cancer was coming from.

Importantly, both of my medical confidants understood and supported that approach. Grant had said, 'I know you're the sort of bloke who's used to being in charge, and having a tumour growing inside you is about as clear an instance as you can experience of not being in charge of what's going on in your life. A tumour does its own thing. So I realise that trying to tell you not to try other treatments is never going to work. But I'm prepared to tell you if I don't think something's going to work, and to give you my opinion if I straight-out think you should not do it.'

Graeme had a similar view. 'Why not try them?' he said. 'You should do whatever's necessary to build up your brain's hopefulness. I will never do anything to undermine hope or sabotage the mental ingredient. The only things I will advise you against is any treatments we know to be counter-productive.'

When talking about these treatments, it is really important to make a distinction between 'complementary' and 'alternative' therapies.

Complementary therapies are used alongside conventional medicine, to improve a patient's wellbeing and enhance their quality of life; these include treatments such as massage, acupuncture, yoga and aromatherapy. By contrast, alternative therapies are used instead of conventional medicine. They are sometimes promoted as 'cancer cures', but their use might be scientifically unproven or not yet thoroughly tested.

Two complementary therapies that I quickly introduced to my lifestyle were meditation and reiki, and I found both to be really beneficial. Meditation quickly became part of my routine and something I enjoyed and valued greatly. I recalled that some of the Sydney Swans football team advocated meditation when they were enjoying success in the mid-2000s. When I researched meditation in relation to cancer patients, I read that studies had suggested it reduced stress in something like one-third of all patients, and mood swings in something like two-thirds.

Essentially, meditation involves concentration or reflection as a way of relaxing the body and calming the mind. I usually tried to do it for thirty to sixty minutes, as close to daily as I could. I would close my eyes while sitting cross-legged somewhere quiet, like the front veranda. Quite often I found that the best time was before the kids woke up. My goal might be to think happy and healing thoughts, or to visualise a goal, which might be simply to eradicate stress. Regardless, the sessions invariably left me in a more peaceful frame of mind.

'Reiki' is a Japanese term that, loosely translated, means the 'spiritual energy' in your body. The practice involves having a therapist place their palms on or above your fully clothed body, as a way of realigning your energy and bringing your body into a natural balance physically, mentally, emotionally and spiritually. My reiki master, Martine Salerno, really helped me to let certain thoughts go, especially thoughts that would otherwise block me up. She had clarity in her own thinking and also offered wise counsel. I can recall her suggestion, at a time when I kept finding myself bickering with the kids, that I should give them five compliments each day. It didn't sound like much, but it required a concerted effort and helped me to have a much more positive inclination towards Matisse and Tiernan. Sure enough, our relationships improved.

While these two methods complemented the medical care I was receiving, another lifestyle change was at the very core of my treatment protocol: my diet. Soon after I was diagnosed with cancer and began researching theories about treatment, I discovered hundreds of people who had found some success in getting the better of cancer simply by changing their diet. For the most part, this revolved around raw foods and juices. In the early months, the first changes I made were to drastically reduce or completely cut out consumption of meat, dairy, sugar, wheat, preservatives and processed foods. My main focus was to move away from animal proteins. All that this really left for me to eat was raw and lightly cooked vegetables, and plenty of fruit and nuts. I was surprised by how easily I adapted to the new diet: the main treats I craved were an occasional piece of chocolate and a beer.

The more I studied the correlation between diet and cancer, the more I began to agree with certain experts. The ones who resonated with me most were those who believed that cancer was caused when our food and environment became too removed from nature. Ian Gawler was from that school of thought. I responded to his gently affirmative nature, his broader philosophy and his approach to food, which was largely based on eating vegetables, grains and fruits. He believed that natural foods helped the body assert itself and heal.

I also readily identified with many of the ideas put forward by the American doctor Max Gerson, who had developed his treatment in the 1920s. His approach was based on the theory that poor nutrition, as well as constant exposure to chemical and environmental pollutants, created a faulty metabolism that led to cancer. Diet was a key part of the Gerson method. Apart from a strictly low-salt, low-fat vegetarian diet, patients needed to drink juice from almost ten kilograms of fresh fruits and vegetables each day. This involved drinking a glass of juice on the hour, thirteen times a day. Supplementing the juice were various vitamins, enzymes

July 2009 At the press conference to tell everyone I had cancer, I took my old number thirty-seven jumper, the one I'd worn when I ran across the mark in the 1987 Preliminary Final. Sam thought it was an omen that I could also overcome this challenge. A few days later, the Melbourne boys really lifted to beat West Coast.

Christmas 2009

My extended family celebrated Christmas day in a spirit of optimism and hope. Up the back: Jamie, Frank, Terri-Ann, Daniel, me and Brian. In the middle: Sammy, Mary, Sam, Sean holding Dylan, Dad and David. In the front row: Tiernan, Matisse, Wayne, Aislin, Sharon, Jacqui, Dearbhla and Mum.

Sam and her wonderfully supportive mum, Mary Williamson.

January 2010

We took the kids on a ten-day boat cruise from Mexico to California, taking in a visit to Disneyland. My health deteriorated and I felt like I was always battling the hangover from hell.

My parents took up Australian citizenship on Australia Day. One by one, their children had left home to live on the other side of the world.

April 2010

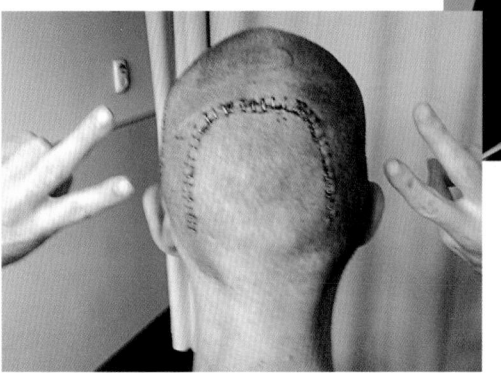

During five-and-a-half hours in the operating theatre, Professor Jeffrey Rosenfeld removed five tumours. He had entered my skull through a 'bone flap', closing it with forty staples.

A couple of weeks later I was back at the G for Richmond vs Melbourne – a win to the Demons.

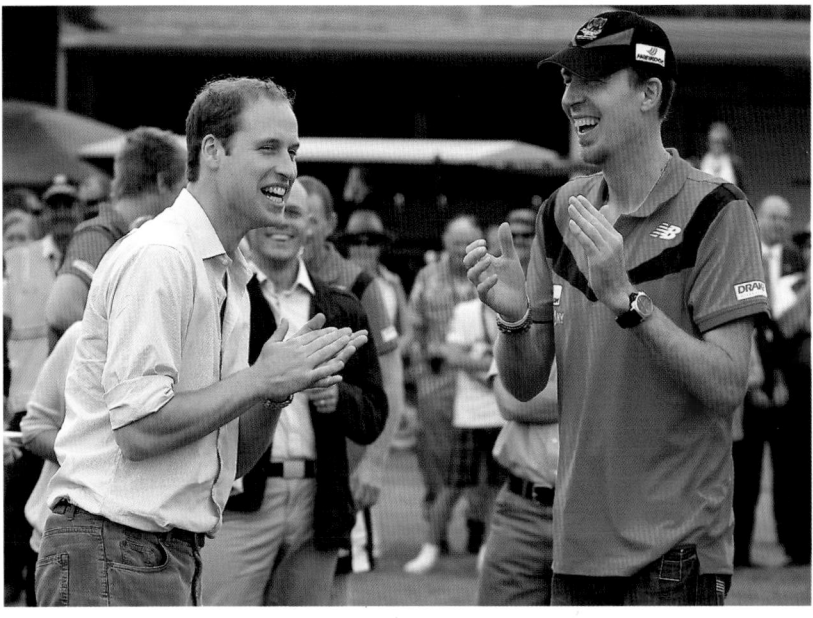

March 2011 In between my weekly visits to hospital, I managed to get out of the house and get on with life. First there was St Patrick's Day, then Prince William was guest of honour at Murrabit, one of the Victorian towns severely affected by floods. I ran him through a few basics of kicking and handballing a Sherrin football.

December 2011

The most important thing of all was my family. Photographer Mark Strachan captured my three most treasured relationships beautifully.

Christmas Day – January 2012

I had often fantasised about sailing off into the sunset, and that dream came true with Sam, Hugh and his wife Cath and all our children. In a church in Portobelo, I got the chance to say a prayer to the Black Christ, a revered wooden statue that was said to be responsible for several miracles.

and extracts, which were intended to stimulate organ function, particularly in the liver and thyroid.

For the first few months after I was diagnosed, I tried to implement a diet that was founded on some of these theories. But it could be confusing and frustrating, because sometimes the systems would contradict each other about which foods were beneficial or damaging. I was learning an enormous amount about food and nutrition, yet the more I learned, the more complex and overwhelming the whole subject seemed.

A chance meeting after that first few months helped me find direction and a dietary approach I could believe in. While wandering down the street in Albert Park, I stopped to take a look at a menu in front of an organic raw-food restaurant, called Le Cru, and happened to bump into a young Reach graduate, Shamila Galbally.

After we reacquainted ourselves, I asked, 'So, do you work here?' I explained that I had recently become a convert to this kind of food.

'I help out sometimes,' she replied. 'You should come inside and meet my sister Nushie and my mum. They're the chefs.'

Shamila's mother, Carolyn, was a delightful woman who empathised with my plight. She had been diagnosed with breast cancer in 1994, and she sincerely believed that changing her diet was a significant factor in her being alive to meet me fifteen years later.

'The problem I have, though,' I said, 'is that there are so many different schools of thought around what is the best diet. About which foods are in and which ones are out. And it also worries me how much weight I seem to drop – whether it's going to leave me strong enough to fight.'

Carolyn explained that their restaurant served food based on the 'Lifefood' philosophy espoused by Dr David Jubb, an Australian who had been based in New York for the past decade. Lifefood involved preparing fresh raw fruits and vegetables that were in season and still had their radiant energy, or 'lifeforce', intact. These were combined with fermented foods to ensure easy digestion. The enzymes in the food were not destroyed by the cooking process.

After that initial meeting, Carolyn offered to come to our house to help Sam and me get our heads around Lifefood and show us how to prepare some simple recipes. She also explained the theory about all types of food having either an acidic or alkaline effect on the body. How the average diet comprised mainly foods that increased the acid levels in the body, making it a fertile breeding ground for chronic illness. It was easy enough to look up an online chart that divided foods into acid-forming and alkaline-forming foods.

It was also through Carolyn that I eventually met Dr Jubb and headed, for the first time, down the path of what would be classified as a genuinely alternative therapy.

David Jubb could be a poster boy for the eccentric genius club. I met him in February 2010, about eight months after my diagnosis, and I wasn't sure quite what I had stumbled upon. He was like a cross between a street busker and a mad scientist. Inescapably, my eye was drawn to his mohawk hair, tied in a knot on his head. His athletic frame and new-age dress sense gave him the appearance of an off-duty acrobat from Circus Oz.

When he spoke, however, it became clear that his brain was constantly working, flitting from one idea to the next, with his mouth struggling to keep up. He was clearly incredibly intelligent, with an extraordinary depth of knowledge about nutrition and the human body, and he explained many of his arcane concepts with simple analogies.

David's was a remarkable story. He told me how he had been born and raised on the Furneaux Islands off Tasmania's north-west coast, and had studied at Melbourne University before heading to the United States in 1980, where he gained his doctorate in physiology at New York University. For more than a decade he had run an organic health-food shop, Jubb's Longevity, in New York's East Village, and a program on Manhattan cable television called *The Universe Inside Our Mind*.

He had strong opinions about how to treat serious illness, and we discussed the methods David believed were most appropriate for my condition. He spoke at length about diet and nutrition, and his Lifefood theories married up with what I had come to understand through Carolyn and her daughters. He suggested that ninety per cent of what I ate should be raw food, which would allow my body to heal properly and replenish its lost minerals.

'There is no pot-boiling in nature,' he proclaimed. 'Have

you ever stopped to consider that no other life form on this planet eats cooked food apart from humans? If we were meant to eat cooked food we would have been born with stoves attached.'

Some of his other ideas about treatment, however, were radical and fascinated me. David suggested applying poultices four times a day and recommended a black paste that would get into my bloodstream and help cleanse it. He advised me to undergo a fifteen-day detoxification program, including the use of coffee enemas, and to consider drinking my own urine to help myself heal.

I mentioned how Mam had been known to slip a few drops of urine to us at breakfast when we were children. 'She must be a very wise woman, your mother,' David said. 'Most people believe urine to be the excess dirty water left over from the food and liquid we consume. In fact, it is a by-product of the blood and abounds with anti-cancer compounds. There are people who don't want you to know about the benefits of urine because it's free, it's abundant and it cannot be patented.'

And yet, he said, urine contained a compound called urea that was an ingredient used in many commercial soaps, skin moisturisers and hair conditioners. David told me about how urine had been used throughout history to help heal everything from broken bones to poor skin, from sore throats to discoloured teeth. Nearly every culture had a reference to urine therapy: Egyptians, Hindus, ancient Chinese, native Americans, ancient Greeks and Aztecs. Even the Bible had a reference to 'drinking waters from thine own cistern' in the *Book of Proverbs*. David told me how Morarji Desai, the prime minister of India in the early 1970s, had declared on his ninety-ninth birthday that the secret to his longevity was drinking his urine every morning.

I was sold on the urine therapy, but David was equally adamant about the benefits of detoxification. I had read about coffee enemas in both the Gerson and Gawler literature. The theory was that the coffee stimulated the liver and gall bladder, causing them to flush toxins from the system, clearing the way for the body's immune system to battle malignant cells.

I decided to squeeze in the Jubb detoxification regimen in before I began another round of chemotherapy. So, for the first fifteen days of March 2010 it was full steam ahead. The regimen required a significant time commitment; there was something to take or do every hour. Castor oil poultices four times a day, prescribed rest periods, and special powders and raw food to consume. Over the first few days I was drinking litres of bicarbonate of soda, as well as tablespoons of olive oil and glasses of my own urine.

The coffee enemas were scheduled for every fourth day, and preparations for the first one involved drinking 400 millilitres of oil and half that of lemon juice, along with the usual glass of urine. Just when I had mentally come to terms with the prospect of the enema, I somewhat sheepishly realised that we had run out of ground coffee, and had to duck next door to the neighbours' house to borrow some. Two litres of room-temperature coffee went in, and after balancing on all fours and holding the liquid in for fifteen uncomfortable minutes, I was free to release it.

The second enema proved slightly less successful, when I failed to hold the coffee in for the whole fifteen minutes and it came gushing out all over the place. My cursing brought Sam to the bathroom door, where she was confronted by a scene from a barista's worst nightmare. 'Jim, I love you, and I'll support you in this,' she said, 'no matter how weird these treatments might be. But I mean, really! We've just had the bathroom painted!' We dissolved into fits of laughter and she reached into the laundry and handed me a mop. 'And, um, I don't think we'll need that back when you've finished.'

I did emerge from that detox feeling considerably lighter and healthier. In fact, whenever I put the time into pursuing a holistic approach to life – diet, meditation and resting – I always noticed how much better I felt. Through Lifeforce foods I came to understand the importance of nutrition, balance and digestion. From that time on, the foodstuffs on our grocery lists and in our pantry changed irrevocably. It gave me the confidence to tinker around with ingredients, to such an extent that I developed a few unique blends of muesli, which I eventually started marketing and selling.

The second time I turned to alternative medicine was a more spontaneous decision. It came a few months later – about seven weeks after my first round of brain surgery – when I took the family for a two-week holiday to Bali in Indonesia.

While there, we marked a milestone of sorts when I reached 1 June 2010 – exactly one year on from learning I had cancer.

Any thought of celebration, however, was short-lived. Just two days later, while swimming in the pool, I ran my fingers over my shoulder and noticed a new lump. It was in precisely the same spot where a tumour had already been cut out. It was even the same size. The one positive was that at least it was close to the surface, and easily accessible for a scalpel. I sent a text message to Graeme Southwick in Melbourne, suggesting he might need to book me in for more surgery.

Once again, I found myself on a holiday with the family but feeling downcast, and therefore guilty about spoiling their fun. We were staying in a guesthouse in Ubud that was owned and operated by Janet de Neefe, a former Melbourne woman, and her husband, Ketut Suardana. They also ran a sublime restaurant and cooking school, and invited us to have dinner with them one night. Both Janet and Ketut impressed me as very generous and spiritual people, and when they suggested that I should make an appointment with a well-regarded local Balian – a shaman, or traditional healer – I had no hesitation in agreeing, hoping it would lift my spirits and rekindle my enthusiasm.

Apparently, there are around four times as many Balians practising their healing on the island of Bali than there are doctors. Some travellers have come to regard a visit to such a healer as a trivial tourist activity, something akin to booking an afternoon of snorkelling or having a spa. But a Balian is regarded as a divine instrument of healing who can never turn anyone away, and visitors are expected to receive the healing with respect and reverence.

When Ketut took me along the next day there was a long queue of local people waiting to see the healer, a huge man who was described to me as a 'black magic doctor'. He treated each person while a crowd of other patients and family members looked on. When it was my turn to see him, he used his fingers to poke and prod my chest, neck, forehead and calves. The process was incredibly painful, but he explained through an interpreter that this was because he was extracting the poison from my body. He began blowing sharp puffs of air on my body and into my eyes, and spat wads of chewed herbs onto my skin. Then he started slapping me on the back. He handed me a beaded wristband to wear, and a container of bright-red oily liquid – apparently from a squid or an octopus – to take with me to drink. He told me to come back in a few days to see him, after which time I would return to full health.

That evening, Ketut had one of his kitchen staff prepare a drink combining the red liquid with ground sandalwood and honey, which made it very palatable. In his quiet and unassuming way, Ketut asked if I would like to visit his cousin, Dharma, a spiritual healer who lived at an ashram about ninety minutes' drive from Ubud.

The next morning, we drove through six or seven towns and some classically beautiful Balinese landscapes. After leaving behind the lush layers of stunning green rice-paddy fields, we arrived at an ashram that was as basic and uncomplicated a place as you could visit. It was the sort of place that would be confronting to some Westerners, yet it disarmed any such thoughts by exuding tranquillity.

Ketut introduced me to Dharma, and for nearly two hours we sat and discussed meditation. His belief was that you could devote as much of your life as you wanted to studying the theory behind meditation, but in my situation it was important to concentrate on developing an effective method of practising it. He suggested that a good technique was to choose a number between one and nine and use it as my 'mantra' – the word that I repeated while meditating to aid my concentration. He also explained his approach to concentrating on the body's seven 'chakras' – its centres of spiritual power – while meditating.

After a while, Dharma asked me to accompany him to the ceremony temple and receive some healing and gifts. He poured water with flowers over my head to cleanse me, and then said something quite moving and powerful: that he would spend the next three weeks taking on my illness, which would heal me. I was not to worry in any way about the outcome, as I would heal. Hearing this left me with such an uplifting feeling on the drive back to Ubud.

All that remained was to return to the Balian a couple of days later. Ketut organised for his driver to take me, and when I arrived it was more chaotic than ever. There was a sea of people, ranging in age from toddlers to the elderly, interspersed with chickens, scrawny dogs and bicycles. There must have been a crowd of close to 100 people huddled excitedly around the healer as he tended to each patient. Men were taking their shirts off and lining up for treatment. The healer was chanting words and throwing water with flowers and rice onto their bowed heads.

My arrival created quite a stir, not only because I was the only Westerner present, but also, I imagined, because I seemed to be twice the height of anyone else there. The crowd melted away and people looked up at me with astonished faces. Upon seeing my wristband, people invariably smiled in recognition, and some of them chuckled, like I was the dag in the group, the try-hard. My driver pushed me through the crowd and told me to take my shirt off and line up.

Before I knew it – and without having a clue what was going on but feeling completely part of it all the same – I was told to bow and drink the water three times as it was splashed into my cupped hands. I had noted that the men before me in the line had all done this with their right hands on top, and I remembered that the left hand was considered unclean. There was a bizarre juxtaposition of thoughts struggling to the forefront of my mind: a random image of Catholics receiving the blessed sacrament from a priest, followed by a fervent hope that the water I was about to drink was clean and would not give me a stomach bug.

After my three mouthfuls of water, the healer began slapping me between my shoulder blades and splashing my head from a bowl of water with flowers and rice in it. Behind me, my driver nudged me and whispered that I should step back and sit down again.

The next thing I knew, everyone was handing out bright-yellow cooked chickens with flowers and burning incense on them. I noticed that each chicken still had a few stray feathers as well as its severed head beside it. I remembered that Ketut had given me a cryptic warning about eating chicken. I was not to worry, he had said; it might give me diarrhoea, but only briefly. Then the Balian spoke loudly to the whole group, and at one point everyone began cackling raucously. I turned to my driver and asked, 'The diarrhoea?' He nodded and began laughing. 'Now you must eat a piece of your chicken,' he said.

It was not the most enticing proposition, but I convinced myself to have faith in the process, rather than trying to question it too much. My philosophy had always been that just because people did not understand something or could not see it, that did not mean it wasn't real. So I started tugging at some of the chicken's skin, only to find that it was as tough as hell. It did not seem to have any meat on it.

Right, I thought. *Turn it over and look for some meat on the breast.* But there did not seem to be any at all, and my hands were becoming slipperier and smellier and I was fumbling awkwardly. Eventually, I found a rubbery morsel on the leg, and gnawed on it until I managed to get it down. Everyone was given a plastic bag and told to put their chicken in it and take it home to eat that evening.

The crowd dispersed and I stood there for about ten minutes, clutching my greasy doggy bag and waiting to see the healer. Eventually, the chance arose and he checked me once more with his prodding fingers, much as he had the first time. He told me that the poison was working its way out of my body and that I would be healed. I handed over an offering the equivalent of about $50 to a woman who I think was his wife. I knew full well that this was a considerable sum for the Balinese, but it was not a lot for the possibility of being cancer-free. It was probably a bit steep for a sorry excuse for a roast chicken, though.

That afternoon, we drove south to Jimbaran Bay, where I met up with Sam and the kids. They had booked in at an exclusive resort, and upon arriving there, in the dusk light, the atmosphere jarred against what I had experienced over the previous few days. It was all swimming pools, ceiling fans and cool drinks. There was none of the authenticity of the ashram, none of the energy of the healer and his crowd of followers.

We moved to a table in the resort's elegant restaurant, and as the waiter seated us and discussed drinks, I glanced down at the plastic bag at my feet. How on earth was I going to incorporate the chicken into my evening meal? Soup seemed a feasible option, and when the waiter left I explained my predicament to Sam, then I opened the bag to show the family the paltry poultry. It smelled so fetid that Sam nearly dry-retched, and the rest of the family agreed that there was no way I could possibly eat it.

In the midst of disbelief and laughter, I told them to have faith; if trusting in the healer's methods meant getting a little sick, then so be it.

When the waiter returned, I explained that I had some local food that I hoped they might prepare in a soup, and he assured me that this would present no difficulties. Only a few seconds after taking my bag away to the kitchen, he returned with the chicken on a plate. In fractured English he asked, 'This what sir wanting to eat?'

I asked whether he believed that would be unwise, and after a moment of hesitation he said he wouldn't know, so I asked him to proceed. The prospect of a dodgy soup was not especially tempting – somehow I could not get Mam's voice out of my head, with her warnings about poorly cooked or reheated chicken – but there was something faintly comical about the whole situation.

After the waiter left, Sam and I agreed that it reminded us of a scene from the television show *Fawlty Towers*, in which Manuel knew he had a suspect piece of veal but served it anyway, hoping nobody would notice. Regardless, I believed eating the chicken was part of the covenant I had made during the ceremony. A stomach upset would be insignificant in the grander scheme of things.

The waiter returned to our table with a triumphant look on his face; the chef had cut up the chicken and prepared it with a curry sauce. The dish looked and smelled quite appetising, although I had never in my life eaten meat that was remotely as tough to chew.

After four or five mouthfuls, I convinced myself that I had consumed enough to have kept my end of the bargain. Nobody had mentioned anything about needing to clear my plate. This was not south Dublin, with Mam warning that you had to eat your meat or you would not get any pudding.

Arriving back in Melbourne in mid-June, to the prospect of more surgery, I was surprised by the sense of freedom that enveloped me. There may have been another lump on my shoulder, but I had no stress, no trepidation. I attributed this to Dharma's promise to carry the load for me over the next three weeks. It was just as well that I had that vow in my mind, because those three weeks would prove to be a time when I definitely needed help.

Just a few days after flying home, I was sitting in the kitchen on a tranquil Sunday when I noticed that my vision was beginning to fail. An incapacitating headache followed, and I was in such a poor state that Sam and her friend Kirsty had to drive me to the emergency department. The doctor prescribed morphine as well as dexamethasone to ease the swelling inside my head, and a CAT scan was organised. When the results came back the doctor announced, somewhat nonchalantly, 'Yes, it's another brain tumour. It's quite deep.'

Beside me, Sam let out a cry of anguish and I saw tears rolling off her eyelashes. While I sat there stunned, Kirsty consoled Sam, who, in between sobs, was railing about how cancer could be so cruel and unjust. Thankfully, I reacted in a way I would never have managed six months earlier. I could hear a voice inside my head saying, 'Now, don't say too much, just listen to her – she really just needs to vent. She doesn't need someone trying to solve the problem for her.'

And, for once, that is exactly what I did. I listened.

'I just think that the doctors have always begun with the best-case scenario,' she said. 'But so far, for us, it's always ended up being the worst-case scenario. It has to change sooner or later, Jim.'

Surely, somehow, some time, I just had to catch a lucky break.

The next morning, I woke up at the Peter MacCallum Cancer Centre contemplating how, only two months after brain surgery, another tumour had shown up on the scans of my skull. Back in April I had emerged from the operating theatre in a fog, vowing that Melbourne would avenge its one-point loss to Collingwood. Now, on the day of the rematch – the big Queen's Birthday blockbuster – I was back in hospital dealing with more brain tumours.

It did not bear thinking about; besides, even thinking was hurting my head. I was in no state to make the journey a few hundred metres across East Melbourne to watch the match at the MCG. I rang Don McLardy to tell him that I would not be at the Melbourne president's lunch; instead, Wayne came to keep me company while we watched the match on television.

We sat there engrossed, as the margin between the teams never seemed to extend beyond one goal. At three-quarter time, with the Demons five points down, I pulled back the sheets and began to climb out of bed. 'Come on, Wayne,'

I said. 'Let's get down there. I can't miss this.'

By the time he pulled into the MCG carpark, there were only a few minutes left. We sat there in the car, listening to the radio, transfixed and afraid to move in case we missed the match-defining moment. First Collingwood, and then Melbourne pulled ahead by six points; just as I dared to believe, the Magpies kicked a goal to level the score. The siren sounded – a draw. I didn't know whether to go through the gates or not, and then I thought, *Why not? The boys will be flat and could probably use a word to pep them up.*

What I hadn't counted on was that when I climbed out of the car, my vision was so poor that I had to place a hand on Wayne's shoulder for help. We negotiated our way to the rooms.

If my failing eyesight came as a shock, there was another one awaiting me inside the rooms. I found myself next to a supporter in a wheelchair and realised that it was one of the club's directors and great benefactors, Peter Szental. He had developed prostate cancer after I had been diagnosed; at one stage it looked to have gone into remission, only to return. I had not realised the gravity of his condition; he had a wan complexion and looked critically ill. He told me that his doctors had declared there was nothing else they could do for him, and he only had a matter of weeks to live. I was so saddened. Here was a man of great energy and drive. He had just turned sixty and was in a position to enjoy more time with his beloved wife and family . . . only to be told it was all over.

It just seemed inconceivable that the same fate could befall me at the age of forty-four. I had to find a way to get well. It looked like I would be lining up for another ride on the medical carousel.

In late June of 2010 I was back at my old haunt, Cabrini Hospital, where Graeme Southwick removed the lump from the hollow near my collarbone. The operation went smoothly and, while I was recovering, my mind felt sharper than it had in months, regardless of the new brain tumour.

As always seemed to happen when I was idle, I started to develop ideas about new projects and ambitions. During one period of convalescence I had devised the concept of Melbourne playing in an AFL-sanctioned Youth Round. This time, I started to think about linking Reach to a secondary school, as a way of showing that our philosophy worked and had a practical application. These musings were, no doubt, a product of my feeling guilty whenever my disease forced me to be inactive. Instead of simply accepting that periods such as this were productive because they helped me recuperate, I tended to see them as inconvenient nuisances that stopped me from achieving other things in life.

In recent months I had begun to learn how to accept help, but I remained determined not to use illness as an excuse for me to sit back and do nothing. I could see how some people could become addicted to being sick, in a way, and to having everything done for them. It was why I believed that hospitals should not be too comfortable or luxurious. Patients should want to be discharged and get on with healing.

Whenever people asked after my health, I realised, it was important that I leave them with a positive experience rather than saying something that created doubt. That way I felt everyone would keep thinking positively about the outcome of my cancer challenge, rather than fearing for the worst and giving me up for dead.

It would be fair to say, though, that rather than seeing myself as sick, I over-corrected in July and August of 2010. During that period, I was denying that cancer could slow me down, and I hurtled headlong at life once more. I was trying to be a better family man, a better husband and father. I was trying to be truer to myself. But at the same time I was looking to ramp up my involvement with Reach, which had just received a game-changing $5 million in grants from the federal and state governments. I devoted time to filming scenes for my documentary, *Every Heart Beats True*, with my good mates Paul Currie and Jules Lund. And I began undergoing another series of radiation sessions for the brain tumour, after which Grant McArthur started me on ipilimumab, the drug designed to enhance my immune system. Thankfully, there seemed to be very few side-effects, just a few cramps and an awful taste in my mouth, particularly when I ate anything sweet.

Feeling so well had also allowed me to become more actively involved in the Melbourne Football Club again, and one event I was determined not to miss was the Foundation Heroes function on the first Wednesday in August. When I had taken on the presidency in 2008, we had set out to demolish Melbourne's $5 million debt, and this 2010 dinner managed to wipe out the final $350000 and put the club in surplus for the first time in thirty years. The function was also the event at which we would unveil our new club emblem.

By the weekend I was feeling fantastic. The Demons could mount a push for the finals if they managed to defeat lowly Richmond at the MCG on the Sunday. When I woke up that morning, the world seemed a better place.

During the drive to the ground, I turned to Sam and said, 'You know, I'm starting to wonder if this new immune therapy might be working. This is the best my head has felt in months.'

Perhaps fate overheard my comment because the very moment Sam parked the car at the MCG, everything changed dramatically. I stepped out of the car and – *bam!* – I could hardly see. The right-hand side of my body went numb and I had pins and needles in my hand. Momentarily, I wondered whether I had suffered a stroke.

Gradually I improved, though, so we decided to go into the ground and head upstairs to the presidents' function. Remarkably, as I walked in I was stopped by one of the staff at the door, who said, 'I'm sorry, Jim, but there is a lady who has been waiting to speak to you. She's been waiting for a while; she's quite insistent.'

Given how poorly I felt, I wanted to protest but I could not bring myself to do so. It would not have mattered, anyway, because as I turned around the elderly woman was marching – slowly, but with a look of great determination – towards me. We had barely exchanged greetings when she began to admonish me for not devoting enough time to my health.

'Now, you might think I'm just a silly old woman,' she said, 'but if you keep this pace up you simply won't get better. Do you hear me? It's time you gave up all this other silliness and put your time into your health and your family. They're the two most important things you've got.'

I knew that she was right, and I agreed. Life had become too hectic over the past fortnight. If a tingling arm was not enough to remind me of that, this woman's stern rebuke had left me in no doubt.

I left the function and sat in an empty corporate box to convalesce and watch the game. When Liam Jurrah kicked a goal to put Melbourne twenty-six points up midway through the final term, I had seen enough and we headed home. For the next two hours the headaches intensified until, mercifully, at about 8 pm, they began to ease off.

The brave woman at the MCG had been right. I could not keep this pace up.

Towards the end of the 2010 football season, I was plagued by intense stabbing headaches. After one especially bad episode at the end of August, I had to be taken to hospital in an ambulance and was confined to the house for a week. More scans were sought; they revealed a second dark spot in my brain, which the doctors seemed to think was not totally unexpected. They remained hopeful that the immune-system treatment might shrink the tumours: two in my brain and two in my duodenum. In the meantime, I had to subject my skull to another dose of stereotactic radiation therapy. The medical treatment was beginning to feel like last-throw-of-the-dice stuff, and it seemed as though the only successes were coming through surgery. I was struggling to see how I could get on top of cancer.

Apart from feeling mentally flat, I was physically wrecked. When I wasn't being knocked about by headaches, I was fatigued. Food held very little appeal and I had lost weight. That September, I seemed to spend all my time cancelling engagements. Not surprisingly, some of them were football functions, such as the Melbourne best-and-fairest count and the players' association awards. Others were more personally upsetting, such as when I had to phone one of my great childhood mates, Ciarán Farrell, to tell him I could not fly back to Ireland to be the best man at his wedding. Some reduced me to tears, like when I had to go to hospital with swelling of the brain on Matisse's ninth birthday.

I felt as though my reasons for living – the things that kept me going and motivated me – were being taken away from me, one by one. When people asked me what kept me going, the answer was always my family. Whenever I felt close to them, I invariably felt stronger and healthier.

The other saving grace during those dark days was the imminent release of *Every Heart Beats True*, the documentary about my cancer struggle. Paul and Jules did an enormous amount of work to have it ready and to promote it, and their enthusiasm for the project touched everyone, including me. Those who saw a sneak preview were bullish about it, which gave us great confidence that it would be successful and raise a substantial amount for Reach through the proceeds from its sales. On the night the film was screened, a gang of a few hundred went to the Dream Factory to watch it. The reaction there, and among my friends and the wider public, really stimulated and inspired me at a time when I needed it most.

There was some brilliant humour that flowed from the footage captured during the detox section of the documentary. My old mate, the Irish comedian Jimeoin, chimed in with, 'If drinking your own piss and cross-dressing helps, then fantastic.' I also had a good laugh about the reaction from the football commentator and entertainer Sam Newman: 'I've not had a coffee enema; I only drink strong lattes. I must order one of those at some stage if you've got a machine here. The mind, or some part of your body, boggles . . . and to cap it off with a nice glass of chilled urine, I mean, could you wish for anything better in the world? So if you'll pardon me now, I'm off to the grocers.'

But my favourite was a text message that arrived from a mate, which read: 'You realise you're now Public Enema No.1?'

13

SMOKE AND MIRRORS

When you get desperate enough in life, something interesting usually happens. In my mind, I had reached a point of utter desperation in my struggle against cancer, a juncture where it seemed like I had nothing to lose.

I had these tumours in my brain and duodenum, but it felt like I had hit the pause button. I had completed more rounds of radiation and immunology, and now I was hoping that scans might show I was ready for more surgery. Yet I was still desperate to find – and to believe in – a cure for my cancer. That cure was nowhere to be found in conventional medicine, or even in conventional thinking, so I plunged deeper into the waters of alternative therapy.

The opportunity to do so presented itself in September 2010, after a conversation between Sam and a dear friend she had known since kindergarten, Danielle. After Sam had recounted my Balian experience, Danielle had mentioned a traditional Indonesian smoke treatment that was advocated by some Australian patients. She and Sam organised to catch up for lunch, and when they did Danielle explained the concept of 'Balur therapy'. She gave Sam some literature and offered to organise a meeting with a Melbourne family who had been through a positive experience at the Griya Balur clinic in Jakarta. The concept piqued my curiosity enough for me to look into it further.

I discovered that the Balur method involved using smoke to detoxify the body. The idea was to reduce harmful mercury and other metals by breaking them down into tiny nanoparticles, which could then be flushed out of the system. This was achieved by having patients lie on a grounded metal table; clinical assistants would then vigorously rub and massage their skin until the pores opened up. At this point the body was totally immersed in smoke to help capture and extract the toxic nanoparticles.

It sounded implausible to my Western mind, but there seemed to be a considerable amount of anecdotal evidence supporting the Balur method, including from patients in advanced stages of cancer. I also heard the voice of desperation whispering into my ear, constantly asking, 'Why not give it a go?' Sam, who by nature is a trusting soul, was cautiously open to the idea, but she was more than a little perturbed about the idea of dropping everything to head back to Indonesia at only a few days' notice.

I was oscillating – determined to go one moment, then convinced it was a ludicrous idea the next – and I couldn't imagine how I would go about it, even if I did decide to try Balur. I discussed my quandary with Hugh. 'What do you think?' I asked.

'Bugger it, mate – why don't you just do it?' he said. 'Even if it's only a one in a hundred chance, you could be that one.' Hugh volunteered to accompany me to Indonesia; Sam and the kids would fly over a week or so later. 'Come on,' he said. 'Let's jump on a plane.'

I wanted to clear it with my oncologist, Grant McArthur. He was sceptical but also reluctant to advise against it, given that it would not interfere with any of my scheduled medical treatment. 'But I really would suggest that you stay close to an international standard hospital and the airport,' he said, 'just in case you need them. You need to have an emergency plan.'

So it was that, just a few days later, Hugh and I found ourselves on a plane flying into the unknown in Jakarta. Naively, we had failed to make a distinction between Jakarta and Bali until we landed. Little may have separated the two Indonesian regions in distance, but in reality they were worlds apart.

Emerging from the Soekarno-Hatta Airport, we jumped into a cab and battled our way through the congested anarchy that is Jakarta. The entire Indonesian capital was gridlocked, and it took us two or three hours to negotiate the thirty kilometres to the hotel at which we were staying. Everyone seemed to be driving, yet I had never seen so many pedestrians. It would be fair to say that Jakarta warrants consideration as the proverbial 'city of contradictions'. It has the extremes of beauty and deformity. It has an officious bureaucracy struggling to mask the all-pervasive chaos. It has glimpses of opulent skyscrapers one moment, then the grimy reality of a shanty town the next.

We were a long way from Ubud now, Toto.

The following morning, we headed straight to the Griya Balur clinic. Our taxi driver had trouble finding the address but eventually pulled into a small side-street, weaving his way past vendors, beggars and alley cats before pointing us to a tidy and unassuming-looking shopfront.

Inside, the reception area consisted of a random collection of vinyl and metal kitchen chairs. Behind the odd drawn-back curtain we could make out the treatment areas, which were elevated copper trays on concrete floors. It was slightly disconcerting that the whole clinic came across as being on the grotty side, and that the air had an unpleasant whiff about it.

I glanced at Hugh, who turned to me, raised his eyebrows and said, 'Well, we're here now, mate. Let's get into it. And remember, whatever you sign up for, I'm up for too.'

Eventually, we were introduced to the clinic's founder, Dr Gretha Zahar, a diminutive bespectacled woman in her seventies. In fluent English she spoke frankly about the philosophy behind Balur treatment and what it entailed. Gretha was a scientist who had a doctorate in nanochemistry from the University of Padjadjaran, in the nearby city of Bandung. For more than a decade she had been researching and developing a variety of specially treated cigarettes, which she believed were true to the region's traditional use of tobacco for medicinal and curative purposes. They were unlike commercial cigarettes and tobacco, which she said had been corrupted by the introduction of poisonous chemicals and filters.

'Mercury is the cause of all illnesses,' she declared. 'In my cigarettes – we call them Divine Cigarettes – there are scavengers that extract the mercury from the body.' She had developed thirty-eight types of Divine Cigarettes; some were for patients to smoke, others were for the clinical assistants, who inhaled the smoke and then blew it onto or into the patients undergoing treatment. Gretha said that, since 1998, she had treated more than 50000 patients, many of whom were stage three or four cancer sufferers. Not all patients could be helped, and some found the treatment too exacting, but many had been cured.

'How long will you need to treat, Jim?' Hugh asked. Gretha replied that, for a patient in my condition, three months would be ideal, but that an initial fifteen-day program should make a consequential difference. The treatment would begin immediately. She left us, saying she would be back to oversee the first session as soon as she had checked on a few other patients.

Despite my initial apprehensions about the clinic, I instantly warmed to Gretha and her no-nonsense approach. She was clearly a very special woman, genuinely motivated by a desire to help people rather than by recognition or kudos. As she worked her way through to another area of the busy clinic, many locals, including some whose children had severe disabilities, stopped her for a few words. She calmly dealt with each query, and the respect shown to her was obvious.

As she moved off, one of her assistants ushered Hugh and me to the treatment area and offered us a Divine Cigarette. It dawned on me that I had not had a drag on a cigarette in almost thirty years, since the days when I was an easily led and mischievous kid in my early teens in south Dublin. As I accepted the offering, it occurred to me how ironic it was that people back in Australia often referred to cigarettes as 'cancer sticks'.

I lit up and began inhaling, only to find that, after about the third drag, I was so lightheaded that I nearly fainted. Only the decision to quickly grab a seat prevented me from falling over. Three puffs and I'd had enough . . . how was I ever going to endure fifteen days of being immersed in tobacco smoke? And would I be required to keep smoking after that? I could not imagine joining the ranks of smokers congregated in a cloud of fumes outside buildings at formal functions. It sure as hell was not a message I wanted to send to my kids, or anyone else's.

That first day of Balur treatment would prove to be the most intense day of my life. I had no idea what I was getting myself into, and the next six hours were as physically and mentally relentless as anything I had experienced. I tried to recall football matches where I had emerged more battered and bruised, but eventually I concluded that none had been as ferocious as the workout I received at the incredibly strong hands of a seventy-one-year-old grandmother.

It began with me stripping down to my underpants and lying on a copper tray, where two clinical assistants began applying some kind of oily solution to my skin, using rubbing and smacking motions to open up the pores. Then Gretha, with great strength and dexterity, spent the next few hours clambering on the table like a cat, working her way around my body and trying to treat every part of it with smoke. The three of them would inhale the divine cigarettes through a hollow bone and then blow the smoke through a rubber tube into each of my ears. They would hold my mouth shut and blow smoke up my nose, until I retched and purged whatever fluid I could bring up. They blew smoke into every orifice. I would hazard a guess and say I had become one of the few people in the world to have had coffee and cigarettes through an enema.

Next, Gretha's assistants blew smoke into dozens of what looked like rubber syringes, and applied them over my body, all the while slapping, thumping and rolling my body around. Finally, I was shrouded in cigarette smoke and wrapped in a foil blanket. Over those six hours, there was not a centimetre of my body that was not pervaded by smoke; Gretha and her assistants must have inhaled more than 100 cigarettes between them.

Every time I thought the treatment must be finished, another hour would roll by. When the end eventually came, I felt like I had been stripped bare, physically and mentally. It was as though I had submitted my entire being, and my body was simply a vessel they were using to make it happen. Towards the end of that first session, I went so deeply into my own mind that I'm not sure whether I actually passed out or not. Afterwards, I was too drained to do anything other than sit in silence. I was simply staring into space as we waited for the taxi to come and take us back to the hotel.

For a long time, Hugh and I did not dare utter a word, perhaps because we were not sure what to say to each other. Eventually, Hugh muttered an oath and spat out, 'Well, that was bloody intense.'

'Yeah,' I replied – it was all I could manage.

Then, with a chuckle, from the side of Hugh's mouth slipped the words, 'Mate, let us never speak of this again.'

Of course, that evening Hugh and I spoke at length about what we had been through. And the more we did, the more I realised how keen I was to get back to the clinic for the next bout of treatment. It felt like destiny, as though it was finally time for me to heal. I told myself that there were just another fourteen more days until I'd begin to emerge from cancer. This had to be the turning point. Throughout that first day, Gretha had often spoken about the divine, and how she had ultimate faith that she would cure me. I desperately wanted to believe, and there was a spiritual quality to the Balur treatment that was enabling me to do just that.

The second day with Gretha was equally potent. I noticed that her assistants were scouring my skin with what appeared to be rock salt. I began to develop a rash on my chest, and numerous beads of blood and small cuts appeared on my skin. Gretha dismissed my concerns, saying that what we were seeing was the pores opening up and releasing the poisonous mercury from my body. She also recommended that I smoke Divine Cigarettes myself, with different types of tobacco that were designed to treat different conditions. As the week progressed, I got to the stage where I was smoking the equivalent of about a pack a day.

After three days, the massage and smoke immersion was becoming more tolerable. 'I'm starting to cope with it a bit better,' I said to Hugh. 'How about you?'

'I have to say, it's still a struggle,' he said. 'Anyway, I'm off to the dental section tomorrow. Dr Gretha wants to pull my metal fillings out.'

Hugh explained that Gretha was staunchly opposed to amalgam fillings, which were most likely an alloy of mercury and other metals. The clinic had a dentist among its staff; apparently, she had come on board after Balur treatment had cured her infertility.

'Besides,' Hugh said, 'I'm not sure that I need any more experience with enemas or smoke up the nose.'

Just then, the expression on Hugh's face changed as something behind my shoulder captured his attention. 'Hey, Jim, look,' he whispered, nodding in that direction. 'It's that American actor. What's his name? He used to be in that show. What's it called? Not *Malcolm in the Middle*. Come on, you know . . . *The Wonder Years*! That's it, *The Wonder Years*. Look. Do you recognise him now?'

'No.'

'Jeez, you can be obtuse sometimes.'

We both tried to suppress our laughter, and I realised how lucky I was to have friends like Hugh who would go to practically any lengths to help me deal with cancer. They gave me the strength to continue when times looked grim. Over the next four days, while I persisted with the smoke treatment, Hugh had each of his fillings replaced.

'How is it?' I'd asked him after the first instalment.

'Not ideal,' he said. 'They don't even offer you the *option* of an anaesthetic. She's in there with the drill, and then she stops every now and then to answer her BlackBerry and to text people. Meanwhile, you're spitting out little bits of tooth and filling. But at least I won't have to worry about mercury anymore.'

Seven days and nine replaced filings saw Hugh out. He needed to head home to Melbourne, and flew back on 15 October, the day before Sam, her mum, Mary, and Matisse and Tiernan landed for their week in Jakarta. Even though we had been in contact through Skype, Sam's jaw dropped when she heard some of the detail of the Balur sessions. Nevertheless, she was determined to be as supportive as possible and agreed to come to the clinic the next day to take part in the treatment.

As idiosyncratic as they were, the Balur sessions seemed to be having some positive effects. My head was pain-free and feeling the best it had since brain surgery. I also noticed some improvement in my ankle, a chronic injury from my football days that was so troublesome I was unable to walk eighteen holes on a golf course. Now the ankle felt the strongest it had in years. The one area that was giving me considerable grief, however, was my abdomen. Gretha believed that this was where the poison was congregating, requiring it to be released through smoke.

When we returned to the clinic the next morning, Gretha treated Sam, while I was placed in the hands of a new therapist. He began manipulating and massaging, and it was considerably more painful than anything I had experienced in the first week. He was using the knuckle on his middle finger to dig into my flesh, but the most agonising moments came when he squeezed in between my toes.

It seemed that whenever I was beginning to get a handle on Balur, a new aspect would arise to shake up my perceptions. And so it proved when I spoke to Gretha that afternoon.

'Your treatment is going well,' she said, 'but we need to change it. I want to take you out of Jakarta.'

Gretha explained that she wanted to continue the treatment at a coastal location. Her intention was to take me to Anyer, a beach town about 160 kilometres from Jakarta in the north-west corner of the island. The prospect of heading to a remote region, away from an international airport and a hospital, was unnerving.

Sam and I discussed the idea that evening. Although she did not dwell on the point, Sam had found her Balur treatment quite stressful. Yet she remained positive about it – I suspect because she did not want to undermine my belief or hope. Nevertheless, we were both sceptical about the idea of relocating to Anyer. Maybe it was our cynical Western minds, but we wondered whether there was a hidden agenda at play. Would we be underwriting a vacation, or a visit to relatives?

In the end, we decided that we had made a commitment to enter into the spirit of Balur treatment. We had come this far, and Gretha had done nothing to make us doubt her sincerity or her motives. She came across as an angelic figure. I had watched local people, so sick that they were turned away from hospital, find solace in the Balur method. There were children who had gone from being severely disabled to being capable of attending school. I could see no reason not to follow her advice.

So the whole Stynes travelling family circus was on the road again. Mary dug into her deep well of patience and loyalty and agreed to come to help with the kids, and Sam and I decided to cross our fingers and hope for the best.

The experience did not begin well when the three-hour drive to Anyer ended with a stretch along a road that was littered with massive bone-rattling potholes. We arrived to find ourselves staying at an underwhelming 'beach resort' that was well and truly faded from its glory days. We felt like foreign correspondents holing up at a crumbling hotel during a civil war.

Offsetting that was the generous and loving nature of the local people we encountered. They displayed unconditional warmth towards us, as had the staff at the Griya Balur clinic. It was also a blessing to get away from the smothering city smog. Anyer has a captivating view across the Sunda Strait, the body of water that famously includes Krakatoa, the awe-inspiring volcano that erupted in 1883, causing a tsunami and killing tens of thousands of people.

Now that we were at the coast, I tried to throw myself into the Balur treatment with renewed enthusiasm. Gretha devoted much of her attention to my stomach, where I was occasionally experiencing severe cramps and spasms of pain. Furthermore, over the next few days I struggled with diarrhoea and dropped a lot of body weight. This did not alarm Gretha. 'I'm breaking down these tumours and you're passing them,' she said. 'We are removing the parasites from your body.'

It was, however, distressing Sam, who could see how bony I had become; she was struggling to maintain her faith in Balur. She had stopped having treatment herself after three sessions and was mightily unimpressed that Gretha had wanted the children to undergo smoke therapy. In return, Gretha was contending that Sam and the family were a distraction and impairing my ability to heal.

Sam was due to fly out of Jakarta at the end of the week, to get the children back to school, and she was determined that I should fly out at the same time. Meanwhile, Gretha wanted to keep me in Anyer for another two weeks to complete an extended cycle of treatment.

'I can't leave you here alone,' Sam said, with exasperation in her voice. 'You're miles from the hospital and the airport and you've got no car. You'll be totally in their hands – you'll be in no position to make any decisions.'

Eventually, we agreed that Sam would, reluctantly, fly back to Melbourne with the kids, leaving Mary to monitor the situation and offer assistance in Anyer.

And that is how the situation would have played out, had not fate intervened. The family's plane back to Melbourne was cancelled, and while Sam and the kids waited for another flight, she decided to check in for a few more days at a Jakarta hotel, hoping to convince me to change my mind. 'At least come back to Jakarta,' she implored me over the phone.

'If I do, Gretha says she'll stop treating me,' I replied.

'Well, how committed to your healing can she really be if she's threatening to stop treating you?'

I had to agree that returning to Jakarta seemed a reasonable compromise, and so I made arrangements to rejoin the family in the capital the next day. But, having endured so much with the Balur treatment, I was determined to at least complete the fifteen-day course at the Griya Balur clinic. My last two sessions were particularly hard work. My bony frame made it extremely uncomfortable for me to lie on the copper tray, and my stomach had started to give me so much grief that I was struggling to eat anything at all. Whatever I did manage to consume was coming out as liquid from one end or the other; I had lost about five kilograms over the past week. Sam resolved that she was not getting on the plane without me.

Unbeknown to me, she had formulated a 'Home Jim' plan in conjunction with family, friends and doctors. She felt that my devotion to the Balur treatment was spiralling out of control – that my stubborn nature meant I had lost perspective and was no longer listening to reason. And she was right.

Fortunately, she had some astute individuals prepared to offer her outstanding support and counsel. Mary, aware that Sam might not succeed by challenging me directly, had advised her that she had to persist and somehow find a way to get me back to Australia. There are times when loved ones have no choice but to step in and deal with a situation, she said, and this was one of those times. We were fortunate to have Mary with us, not just to watch out for Sam and me but also to look after the best interests of the children.

Grant McArthur, meanwhile, had stayed in contact with Sam by phone and offered his advice. 'Sam, you have to get Jim out of there,' he said. 'But do it in a way that doesn't destroy his spirit, because he'll need it to maintain the struggle when he gets back.'

When Sam was confident that I was actually going to board the plane home, she organised for Hugh, Jules and Wayne to greet me upon my arrival at Tullamarine, with orders to drive me straight to hospital. No argument.

When the plane touched down, I was taken aback to find those mates waiting for us: Jules, loud and funny, Wayne, with his mop of curly hair, and Hugh, who had the hint of a frown as he issued instructions. Without trying, they could have passed for the Three Stooges. After greeting me at the crowded terminal, they swung into action. Wayne drove Mary and the kids home, while the other two whisked me off to the Peter MacCallum Cancer Centre.

It turned out that the intense pain in my gut was being caused by two new tumours in my intestines. One was blocking my bowel, prompting my body – which thought the blockage was food – to keep trying to flush it through. As it kept failing to do so, the bowel was turning in on itself. Surgery would be needed to remove a section of intestine and stitch it back together, minus the tumour. The positive news was that the original tumour in my duodenum had not grown, which was important, given that the doctors were uncertain about how to remove it surgically.

Before I got anywhere near an operating theatre, however, I needed to spend at least a week recovering in hospital. The doctors were pumping me full of drugs to stop my diarrhoea, and they had me on a drip to get my fluids and nutrients up. While I was waiting for surgery, Hugh dropped in one evening. 'So what do you think about the old Balur now?' he asked.

I had spent hours lying in the hospital bed, thinking about that very question. 'Well, I guess I've been impulsive throughout this cancer journey, and this was my most impulsive decision yet,' I said. 'It didn't work out, but it gave me hope when I needed it, and you can't knock that. It was an adventure and I'd do it again.'

'So would I,' replied Hugh.

We agreed that the Griya Balur clinic was run by beautiful

and genuine people, who were in it for no other reason than to try to help others.

'In the end,' I said, 'I don't want to lose trust in people who genuinely believe they can help. I don't want to trade in hope for cynicism. But I think I'll have to put the Divine Cigarettes away for a while.'

14

PRECIOUS STONES

I was feeling flat, I was feeling stupid and I was feeling a lot of pain. I spent the first week of November 2010 in hospital, recovering from stomach surgery and trying to recover from a bout of self-pity. The surgeon had successfully removed the tumours – as well as two sections of small intestine – from my stomach, but for the next few days my digestive system practically shut down. It had me in such agony that I barely managed to do anything more than sip on water and suck on ice cubes.

That explained the pain. I was feeling flat because it was such a struggle to cast my mind forward with any optimism. Tumours remained in my brain and duodenum, and it was disheartening that new spots seemed to appear whenever I checked in for my regular scans every two or three months.

As for feeling stupid, well, that was caused by further reflection upon my Jakarta experiment. I did not regret the Balur experience, and I was untroubled by having put my faith in a venture that had not worked out. But I did regret my decision to disrupt the family's life and drag Sam and the kids around in a cloud of smoke and selfishness for almost two weeks.

Matisse and Tiernan were starting to show signs of the eighteen-month cancer ordeal. Teachers at their school, Wesley College, were exceptionally supportive but were expressing their belief that both children needed to have some continuity and routine. I may have had the scope in my life to make spontaneous decisions about treatment and timetables, but the kids needed structure and certainty. It might be something as simple as Matisse wearing her school uniform on a casual-clothes day, or not having the right shoes for a sports class. One night she became upset because other children had been teasing her about how often she had put in a lunch order over the past few years.

These issues could not be dismissed as excusable memory lapses by busy parents. The guilt ripped at us when our nine-year-old daughter was caught wagging orchestra because she had missed so many rehearsals that attendance struck her as a futile exercise in embarrassment. It ripped at us when our little boy was heartbroken because he was the only one without a parent showing up at the kindergarten portfolio presentation. The reminder notice was in a hospital room, forlornly tucked into the back pocket of my jeans.

Cancer may have served as a reminder of just how important my family was to me, but I had to keep adjusting my approach to cancer with them in mind. There needed to be a framework in place for them to get on with their own lives. During my football career, recovering from injuries had been a very personal, obsessive pursuit. I realised I had been taking a similar approach to cancer, disregarding the fact that I was surrounded by family and friends who wanted to be supportive. The children were always exhausted at that time of year anyway, without the extra emotional and physical weight I was adding to their load. To their minds, my cancer journey had become like tedious background music. They had begun to ask questions like 'When is this cancer going to go away? Are you nearly better yet, Daddy? When can you stop going to boring old hospital?'

In the last eight weeks of 2010 Sam and I made a conscious effort to do less and try to recharge our batteries. Initially, I had to rebuild my strength, physically and emotionally. For a week after surgery I could not manage any food, and my weight dropped to seventy-eight kilograms. Eventually, I could handle soup, then I was able to progress to easily digestible fare such as porridge and gnocchi. By the end of November I was healthy enough to return to something resembling my usual routine.

The enforced rest ensured that, in more ways than one, I was taking care of my inner self. I was thinking deeply about life. Cancer brings everything up. I had found, over the past eighteen months, that anything I was unhappy about or troubled by slowly rose to the surface. One by one, maybe every month or so, these light-bulb moments about life would come to the front of my mind, and I would stop and say to myself, *There's another one*. I began to think of them as precious stones that simply needed to be gathered up and polished to help lead me to a better life. Sometimes they forced me to confront parts of my life that I was not especially comfortable with, or would otherwise push to the background. There were stresses that I had carried around with me for years. So, as they occurred to me, I started to knock them off, one at a time.

It might be a fractured friendship. One mate and I had fallen out and not spoken for the better part of ten years. So I rang him up and said, 'Let's get together and just let it be.' And it wasn't until I spoke to him that I realised I was causing him a lot of hurt. I realised that, in a way, we were both grieving over the relationship that had broken down, which was not doing either of us any good. We did not have to become best mates again, but it was worth resolving the fracture so that neither of us was carrying unnecessary angst.

Some of these precious stones had been found in more oblique ways, such as when I learned that I didn't have to be in control all the time – that it was okay to compromise and to accept help. One of the most important stones was that of understanding the art of 'being there'. By that, I mean paying attention, listening, focusing when you are with another person. Learning to be present, rather than being distant because your mind is on what happened earlier that day, or on the next appointment. Not thinking about solutions to unrelated problems while you're having a conversation. Not sending a text message while someone else is talking to you.

I knew that my tendency to be mentally absent used to drive some of my old friends to distraction. They remembered what I was like in my teens and twenties, when I was more carefree and prepared to live in the moment. In recent years I had become so busy, so often in a rush, that I had struggled to carve out any quality time with people. I was always running. One great mate had stopped me one day as I was mentally scurrying from one topic to the next. He grabbed me by the shoulder, forcing me to look him in the eye, and said, 'Hey, idiot! It's me. Cut the crap. Slow down.'

That summer of 2010–11, I loved working on being there. On having less on my plate and better conversations. I found that having times like that cleared my mind and lifted my mood.

One evening, while I was in hospital, Phil Gregory, an old friend who had helped me greatly in the early days of Reach, dropped in and sat next to my bed for a while. He drank a couple of beers, and we just laughed, spoke about old times and caught up on each other's lives. There was no agenda, and we weren't trying to achieve anything in particular. It was simply a good old chat, a quality connection. It reminded me how easy it is to forget to have those kinds of moments with friends when life is dragging you in so many other directions. I could see how I had spent a lot of time in my life chasing ambitions and dreams, but before I had realised them I had already moved onto the next one. By doing that, I had not been experiencing the present; in a way, I had missed out on my own life.

I had been paying lip-service to the concept for eighteen months, but now I knew that I had to discover a way to disconnect from some of the pressures of life. To slow down, get back to basics and prioritise what I valued most. I needed to cut back on all the talks I was doing and scale back my involvement at the football club, as well as my business commitments.

Medical scientists might argue otherwise, but I genuinely believe that my stressful lifestyle was a major contributor to where I was at with my health. I needed to restore my regimen, with renewed dedication, and not simply adhere to it when it suited me.

In December I had some more sessions of targeted radiation for my brain tumours, and there was the ongoing long-term course of the immunology drug ipilimumab. But I also needed to stick to my diet, get my fluid intake right, meditate daily and find a balance between exercise and rest. In football terms, they were all one-percenters. It had taken me eighteen months to comprehend that no individual aspect was going to make a difference on its own. I had to make an extended commitment to all the little details.

That summer was bliss. It began with a return to my Irish roots. Arguably the world's greatest rock band, U2, was touring Australia and playing concerts at Melbourne's Etihad Stadium in early December. The promoters contacted me, asking if I would like to go, with the promise of prime seats and the possibility of meeting the band afterwards. They did not have to ask twice. Growing up in Ireland, there were certain songs that had gripped my gang of friends and always got us singing along. As a younger teen, it was Thin Lizzy's version of the Irish standard 'Whiskey in the Jar'. But as I got older, U2's stirring 1983 anthem 'Sunday Bloody Sunday' always had us up on our feet and belting it out within seconds of the distinctive snare-drum opening.

The show was brilliant; it was enough in itself to raise my spirits. But getting to meet the band afterwards was an unforgettable experience – not just because they were my musical heroes, but also because there proved to be an easy connection between us. In particular, I found guitarist The Edge – whose real name is David Evans – to be a really natural and unaffected guy.

We spoke for about an hour, and a decent chunk of that was a discussion about cancer. I had not known that one of The Edge's daughters, Sian, had been diagnosed with leukaemia when she was nine. 'That was a few years ago, when we were doing the Vertigo tour,' he said. 'We ended up postponing some of the concerts here and in Japan so I could spend time with her. In the end, she was the one who actually kicked me out of the house and told me to get back touring again.'

He spoke about how Sian had recovered, and attributed her recuperation to the work of the Angiogenesis Foundation, a non-profit organisation in Boston. In fact, the foundation had so impressed him that he had joined the board of directors.

Angiogenesis, he explained, was the growth of new capillary blood vessels in the body; around seventy diseases could be explained by either having too much or too little growth. In the case of cancer, these extra capillaries fed blood to tumours, enabling them to grow and spread. He said that certain foods – such as berries, soy, parsley, grapes and garlic – were found to help inhibit angiogenesis. More food for thought.

Another thing The Edge said that night also stayed with me. 'When you have cancer in your life you really live, because you don't want to take anything for granted.' On the way home, with a skip in my step, I said to Sam, 'That was one of the best moments of my life.'

I was certainly not taking anything for granted when the 2010 Christmas holidays rolled around. It had always been special to have that festive time with the family, and that year it was all the more so because I was active and well. The highlights of Christmas Day included Tiernan's reaction to getting a Wii computer game from Santa – he ran around the living room jumping and screaming, occasionally stopping to look at the box and then setting off again – and the lavish desserts at Mam's dinner that evening, which successfully tempted me to break every dietary rule I had.

For the next two weeks we headed out of town, lazing around down at Rye in shorts and T-shirts. Our biggest stress was shaking grains of sand from our hair and from whatever novel we were reading. Friends visited from Ireland; first Ciarán Farrell, whose wedding I had been so upset to miss, then my former Ireland teammate Bernard Flynn. His son,

Billy, spent hours with Tiernan, leaping off rocks into the sea. For a whole afternoon, as I watched them derive pure delight from one of nature's simple pleasures, I forgot that life was anything other than perfect.

New Year's Day had stopped being about resolutions for me. It was cause to celebrate making it through to another year. The first few days of 2011 gave me reason to believe that this might just be the year that turned my life around. I had rediscovered my optimism and regained weight. My body felt strong and, apart from the odd struggle with poor peripheral vision, there were very few issues with my head. The headaches were increasingly rare.

I was scheduled for one of my regular brain scans on 7 January, and I headed back to Melbourne with a hint of apprehension. I was nervous about having some of the air taken out of my ballooning zest for life. Instead, for what felt like the first time in eighteen months, I finally caught the break I was always summoning.

After an anxious weekend, the scan results came back on the somewhat intriguing date of Tuesday 11/1/11. They showed that one of the two brain tumours – the one that was causing trouble with my vision – had not only stopped growing but also appeared to have withered and died. It still remained in a delicate area but could now be removed through surgery. My sporadic headaches could probably be attributed to brain swelling.

The news was so uplifting. Could I finally be on the verge of the miracle I had been praying for? It was incredible that, only two months ago, I had been a scrawny and dismayed figure, unable to eat and feeling like I would never manage to get out of my hospital bed. Now, here I was, wondering if I was on the cusp of never having to sleep in a hospital again.

The heavens were absolutely pelting down with rain as I headed to my car. But I was so delighted that I did not even rush. A thought occurred to me. No matter how dismal the clouds seemed during the storm, they might yet produce a rainbow.

I have had some memorable weeks in my life, but that one will take some beating. Not least because, the day after my scan results came through, Jules was on the phone. 'Mate,' he said, 'I'm just wondering . . .' He paused for effect, and I wasn't sure whether this was a good sign or he was gently trying to break the news that he had roped me into some hare-brained scheme. 'What do you think about . . . the prospect of meeting . . . Lance Armstrong?'

Was he joking? That was the first thing I had to establish. But, no, he wasn't. Armstrong, the seven-time Tour de France winner, was in Australia to compete in his final overseas professional cycling race, the Tour Down Under. A representative from his foundation had been in contact about me heading to Adelaide for a meeting on Friday.

I was blown away. First U2, and now this. I regarded Armstrong as the most inspirational person alive today. At age twenty-five, he had been a world champion when scans revealed that he had testicular cancer, which had spread to his lungs and brain. But he overcame the disease and returned to the bike, where he established himself not only as the greatest cyclist in the world, but arguably also the greatest in history. He leveraged his profile as the planet's highest-profile cancer survivor to establish a foundation to support the cancer community, and to be an advocate on their behalf. His distinctive yellow Livestrong silicone wristbands, launched in 2004, had raised tens of millions of dollars.

Jules and I flew to Adelaide and met Armstrong in his hotel room, with no agenda other than to connect. Lance explained that he had seen a trailer for *Every Heart Beats True* and had heard some impressive stories about the success of Reach. Nevertheless, I felt slightly awkward about dropping in on him out of the blue like this. My self-consciousness quickly dissolved when we began discussing our young families. He spoke about his five kids, including twenty-month-old Max and three-month-old Olivia, who were with him in Adelaide.

We also found common ground when discussing physical fitness, aerobic capacity and stamina. 'They tell me that you were a pretty resilient football player,' he said, and I explained about my 244-game streak. 'Okay, so you're like the Brett Favre of the AFL,' he chuckled.

It was a pretty cool compliment. The former Green Bay quarterback had been a starter in 297 consecutive games, and was regarded as one of the greatest players to have pulled on a helmet.

'That was one of the reasons why I struggled so badly to get my head around it when they told me I had cancer,' I said. 'Because I'd lived such a healthy life. Never missed a beat.'

'I was the same,' Lance said. 'No sick days off school as a kid – same on the bike – and then all of a sudden, *whack!* Cancer is like that.'

He asked how I was tracking with my health now, and I explained about needing more surgery in a few days to remove the dead tumour in the brain.

'Well, better to go in and get a dead one than a live one,' he said. 'You just have to take these baby steps, and at the end of it you will have walked the whole journey.'

I was interested to know what he thought about the idea of finding a cure for cancer.

'People talk about the day that we cure cancer,' he said. 'There won't be that day. There'll be the day that we cure melanoma. There'll be the day that we cure testicular cancer, which I tend to think that they've done. There'll be the day that they cure lung cancer. And there are a lot of different ways to cure this disease. People don't talk about "prevention" as a word that means "cure", but to me it does.'

His philosophy was that if we could educate a seventeen-year-old about the dangers of smoking and prevent them from ever taking a drag on a cigarette, we were effectively curing them of lung cancer down the track.

Mentioning teenagers led us to a discussion about Reach, and Lance was genuinely absorbed. He spoke about how his own foundation had also flourished, despite evolving from such modest origins and ambitions. 'We started out thinking we could maybe organise a few charity rides,' he said. 'Now it's massive. We have eighty full-time staff in Austin.'

I started to wonder if there might be a way to link the two foundations.

'Sure,' he said. 'Let us know what we can do to help you. Maybe we can partner up on some stuff.'

Meeting a man who had been riddled with cancer and yet came out the other side gave me great confidence when I was back at the Alfred Hospital five days later for more brain surgery. I was sitting with Wayne in the neurosurgery ward, waiting for Professor Jeffrey Rosenfeld to come in and talk me through the operation.

Hearing his voice drifting down the hall, I turned to Wayne and said, 'Remember Elliot Goblet?' When Jeffrey arrived, I simply turned to Wayne and smiled knowingly, and he was gone. Wayne tried to suppress it, but a belly laugh erupted through his nose and he had to get up and leave, shaking his head and wiping tears from his eyes.

Jeffrey, totally nonplussed, watched him go. 'Irish joke,' I explained, and we got down to discussing the surgery. I wanted to know whether the fact that the tumour had perished would make his job any easier. He explained that the issue was not so much with the tumour as with the healthy cells, especially because he would be operating in the visual cortex of the brain. 'But we are confident that it will go well,' he said. Then, with a chuckle, he added, 'We wouldn't muck it up. You're a high-profile man. The hospital's fine reputation is at stake.'

When I awoke from surgery hours later, the pain in my head was intense, yet it couldn't make a dent in my overall peace of mind. While I recovered over the next few days, I found that I was in a great place emotionally; I knew there were more tumours that had to come out but I actually felt fully healthy. It was a weird feeling. I was daring to dream about remission, about how I would leave cancer in my wake and sail off into the sunset.

Sam and I fantasised about doing just that. We talked about how, at that very moment, Hugh was on board his catamaran, sailing around the Bahamas with his wife and two daughters. I would get better and we too would sail off in search of paradise. We began to look up Caribbean islands, places like Grenada, Antigua, Montserrat. We began to pencil plans in our diary, began to look up school holiday dates to see how they matched up against airfares and weather conditions.

'I can do this, Sammy,' I said. 'I just have to be really committed to the lifestyle and the diet. And Grant wants to try me on this new trial drug he's been talking about. I feel like I can see a way out.'

I spent the last week of January 2011 with the outstanding rehabilitation staff at the Epworth Hospital, making sure my brain was still sharp and easing my body back into some physical exercise. The one disappointment was that I continued to struggle with my peripheral vision, to such an extent that it became obvious to me that I would never drive again. I was not thrilled by the prospect of indefinitely using taxis and public transport and being driven around, but I figured that if that was what I had to sacrifice to overcome cancer, it would be a small price to pay.

I stuck to my vow to be disciplined with my diet and lifestyle choices, even pulling out of a commitment to attend a Reach Crew camp, which really tore at me.

There were, however, two important meetings in February I was certain I would not miss. One was an appointment with Grant to have series of scans to determine whether I was ready to commence taking a trial drug. The other was a sit-down with the Melbourne Football Club's gun young midfielder Tom Scully, who had played one season with the Demons since we had selected him with the number-one draft pick. Football's jungle drums were suggesting that the AFL's new expansion club, the Greater Western Sydney Giants, was making a pitch for Scully to join its ranks for their debut season in 2012. Scully was telling Melbourne he had not been approached but was simply putting off a decision about his future until after the 2011 season.

Don McLardy had made a good suggestion. 'We need to know what's going on with Tom,' he said, 'so that we can work out our position as a football club. There are a lot of other things riding on it as well. He's got a lot of time and respect for you, Jim. Why don't you have a chat with him? If he tells you eye-to-eye that he's not going, well, that should be good enough for anyone. Then we can all get behind him and support him to the hilt. This issue is not going to go away. We're going to have to deal with speculation about it all year.'

So I invited Scully over to my house for a chat. Knowing that he was just nineteen years old, I was mindful of coming across as though I was heavying him in any way. When he sat down at our kitchen table, I began by telling him that we regarded him as a vital part of Melbourne's future, someone we thought could help the club continue to build both its culture and its on-field success. I also suggested that Melbourne was ideally placed to help him develop both as a leader and a footballer, and that the club was a great institution to have behind him after his playing career ended. Then I outlined the situation from the club's point of view.

'I understand that you're under a lot of pressure, Tom,' I said. 'All I ask is that you be honest with us. If you make a decision to leave, then you make that decision, but I need to know so that the club can make some plans. Don't make us look like fools.' I explained that whether he stayed or left would impact on other aspects of the club, such as our contract negotiations, recruiting and marketing. Then I asked him, directly, whether the Giants had approached him.

'I'm not sure where all the rumours have come from, Jim,' he replied. 'But GWS hasn't approached me, or my manager. There hasn't been contact with them in any shape or form.

I agree with everything you're saying about Melbourne. I love the club and want to play out my career with Melbourne.'

He spoke simply and with conviction, and I believed him. When he left, I turned to Sam and declared enthusiastically, 'That's fantastic! It looks like he's staying.'

She shrugged. 'Hmm . . . maybe.'

'What do you mean?'

'I got a bad vibe when he walked in,' she said. 'He wouldn't look us in the eyes. He kept looking down.'

'Nah, he was just nervous, that's all.'

'Maybe.'

In retrospect, Sam could have been right. At the end of that season, Scully announced that he had decided to sign with Greater Western Sydney, and it later emerged that his father, Phil, had been offered a lucrative six-year deal to join the Giants' recruiting department. That offer had been made three months before Tom and I'd had our chat.

Grant McArthur was as ebullient as ever. He was enthusiastic about the new trial drug. He was enthusiastic about my feeling healthy. He was enthusiastic about my being enthusiastic.

I had immense respect for him. There had been times when I was feeling low, lying in my hospital bed and looking out the window on a grey afternoon, and he had popped his head through the door and lifted my mood immeasurably. I appreciated what it meant for an incredibly busy man like him to find the time to visit me on a rare day off.

Before meeting with him on this day, I had been for PET and CAT scans to determine whether it was still appropriate for me to trial this new drug.

'You'll be one of the first patients to try this, Jim,' he said. 'It's a drug called EnGeneIC from a research team in Sydney. What it does is load up nanoparticles with chemotherapy and deliver a high concentration to precisely where it's needed. The EnGeneIC drug looks like it may have managed to side-step two of the problems that we find with standard chemo: it directly attacks the cancer cells without hurting the normal cells, and it doesn't look like cancer cells are able to develop a resistance to it.'

Grant said that if we proceeded, it would only take about thirty minutes to administer the drug, but that I would need to stay in hospital overnight for observation.

I left his office wondering if this might be the final piece in the puzzle, the drug that could help me get rid of the last few tumours and be cancer-free. My jaunty mood was tempered, though, when I discovered that, on that same day, my good friend and former teammate Sean Wight was also in hospital having a PET scan. It revealed a tumour the size of a tennis ball in his lung, three more near his spine and one in his adrenal gland. A flash of abject sadness surged through me. I knew precisely how Sean would be feeling as he set out on his own cancer journey. It was staggering how similar his condition seemed to mine when I was diagnosed twenty months earlier. Our names were already forever linked as two pioneers of the 'Irish experiment'.

Sean, who was actually born in Scotland and spent some of his childhood in England, had come out to Melbourne a couple of years before me with another talented Gaelic footballer, Paul Earley. He was as talented as any athlete I have ever seen: he had represented Kerry in an All-Ireland minor final, trialled for English soccer club Fulham and lowered his golf handicap down to a few shots. He had played AFL football for a decade and represented his state and his country. About the only time I had ever seen him struggle at sport was in the pool, where he swam like a watermelon.

Sean was one of the first people I had got to know when I came out to Australia as an eighteen-year-old. We met at the old Melbourne Football Club offices in Jolimont Terrace, and he had impressed me with his self-assuredness. He was his own boss and knew exactly where he was going. More importantly, he was twenty, had a driver's licence and a car.

As a footballer, he was spectacular, skilful and balanced. He had a remarkable leap and was unfalteringly courageous. It occurred to me that Sean had a physique like a modern midfielder: he was only a couple of centimetres taller than Tom Scully yet he'd taken on some of the game's great key forwards, such as Tony Lockett, Jason Dunstall, Gary Ablett and Dermott Brereton. The other hallmarks of Sean's time at Melbourne were his loyalty and integrity.

I spoke with Sean and offered to help in any way I could. 'I just don't get it, Jim,' he said. 'You know me – I've never smoked, never been a drinker; I've looked after myself. And now they tell me I've got lung cancer. How does that work?'

He felt like he had fallen off a cliff, and was worried about the months ahead. The doctors didn't think surgery was an option, and the prospect of chemotherapy and radiation made him anxious. I spoke about some of my experiences and recommended he have a chat with Graeme Southwick.

Sean was also concerned about his support network; his marriage had ended about twelve months earlier, and his mother and sisters lived overseas. I assured him that the club and his former teammates would rally around him. In the weeks to come, the former Melbourne player and president Stuart Spencer and his wife, Fay, would take Sean and his mother, Peggy, into their home. The club would help him with medical bills, transport and nutrition. Nevertheless, it troubled me how powerless I felt to really help Sean. It gave me an understanding of how challenging and frustrating it was trying to support a cancer patient.

When I returned to Grant McArthur's office on the last day of February, my mind was racing through the full spectrum of possible scan results. Would I be cleared to start the trial drug? Or devastated by more fiendish little dark spots? Surely the fact that I was feeling so well had to mean a positive report?

After Grant delivered the news, Sam and I were unsure whether we should giggle or cry. He informed us that the scans showed no new activity, and that the tumours in my brain and duodenum had stopped growing.

I could begin the EnGeneIC trial within a few days.

When he had finished speaking, we tumbled through the door like kids who had been let loose in a lolly shop. Had it not been for the fact that we were in a hospital, I think we would have whooped and hollered. Outside, we hugged silently; that communicated what we were both thinking better than any words could have.

Eventually, we let each other go and spoke about the need not to get too far ahead of ourselves. It was another lesson I had learned about the cancer rollercoaster: don't allow yourself to rise too high on the highs, or fall too low on the lows.

15

CHALLENGES

Imagine lying naked in the Arctic Circle, shivering and writhing because every one of your joints is aching. That was me on the first day of the EnGeneIC drug trial. This was supposed to be my saviour, and instead I was moaning and groaning and wondering when it would all end. For about seven hours it went on, before halting abruptly that evening. During the night, though, the freezing sensation returned, and with it awful dreams from which I woke up feeling a touch paranoid. I drifted in and out of delirium that night, and woke the next morning with a high temperature and extremely low blood pressure.

My body's reaction to the drug stunned Grant McArthur. It was more severe than anything the EnGeneIC scientists had seen. 'The positive, for me, is that it suggests your body's immune system is working well,' Grant said. He wanted to keep me in hospital for another day to monitor my health, which included hooking me up to an electrocardiogram to record my heart's activity while I did some light exercise in the gym.

'But I've already got some light exercise planned, Grant,' I said, half-jokingly. 'I wanted to head over to Carlton to see how some of our young guys go in the practice match against the Lions.'

He suggested that if I could forego the practice match, he would do his best to make sure I was ready for the start of the season proper in a few weeks. In the meantime, he was proposing reduced doses of EnGeneIC – and, we hoped, reduced side-effects – during weekly hospital stays throughout March.

My second experience of the trial drug at the Peter MacCallum Cancer Centre was not as physically exacting, but it did provide me with one of the most surreal memories from my time spent in hospitals. Mercifully, that night I fell asleep without any of the chills I had experienced the first time, only to be woken at about 1 am by a minor commotion in my room. The curtain around my bed was half-drawn, revealing a huddle of about eight doctors and nurses examining the floor and conferring gravely.

What is wrong with me now? I wondered, thinking they were scrutinising my chart. 'Do you think we should get an ambulance?' one whispered, simultaneously alarming and totally baffling me. Weren't we already in a hospital?

It was only then that it started to occur to me that the whole cluster of white coats seemed oblivious to my presence. I propped myself up on an elbow and peered down at the floor, where I saw a nurse lying flat on his back. It turned out that he was a diabetic; his sugar levels had dropped so low that he had passed out.

Nevertheless, in my half-awake state it took me a while to work out what was going on. Furthermore, I was busting to go to the toilet but could not get to the en suite without disrupting the group. I wheeled my intravenous drip into the corridor, intending to use the bathroom in the vacant room next door. In my haste, I left the bathroom door open, only to realise – midstream, so to speak – that the room was no longer vacant. I was in the clear view of a woman lying in her bed a few metres away.

Thankfully, she was asleep and I was able to finish and creep out undetected, returning to my room to find the nurse sitting up against the wall with a sandwich in one hand and an orange juice in the other. I clambered back into bed, chuckling to myself about how I would probably imagine this was all a drug-induced dream when I woke up in the morning.

In between my weekly visits to hospital, I managed to get out of the house and get on with life. On St Patrick's Day, the team at Reach launched a great initiative called the Open Book Project. The idea was for people over eighteen years old to digitally upload pages from their teenage diaries, to show young people that they had been through similar challenges and anxieties when they were teens. We described it as going 'inside the minds of yesterday's teenagers', and we'd enlisted the help of several celebrities.

Some of the entries were priceless. There were heart-wrenching pages, such as when former Australian rugby captain John Eales lamented, 'It's so unfair,' after his sister had died at age twenty. Singer Kate Ceberano wrote at age fourteen about being 'the wrong colour. I'm not Aboriginal enough, not white enough, not black enough'. Then there were some goofy scribblings, such as when comedian Tim Ross wrote in Year 9, 'If my brother keeps growing his hair to look like Bono I'm going to stab him in the head with a fork.' Mine, written when I was fourteen, was a tender account of breaking up with a girlfriend. It ended: 'There was a huge argument and I hurt her feelings etc. Then I went to watch a James Bond film.'

Another project, a few days later, also helped take my mind off my own troubles. I joined a group of Melbourne footballers who travelled to Murrabit, one of more than sixty Victorian towns severely affected by floods that January. Flying in by helicopter two months later, you could see that several properties were still underwater. While we were there, we conducted a football clinic as part of the day's festivities, and the positive and spirited approach the locals had towards recovery was marvellously energising. They held a huge community barbecue; the guest of honour was Prince William, who impressed all with his down-to-earth manner. He listened carefully when I ran him through a few basics of kicking and handballing a Sherrin football. I reckon he handled it better than I had at my first attempt, twenty-seven years earlier.

I returned to the city that evening optimistic about the various aspects of my life. Although the AFL season began with me back in hospital – watching on television as Carlton overran Richmond at the MCG – the side-effects of the trial drug had become more bearable, partly because Grant had eased the dosage down. The overnight stays now seemed little more than a nuisance precaution. I would know more about any effects the drug might be having on the tumours when I checked in for another regular set of scans in mid-April.

Our family had settled back into a comfortable routine, and it pleased me to be able to spend some quality time with the kids. Having celebrated Tiernan's sixth birthday down at Rye, we managed to set aside a day of father–son time in St Kilda. We went to the cinema and had a meal at a restaurant, and by the time I had read him the first page of a bedtime story that night he had nodded off to sleep, with the trace of a smile on his face.

Then there was Reach. I was buoyant about how it was developing now that it had federal and state government grants under its wings. From what I had seen and heard, a fine Crew of new young leaders was developing too.

At the football club, our expectations for the season ahead were bullish. There was a perception that we were a team on the march, on the verge of making the finals for the first time since 2006. I was feeling clear-minded and confident enough to publicly buy in with opinions on a range of football issues: from troubled forward Brendan Fevola signing up to play for our feeder club, the Casey Scorpions, to ways for the AFL to bridge the gap between its richest and poorest clubs.

It all added up to an impression of smooth sailing, and Sam and I began to turn our minds to the Caribbean again. But over the next four months my health and the football team would spiral downwards, creating a perfect storm that would culminate in the lowest week of my life.

It began with a health setback. Results from a full set of scans in mid-April showed that the tumours in my head and gut had both grown. Worse still, a third tumour had appeared, on the right-hand side at the front of my brain. I was crushed. I had been so certain of receiving good news.

At home that evening, I moped around in the kitchen, wondering how to stop myself from sinking into despondency. I stood at the table, looking at the mobile that had hung there for almost two years, a wire frame adorned with cards, letters and photos that had been sent by friends and family. It twisted slowly in the breeze, like a chandelier of hope. I began to read a few of the messages.

One was a note from Trisha Silvers, an early Reach graduate who had become one of our dearest friends. We had spoken often over the years about digging deep, most notably after she had survived the Boxing Day tsunami in Thailand, which tragically killed thousands, including her husband, Troy Broadbridge, a Melbourne footballer. They were on their honeymoon at the time, having been married just eight days earlier. Matisse had been a flower girl at the wedding, and I had hired a vintage car to drive them from the reception.

I read her message and smiled. It included a familiar passage from the book *The Survivor Personality*, by Al Siebert, which asked people how they would respond if their lives were hit by adversity or disrupted. They could choose to feel victimised or blame others for their difficulties. They could allow themselves to feel helpless and overwhelmed, and simply shut down. Some would allow anger to take over, and lash out, trying to hurt others. But there were a brave few who somehow managed to reach within themselves to find ways to cope with their plight. Siebert described them as 'life's best survivors'. They were the people who were resilient and durable in adversity, the ones with the capacity for surviving when times were extremely difficult, or when they were hit by a crisis. They were characterised by a capacity to regain emotional balance quickly. They had the ability to adapt and cope well, to gain strength from adversity. They might even find a way to view their misfortune as an opportunity. These were the people most likely to make things turn out well in the end.

It reminded me that I had spent years championing the message that 'adversity is often our greatest teacher'. I could not change what the scans showed, but I could change my attitude from mope to hope. It was time to get on with the next part of the journey.

Grant had said it was worth persisting with the trial drug to see if there was any improvement when I had completed the full course. And I had arranged a catch-up with David Jubb to begin another detox course.

By the middle of May it had become clear that neither the intravenous drugs nor the coffee enemas were stopping the tumours from growing. The doctors were leaning towards more brain surgery, followed by another bout of chemotherapy or radiation to keep the duodenum tumour under control while they worked out a way to tackle it.

I had another appointment with Professor Rosenfeld. He believed the best way to remove the brain tumours would be in two separate operations, spaced weeks apart to reduce the stress on my brain. He warned me, though, that there was a real possibility of losing my eyesight.

'You mean losing even more of my peripheral vision?' I asked.

'No,' he replied. 'I mean, you could be blind.'

That shook me up, but seemed to be no other option. So, towards the end of May, I was back at the Alfred Hospital to have tumour number twenty-one removed. It was such a relief afterwards, in the recovery room, to remember that the sight of a drab wall, a door, the ceiling, meant that I would get to once more lay eyes on my beautiful wife and children.

My brain was a bit cloudy, but the most pain was actually in my stomach, where they had given me a huge injection to thin my blood. Coming through the surgery so strongly meant I was already starting to think about signing out of hospital and getting along to the next Demons match, which was three days later. It was not simply that I wanted to watch the game. Melbourne was scheduled to play a rare Friday-night match, and the occasion was being used to raise funds for the Olivia Newton-John Cancer and Wellness Centre at the Austin Hospital. There were plans to open the centre in about twelve months' time, but another $10 million in public donations was needed to reach the necessary $186 million in project funding.

Olivia planned to sing a few classics with my former Melbourne teammate Russell Robertson. Before being booked in for surgery, I had hoped to get up on stage and annoy them. I fancied myself as a bit of a keyboard player, but when it came to singing I was a good pianist.

The chance to share a stage with Olivia and help raise money for an exemplary project was too tempting to miss. At about the same age that I was breaking up with girls and scooting off to James Bond films, I had a crush on Sandy from *Grease*. I could recall taking my younger brother Brian to see the film at the local cinema. We got there so early that we managed to sneak in and see about an hour of the previous session before we watched the film.

The day after my surgery, Olivia and her husband, John, visited me at the Alfred, and we discussed her project. Having been diagnosed with breast cancer in 1992 – on the same weekend her father died from liver cancer – Olivia had been in remission for almost two decades. Rather than being a cancer survivor, she described herself as a 'cancer thriver'.

'I've heard lots of stories about your positivity, and how that's having an effect on other people,' she said. 'Also that you're trying a lot of different therapies. I was curious to get your thoughts on them, because that's a big part of the wellness centre.'

I told her that, for the most part, the treatments had been overwhelmingly beneficial, but that it would make an enormous difference to patients and their carers to have complementary therapy integrated with conventional medicine under one roof.

I promised to join her in promoting the cause a couple of nights later at the MCG, and I managed to honour that vow. The goodwill in the stadium that night was almost tangible; it even extended to excusing my vocal efforts during our rendition of 'You're the One That I Want'. Still, I maintain that my occasional contribution during the chorus was superior to Meatloaf's performance on that same spot a few months later, during the Grand Final.

Tumour number twenty-two was obviously a dogged little beast, because having it removed a few days later really knocked me around. Maybe Jeffrey Rosenfeld was practising his deadpan comedy routine, but he maintained that I woke from surgery softly warbling 'You're the One That I Want'. 'I don't think you'll be dancing with Olivia Newton-John in the next few days,' he chuckled, 'but remember, that's two brain operations in the space of about a week, so even you are going to need to take it easy for a while now.'

I spent that week in early June slowly recovering in hospital, snoozing and watching DVDs. About all I could manage was a little rehabilitation work at the Epworth. I got a good laugh when I heard that Tiernan had told his prep teacher, 'My dad is in hospital because they took his brain out.'

One of the rare times I ventured out was to attend a fundraising evening for Sean Wight that the football club had helped his family to organise. When we arrived at the Bentleigh Club I was shocked to see how much his health had deteriorated since I had last seen him, a few weeks earlier. Frail and wan, he was confined to a wheelchair. This man had once been one of the most gifted athletes I had ever seen. It was terribly sad – more so because he knew the end was near.

That image remained with me, and became even more evocative when Sam and I met with Grant McArthur in his office three days later, after the Queen's Birthday long weekend. For once, there was little enthusiasm in his voice, and he delivered the biggest blow of my life. Unfortunately, it appeared that the two operations had failed to remove all of the malignant growth from my brain. Jeffrey Rosenfeld was reluctant to go back in, not just because he feared for my vision, but also because he feared I might not make it off the operating table.

Furthermore, Grant believed that after almost twelve months of immunotherapy, it was time to accept that the ipilimumab was not working and should be stopped. The tumour in my duodenum was still growing, and surgery remained problematic. Grant had some thoughts about treatment that would prolong my life, but essentially he was telling me that, at this point, I had to choose quality of life.

I slumped in my chair. Beside me, Sam put her head on her knees and began sobbing. As determined as I was to maintain my surrender, to maintain hope, this was the biggest blow yet. It was going to take enormous resilience to push onwards. The terrain had become unforgiving; I was definitely beyond Hell Fire now.

Throughout June, I felt physically and mentally drained. The fatigue often forced me to have one or two sleeps during the day, and I occasionally struggled with sharp pains in my skull.

With the help of Graeme Southwick and Grant McArthur, I did manage to maintain a slither of hope about a treatment option. There were three cutting-edge immunology drugs in the United States that were worth exploring: one drug company was from Texas, another was nearby and a third was in Boston.

The doctors felt that my chances of success with these drugs was only in the range of ten to thirty per cent, but that appealed to me more than zero. We began to pursue the PD-1 antibody, which had produced some successful results in clinical trials involving people with advanced melanoma. Unfortunately, the company producing PD-1 in the United States was blocking any attempt to use it in Australia.

In the meantime, I would undergo more chemotherapy in

an effort to stall any malignant growth. While I was at Peter Mac having treatment, the news came that Sean Wight had passed away. This hit me hard. In the two years I had been living with cancer, there had only been occasional moments when I had become a bit weepy. But that day I wept freely when I learned that Sean had been taken from us at the age of forty-seven.

That grim day bolstered my resolve to somehow find a way to come out the other side of cancer. Remaining positive was imperative, and complementary therapy again proved beneficial. My meditation teacher, Paula Armstrong, was inclined to chastise me whenever she sensed any hint of negativity, always maintaining great faith in my recovery. She suggested that I invite friends and family along to a group meditation session.

It was an inspired idea, and on the first Sunday in July, about 150 people from diverse parts of my life – from toddlers to an eighty-three-year-old – gathered at the Dream Factory in Collingwood and meditated to channel energy towards improving my health. It was humbling that so many turned up, even those who came secretly believing it to be a load of new-age nonsense. In the end, I believe that they all took something positive away from the experience, as I did.

While my mind was bouncing back as I moved deeper into July, I wasn't so sure about my body. I was beginning to get ominous stabbing pains in my gut.

It was in this context that another struggle was being played out, albeit under greater public scrutiny: that of the Melbourne football team.

It was a massive year for the club. Being debt-free, with a record membership base and settled training, administrative and social facilities, meant that the attention was squarely on how the team performed in 2011. By extension, the focus was on the coach, Dean Bailey, who was in his fourth year at the helm and the final year of his contract.

In his first two seasons Melbourne had been in turmoil and had finished last, the by-product of introducing and developing young footballers, which had to be done. Finishing in twelfth place in 2010 had been difficult to assess because we'd had injuries to key players for sustained periods. Going into 2011, then, the expectations were high. Supporters were talking finals and the media was suggesting we had the talent to develop into an emerging power. My own expectation was that we must keep improving; we had won eight games the year before, so at least ten wins seemed a reasonable pass mark.

I found Dean to be a difficult man to read. He struck me as a decent and affable guy, but I went into the season uncertain of his capacity to deal with the politics of the football department. On a very basic level, did he have the strategies and a game plan to help this group of players hold its own against the elite teams? More broadly, was he a leader who could impart values and principles to these players, not just as footballers but also as people? Being such an influential person in their lives, was he attempting to create a strong, respectful and sustainable culture among the group? As we aspired to rebuild Melbourne as a great club, that was the sort of leadership our football department needed. At times I thought that if I'd been well, I might have mentored him through this difficult period.

Dean was a central figure but the responsibility was not his alone. Over the summer we had commissioned a management consultant, Ray Andrews, to review the internal workings of our club, taking in the administration, the board and our football operations. We wanted to incorporate the findings in a long-term strategic plan, to ensure that our players had the best possible platform from which to thrive and succeed.

The season began with a frustrating draw against Sydney, followed by a disappointing forty-five-point loss to Hawthorn. What was most disturbing was that we had led the Hawks by three goals in the second quarter, only to allow them to score the next sixty-three points unanswered. Good teams, with good on-field leaders and good coaches, simply did not allow that to happen.

That was to become a feature of our season, unfortunately. In Round 8 we allowed North Melbourne to steamroll us in the second half; in our Friday-night match against Carlton we were accused of playing 'bruise-free football'; on the closely watched Queen's Birthday stage we were humiliated in an eighty-eight-point loss to Collingwood, who managed twenty-five scoring shots to our seven after quarter time.

In another Friday-night match, in Round 15, the Western Bulldogs crushed us by sixty-four points; we managed just two rushed behinds in the last half-hour, while the Dogs piled on six goals.

The concern was not our win–loss record. We had managed to win most of the games we were expected to win, and we were hovering just outside the top eight on the ladder. Rather, the problem was that we were simply not competitive against the better teams. Worse still, we were capitulating and seemed powerless to hold teams up, once they got on a roll. It seemed to me that the coach was struggling to have any influence on the outcome of games.

Meanwhile, there were other causes for concern within the club. It became increasingly clear as the season got underway that the football department had become dysfunctional. One of the findings from the off-season review was that the football department had to become more professional and better resourced. Inadvertently, that seemed to have created jostling within the department, as staff from areas such as recruiting, player development and sports science all pushed their cases for more resources.

Chris Connolly is one of the greatest blokes you will ever come across, and is extremely loyal to the Demons. But I was not certain that, in his role as general manager of football, he had the football department under control. Meanwhile, Dean Bailey, perhaps feeling under siege and wanting a bigger say in proceedings, seemed to be pushing for more control of the department, arguing that the coaches and players felt compromised by some of its shortcomings. I had asked our chief executive, Cameron Schwab, to delve into the situation and report back to the board. He needed to either resolve the issues or come back with recommendations. It was only a couple of months into the season that I learned he had ignored that request. He believed the football department was fine and that the coach was the real area of concern.

That was why, in early May, I resolved to become more involved in the role of football director. Having spent more than a decade inside an AFL football department, I felt I could closely examine the 2011 model and brief the board. Unfortunately, the best part of the next two months coincided with my being sidelined by brain surgery. In that vacuum, the football department continued to fracture. I began to explore the idea of finding someone else to take on the director role. It would have to be a respected football figure whose opinion would carry weight. Two names that came to mind were those of my former captains, Greg Healy and Garry Lyon.

Melbourne could have struggled through to the end of the season had circumstances not conspired at the end of July to create a perfect storm.

The board had to make a decision on Cameron's future as chief executive. He was contracted until the end of October but had a clause stating he needed to know three months before that date what Melbourne's intentions were. We could either activate a two-year extension or opt to let his contract lapse at the end of the season. As coincidence would have it, the deadline for that decision fell on 30 July, a Saturday on which the team was due to play in Geelong.

On the Friday before the match, the board discussed whether to offer Cameron a new tenure. I felt that some aspects of his work were first-class, and that perhaps two-thirds of what he did overall was good. But I was frustrated by the fact that he was choosing to ignore the board and seemed determined to run his own agenda. Some of his behaviour was proving destructive, and it was clear he had lost the faith of the coach and the playing group. I did not believe he should be offered the extension, and on the Saturday morning we informed him.

Cameron rang the Cats to excuse himself from their luncheon but drove down the highway later in the afternoon, while I was feeling so unwell that I stayed at home and watched the game on television. What unfolded was an insipid and totally unacceptable performance from Melbourne: a 186-point loss, the second-biggest losing margin in AFL history.

My phone was lighting up with calls and text messages, and the board agreed to gather the next day to discuss the situation. On the radio, Garry Lyon described the loss 'a disgusting and disgraceful scoreline that should never, ever be tolerated or accepted'.

Greg Healy and, later, Garry dropped around to my house the next day for a chat about the state of the club and to discuss ways they could assist. Garry was still there when the club's two vice-presidents, Don McLardy and Guy

Jalland, arrived ahead of the board meeting. We were all a little shell-shocked. The thorough nature of the team's submission to Geelong meant that we simply could not walk away from the situation. We had to act, but we were conscious of not overreacting.

That morning, Don had spoken to Dean, who knew there was no way to explain away the thirty-goal loss, other than to acknowledge that it was humiliating and embarrassing. But he had not lost faith in his ability to coach.

The four of us spoke about whether Dean was strong enough to lead the club to a Premiership. He had begun to get closer to the players that year – maybe in an attempt to strengthen his position. They thought he was a terrific guy, but there was a view that they were now walking all over him. On one occasion, they had even cancelled their own time-trial run. My feeling was that if we did not think Dean could take us to a flag, we would be best served to take action now, with five rounds of the season remaining.

I asked Garry, who had been part of the advisory panel that had recommended Dean's appointment at the end of 2007, whether he agreed. 'Don't expect me to try to talk you out of it,' he said. But Garry was of the very strong opinion that the club would be seen to be imploding if it announced the removal of both its coach and its chief executive.

After Garry left, we drove to Don's home in Malvern, where the board met to discuss the situation. There have subsequently been suggestions that our board was divided; that is categorically untrue. There was a rift in the football department, but the board remained united. It was a group of high-powered, successful people who shared an incredible passion for the Demons. We often had differing opinions but we always reached a consensus. In my time as president, I could not recall one instance when we needed to take an issue to a vote. That Sunday, there were some who believed Dean should coach on. The majority of the board agreed with the view that removing two key personnel was an overreaction. I believed that we should make both changes, take our medicine and move on.

Eventually, it was proposed that we should give Cameron his three months' notice but simultaneously offer him a new one-year deal. But first he would need to hear some home truths about aspects of his job that he needed to agree to improve on. They mostly involved his approach and attitude, not a lack of ability. He was called to the meeting, and once his situation was resolved, we reached a consensus that Dean had to go.

It was not about the prospect of missing the finals, or Dean's record of twenty-two wins from eighty-three matches. We were troubled by the team's lack of hard-edged competitiveness. By the fact that Melbourne seemed to have rolled over three or four times against the elite teams that season. And the situation seemed to be deteriorating, culminating in arguably the meekest surrender in the game's history, against Geelong. We all had respect for Dean Bailey as a man, but it was time to remove him as our coach.

'He deserves to hear it from me, though, face to face,'

I said. 'Can someone take me over to his house? Where is he? Essendon, isn't it?'

'Strathmore,' Don replied. 'But the problem is, Jim, that the TV cameras have already followed us here from your place. If we jump in a car and drive over there, the whole thing is going to degenerate into a farce.'

There was no back gate at Don's house, and we quickly ruled out ploys and decoys to fool the media. And anyway, by that stage I was fading so badly that I was not even sure if I could manage the drive across town. It was about 8.30 pm when we decided that the best option would be to ring Dean.

'Mate, I'm sorry,' I began, 'but I've got some bad news . . .'

Don McLardy was awake at 6 am the next morning and organising the media conference to confirm Dean Bailey's sacking. Having seen how drained I was the previous evening, he was working on the basis that I would be absent, but I told him to factor me in. Still, I was not full of confidence when I arrived at AAMI Park.

'Listen, I'm not sure about this,' Don said. 'I mean, you look orange . . . that can't be good. How about if you sit in on it but let me do the talking.'

'No, I need to front this,' I replied. 'It needs to come from me.'

When we got underway at about midday, I could barely make out the words of the statement I had prepared to read out. I struggled through and was determined to convey that everyone at the club needed to share the blame for the season going off the rails, rather than just making Dean the scapegoat.

'I haven't been that well,' I said. 'I haven't been able to carry the load I should have been carrying. When you are not well, it is hard to carry the load. I wish I could be doing more, but I just can't.'

I remained at the club for a while after the media had left, but by mid-afternoon was in such a lacklustre and feeble state that I had to be taken to hospital.

The doctors there used a gastroscopy – a tiny internal camera – to discover that the duodenum tumour had grown and that I was bleeding internally. My blood count was down to sixty-five, whereas the normal count for adult males is in the range of 130 to 170. The next twenty-four hours or so was probably the most critically ill I had been through the whole journey; even after six blood transfusions over two days, my blood count had only reached the eighties. I made a mental reminder to myself that whenever people asked if there was anything they could do to help, the answer should be to make sure they were blood donors.

More scans revealed that there were no new tumours, just the troublesome one in the duodenum and the existing specks in a difficult-to-reach part of the brain. Over those few days in the first week of August, I had numerous conversations with specialists and surgeons and a plan was formulated to attempt surgery to remove the tumour. Grant McArthur was of the opinion that it would require the involvement of two surgeons and a specialist on the pancreas. The upside was that, if successful, it would make me tumour-free again. If it was unsuccessful, though, I could die on the operating table.

About the only redeeming feature of that tough week in hospital was that I was largely oblivious to all the speculation and analysis swirling about the football club. I was delighted that Garry Lyon agreed to become our interim football director. Quietly, I began sounding out the doctors about whether there was any prospect that I might be allowed to get to the MCG on Saturday to watch Melbourne under our new caretaker coach, Todd Viney.

'If the bleeding stops and you get your blood count up above 100, then we'll talk about it,' Grant said.

Remarkably, when it came to the crunch, my blood count shot up from eighty-five to ninety-nine. A seventh bag of blood got me above 100 and into a position where I could negotiate a day trip to the football. At the stadium, I was circumspect enough to limit myself to watching quietly from the stand, where I sat and chatted with Greg Healy. We were playing Carlton, but there would be no dancing with Olivia this time. Melbourne produced an impressive first quarter before – much to everyone's chagrin – again conceding eleven unanswered goals to lose by seventy-six points. I wondered what Dean Bailey would make of the result.

Four days later, I went under the knife, hopeful that the specialists might be able to remove this tumour that had dwelled inside my gut for the past twenty months.

They could not.

Having made a large incision just under my ribcage, through some of the stomach muscles, the surgical team did not like what they found. The tumour was in an incredibly difficult spot, entwined around the pancreas, the main aorta that supplies the lower legs and the main blood vessel that supplies the bowel. Their main concern was damaging that blood vessel, which would mean that the bowel was irretrievably damaged and I would die. So they closed me up.

The repercussions did not hit me immediately after surgery. But the pain did. The epidural that was supposed to reduce my pain only blocked fifty per cent, and for the next few days I endured some bouts of excruciating pain. For five days I could not eat. At times, the cocktail of painkilling drugs gave me hallucinations.

I spent most of August in hospital with a sore gut. I was nauseated, vomiting, losing weight and unable to eat solid food. The doctors were floating the possibility of micro-surgery to remove the tumour: cutting the aorta and vein, removing the cancer and then reconnecting them. In the meantime, they planned to put in a stent to keep the duodenum open, which would allow me to digest solid food. I needed the nutrition and the energy to keep my spirits up.

To stop myself from stewing in my health problems, I managed to get to one last football match that season. It was Melbourne's last home game of the season, and the boys had a thirty-point win over the Gold Coast.

Afterwards, as the team came from the field, I paused at

the top of the players' race and cast my eyes around the grand colosseum. So many memories. I hoped that in my lifetime I would see a jubilant knot of Melbourne players jogging around the boundary and holding aloft the Premiership Cup.

I turned and walked into the dressing rooms so I could be there when the team belted out the club song.

16

PEACE

The Peter MacCallum Cancer Centre is a grey, funereal building. Its exterior provokes a sense of disquiet. Inside, it is clear that the funding has been spent on expensive medical equipment and patients' facilities, meaning that most of the common areas or staff spaces are outdated. It's like being in a house that has the latest swish TV, computer and sound system, but whose rooms have tired 1960s linoleum and wallpaper.

All the patients are somehow touched by cancer. There are no chirpy teenagers heading back to school with their arm in a sling and a funny story to tell. It should be a grim place, but the miracle of Peter Mac is that the staff members are so upbeat. That's hugely important, given that the visitors are constantly on the lookout for positive energy.

I loved the fact that a woman in a bandana might stop me and wish me all the best. Other times, I thought about how greatly I admired some of the people who were on their own, doing it tough, maybe down from the bush. They were always up for a yak. One teenage girl with a facial piercing said to me, 'Oh, yeah, you're that Reach guy,' before adding, 'Didn't you play football too?' It was the best thing anyone had said to me in weeks.

For all that, it still upset me that at the start of September I was so unwell we had to have Matisse's tenth birthday in the hospital's games/family room. Things started slowly but, as all the cousins and uncles and aunts arrived, our spirits lifted. There is a chaotic energy about a big extended family that I have always cherished. I loved the fact that there was this crazy, pliable dynamic that seemed to shift every time we gathered. There might be a little spat between two members of the family, and the consequences would ricochet around the group, but in the end we all knew that we could rely on our parents and brothers and sisters for that unconditional love.

I had been encircled by that love and support for my whole life. I would not be the person I am today without them. Some people are lucky to have a special bond with a brother or a sister. I had five exceptional relationships like that. How remarkable it was, I thought, that twenty-seven years ago, Sharon, Brian, Terri-Ann, David and Dearbhla had been all whispers and excitement, hearing snatches of a conversation as strange men from Australia spoke to Mam and Dad about taking their eldest brother to the other side of the world. Now, all of the family lived in Melbourne.

My parents took up Australian citizenship in 2010. To think that, one by one, their children had left home, not to set themselves up across town or in another corner of the country, but 17000 kilometres and a day's travel away. And not once had I heard a negative word about it. Just constant love and support. I will never be able to thank my family enough for that.

The following day, a group of medical experts gave up their Saturday morning to gather at Peter Mac for a round-table discussion about the tumour in my duodenum.

Graeme and Grant were both there, along with two upper-gastrointestinal surgeons, a vascular surgeon and a plastic surgeon. Jeffrey Rosenfeld joined in the discussion via a phone hook-up. For more than an hour they discussed my condition, and whether microsurgery was viable. Then they called me into the room.

'We've had a fairly detailed technical talk about what would be needed to remove that tumour,' Grant said. 'And the bottom line is that the microsurgery could potentially be done, but we're reluctant to do it. There would be a six-month recovery period and a lot of time in hospital, and we're worried that, in the meantime, you would have problems with the activity in the brain.'

I could not fathom a six-month recovery period.

'Well,' Grant continued, 'to remove the tumour, they would have to remove your whole pancreas – that's the gland that puts enzymes into the bowel to dissolve your food, and that makes the insulin hormone you need to control your blood-sugar levels. Then the blood vessels would have to be rejoined. There are some life-threatening risks technically,

but potentially it would be feasible. You would be made diabetic. You would have to go onto insulin and start taking
enzyme tablets by mouth.

'So, the consensus in the room is that if there was no malignant growth in the brain, we would be willing to have a go at
the duodenum, but because of the brain there is great reluc-
tance. We don't think it would be the right decision, from a
quality-of-life perspective. Is that the best way to spend the
weeks and months ahead of you?'

One of the surgeons said, 'What we don't want to do is
shorten your life. Or to create a situation where you spend
the rest of your life bed-bound.'

I took a few deep breaths. I had to let the gravity of what
they were saying sink in.

'Would it make a difference if we could get on top of the
specks in the brain?' I asked. 'I've been hearing a lot about
CyberKnife technology in India, where they deliver higher
doses of pinpoint radiation. Is there any benefit in looking
at that?'

Grant suggested that there was no harm in sending my
scans to Bangalore for the CyberKnife experts to examine.
'But from what the scans show,' he said, 'it's going to be very
hard for them to know exactly where to treat. The spots that
you have are in a very difficult place to access, and there are
likely to be other cells that the scans don't show.

'Jeffrey's view is that, to tackle the growth as it is, the min-
imum outcome would be blindness, and even then we could
not be sure that we would get all of the cancer out, whether

through conventional surgery or radiosurgery. It might be possible to get some of it, but not all of it.'

I felt like I had reached a cul de sac. 'What steps do you guys think I should be taking next? If you were in my position, what would you do?'

Grant said that more radiation was an option, to prevent future bleeding and at the same time kill a few malignant cells. He had also not given up on getting access to the PD-1 antibody. The American supplier would not look beyond the United States, and the Japanese company that had the license for the rest of the world was not budging. But there was one last option. Grant had been in contact with the chief executive of an Israeli company and was hopeful that it might release some to us. If not, Graeme was heading to Israel in a couple of weeks and could appeal to them directly. There were also philanthropists in Melbourne who helped finance the company and they might be prepared to make a case on my behalf.

Getting access to PD-1, then, would be my last throw of the dice.

With that, the meeting broke up. 'I appreciate your time and energy, guys,' I said. 'There are a lot of other people in this building who need it too, and I'm conscious of not taking you away from them.'

My time over the next two months was largely split between looking after my body in hospital and my mind down at Rye.

The only directions I wanted to channel my energy were towards my family and healing, and being at the beach house was therapeutic for both. Just spending time with the kids had such a relaxing effect on me. In the evening, I would sit in front of the fireplace, an arm around Sam, soothed by turning my face towards the warmth.

In the city I would be too busy to stop, to look around and listen. At the beach there were times when the only noise was the birds calling, or the waves lapping at the shore. I noticed how much the treetops stooped in the wind, the patterns of the tides and the clouds. There was time to think deeply, to contemplate what it all meant.

Having spent months banishing any kind of doubt from my mind, I opened that door and allowed myself to contemplate that it might not be possible for me to live through this. Cancer had already led me to a better life; now I needed to hear what it had to say about death.

When I did look closely at death – really studied its face and felt its cold eyes upon me – I realised how many truths about life could be found there. It reminded me of the old adage that the best view of one's soul is from beyond the edge, looking back.

I really believe that life is a constant duel between ego and spirit. When it's allowed to run free, ego is that part of you that wants you to be the best at what you do, be the richest, the most popular, have the best job, the most beautiful house and the most gorgeous woman on your arm. Ego aspires to greatness, without caring whether it's good for your soul – or, more importantly, whether it's bad for your soul. Ego wants adulation, attention and recognition.

Your spirit, on the other hand, is your essence, your nature. When nurtured, it helps you discover the greatness within; it helps you to become all you can be, not all that everyone else wants or expects you to be. Your spirit helps you to learn more about love, compassion and emotions.

I found that when faced with death, my ego just dropped its barriers. And when that happened, my spirit had room to breathe.

Before I was diagnosed with cancer, the balance in my life was tilted too heavily towards ego. I would go so far as to say I had lost my way. I was losing touch with my family and my friends, and losing touch with what was important in my life. Reconnecting with my spirit had helped me look deep within myself and grasp some important principles about life and, now, about death too.

Very early on, I could recall Mam saying, 'I pray that you beat the cancer and that you are there for other people who have to go through this.' Regardless of whether I'd beat it or not, I felt that I had an important message for anyone diagnosed with cancer or any other serious illness. The element of hope has to be the starting point in your journey. There is life after diagnosis, and it is crucial that you live it with hope. It will improve your experience of life with cancer. You will be more likely to find happiness and less likely to feel anxious. It will improve your chances of recovery.

There is a wonderful line written by the great Irish poet

Seamus Heaney that is worth keeping in your thoughts: 'Even if the hopes you started out with are dashed, hope has to be maintained.'

As my own condition became more serious in the first few months after diagnosis, one device I used to rouse my hope was a bell curve. This was a chart that showed how long people lived with advanced melanoma, a 'terminal illness'. For some people, shown on the upward line, it might not be long. For most it was near the top of the bell, and for others it was beyond the norm, as the line came back down. But it dawned on me that the bell curve never came back down fully. *Because not everyone died.*

Instead, the line plateaued and reached onwards, signifying that people lived for months and years longer than expected. The further that line went, the more time they were spending living life. Sharing time with loved ones. Enjoying the moments.

That gave me hope I would be one of those people who escaped from the bell. And I felt like the longer I survived, the longer I was going to continue to survive. And the longer I survived, the more I appreciated what an incredible thing life was.

As sinister as cancer might be as a disease, and as harrowing as the treatment could be, there was still beauty in the experience. I thought of all the wonderful moments I would have missed had I simply given up and allowed cancer to take me. I understood that not every cancer patient was going to get to meet U2 and Lance Armstrong, but they too would enjoy magical days.

I could still picture the smile on Tiernan's face as he stood in the kitchen waiting to be taken to his first day of prep. I could hear the naughty giggling that I shared with the kids when, for once, I was the one lying on the bed talking, keeping them awake too late, pulling faces as we were told off by Sam.

I thought of the night that I walked around the boundary at the MCG to do a television interview, and the 15000 women who were waiting to form the shape of a Pink Lady all stood to applaud me. It was the most humbling moment of my life.

I remembered the privilege of accompanying one of the Melbourne footballers, Liam Jurrah, to his home town of Yuendumu, and being treated with such warmth and respect by the Warlpiri people. I got such energy from seeing kids there who were just going for it and loving life.

One of the most powerful moments came when I was a bit low after brain surgery. The Reach Crew organised for a bunch of kids to gather around and deliver positive messages to help lift my spirits. To restore my hope. I looked around that room, and every face had a story. So many wonderful memories. And I began to bawl like a baby. It was very healing. Thousands of young people had been through a similar exercise, but I never had before. That gave me a compelling reminder of the power of Reach.

And that is the importance of making sure you live your life with a terminal illness, rather than just allowing it to drain away. From the moment some people found out I had cancer, they started to look at me as a man who was dying.

But we will all die.

So why think of cancer as dying?

Why not think of it as living?

While I had time to think, I needed to find where I was at with my religion, my spirituality, my belief systems. Initially, I was really lost and confused. For most of my life I had been a staunch Catholic, but as I grew older I had trouble accepting that I had to subscribe to a strict interpretation of faith. I did not like being told how I had to honour God, and that if I did not do it in a particular way, there would be guilt and damnation.

I had to form my own understanding. I did not doubt Christ's teachings – in fact, at times I turned to them to cope more effectively with my illness and to find meaning – but I had trouble with how some people interpreted them. I believe there is something to be gained from learning about the religions of the world. I could not understand why people would close their minds to something like the Bhagavad Gita, for example, the Hindu scripture that some scholars believe to be twice as old as the Bible. It is one of the reasons I was open to the Balian experience in Ubud, and to the reiki sessions. Various religions and spiritual practices explore ways to become a better person, if you're open to accepting their wisdom. And being open-minded to such learning is infinitely more important than focusing on how the devotees worship, dress or sound.

I don't see religion as having to fit in with someone else's definition. To me, it makes sense to learn as much about other faiths and ideologies as you can. I would venture to say that people have learned more about each other's religions over the past fifty years than throughout the rest of history. Ideally, that trend will continue and foster understanding and tolerance.

For all of these reasons, I did not have a conventional belief system. But I did feel the need to be connected to God and to pray throughout my illness. It helped me find peace.

At times, I did contemplate the afterlife, but the way I saw it, there was no point dwelling on it. Everyone would find out eventually. But I did not want to rush towards it.

The dice for my one last roll was handed to me in October 2011.

Getting access to the PD-1 antibody had been no small task. The Israeli company had nearly all of its stock tied up in clinical trials and was reluctant to release any to Australia.

Grant and Graeme had almost given up pursuing the treatment, but they enlisted the help of Melbourne board member David Thurin, whose extensive medical background and close links with the philanthropic Gandel Group helped enormously. In the end, we argued that my situation could benefit their research and help open lines of communication for future use of the treatment in Australia. The Israeli firm managed to find some spare PD-1 and I began to receive fortnightly doses. I had peace of mind from knowing that we had pursued every type of cancer treatment possible.

It was more difficult to be at peace with the idea that the treatments might not keep me alive.

Dying did not scare me. I was proud of what I had managed to achieve in my life. I had tried to live a strong life, one with purpose, with meaning. I had not just meandered along the path I travelled; I had tried to extract the most out of myself. And I believe that I did so with integrity.

I had always believed that life was about becoming all you could be. It was about opening yourself to opportunities to learn and experience new things. Two of the greatest men ever to have lived have summed this up better than I ever will. Abraham Lincoln, the great American president, said, 'In the end it's not the years in your life that count; it's the life in your years.' Leonardo da Vinci, Italy's Renaissance genius, expressed the sentiment elegantly: 'As a well-spent day brings happy sleep, so a life well spent brings happy death.'

But the words that gave me greatest solace came from another great man: my father. When he was interviewed for the documentary, he said something that gave me enormous pride: 'Jim will never live long enough anyway. No matter what age he goes down at, he will have an unfinished business sheet in front of him. He never closes the door, but he's always opening a new one.'

Dad had summed it up so concisely. There would never be enough years in life. I would always have more doors to open. In the end, all we can hope for is that when we die, the people who knew us will look at our life and say, 'But, oh, how he lived!'

I was at peace with the concept of leaving this world, but not with the thought of leaving my family. It was the one aspect of cancer that had haunted me and hurt me throughout the journey. The only way to ease the pain was to think about how blessed I was to have shared quality time with Sam and the kids. I couldn't let myself think about the time I would miss out on.

I was blessed to have fallen in love – body and soul – with a woman of such astonishing beauty. And then to have fallen in love with her all over again, when adversity had revealed the depth of her greatness. I had watched her become a stronger, more purposeful woman, and at the same time I had grown to appreciate more fully her caring and generous spirit. It takes love to see the beauty in anything, especially life itself, and I had been blessed to have Sam to open my eyes to absolute love.

I was also blessed that our love had embraced two wonderful children. Their spirit, their verve and their caring nature made me enormously proud and confident about what they would find in life. I was convinced that they were resilient enough to overcome adversity, and I knew they were surrounded by genuine people who would love and support them.

The children would not be afraid to be who they wanted to be. It deeply pained me that I might not get to see that growth, but I hoped I might still influence it. I hoped that there would always be a picture of their father in their hearts, a picture that would make them proud. I hoped it would lead them to believe that I stood for something, and make them in turn want to pursue a life that stood for something. I believe that the best way to influence what our children will become tomorrow is by helping them grow today.

And that is where I searched for peace: in knowing that, as long as I lived in their memories, I would always be alive.

I might have been preparing for death, but that did not mean I was prepared to die. There were new challenges to take on. For six weeks in October and early November, while the doctors administered the PD-1 antibody, I worked on two projects: this book and the launch of Jimbo muesli.

There were times when I felt quite frail and lethargic, but it was a great salve to my spirits when I saw a Twitter post from Lance Armstrong that read: 'Jimmy Stynes, we are all thinking of you and are sending healing energy your way from all around the world!' I would need every bit of that healing energy because my body was beginning to fail me.

I was having trouble with language again too. I would have to pause and grasp for the right words during conversations. There was also a persistent numbness down my right arm. The symptoms were causing Sam real angst, but the tipping point came in mid-November, the day before the Reach Breakfast, an annual event that brought together inspiring teenagers, corporates and celebrities.

Sam noticed that I was particularly scatty, and I had pains

shooting down my arm and also occasionally in my gut. There was a brief but frightening episode when my eyesight temporarily deserted me. Sam rang Grant, who urged her to bring me into hospital the following morning.

The next day, after changing our minds half a dozen times, Sam and I made a low-key appearance at the Reach Breakfast before heading across the city to see Grant in his office at Peter Mac. We spoke about the various symptoms, which alarmed him, and he organised for me to have a brain scan.

When we reconvened later in the day, the mood was grim.

'It's not good news,' Grant said. 'The tumour in your brain is growing again. It's going to be very, very hard to treat it. In fact, with the way it's positioned, I suspect it's going to be inoperable.'

He explained that a more comprehensive set of scans would be advisable, but at this stage it looked as though there was no point persisting with the PD-1 treatment.

'Is there anything we can look at?' I asked. 'Do you do a line in miracles around here?'

'I can prescribe one,' he said, smiling weakly. 'We're at the stage where we've pretty much run out of options. We could perhaps look at whether there might be some more focus radiation, but to be honest I'm not sure that's the best way to go at this stage.'

There was a long silence.

'Now,' he began slowly, 'some people want to talk about the end and some don't, but throughout this you have always wanted to be upfront.'

'So . . .' I had to find a way to get the words out. 'What you mean is that I've only got a few weeks to live?'

'No, but in the coming weeks you're probably going to get sleepier more often. You might drift away. I can't tell you what the timeframe is, Jim. The tumour might bleed into the brain and things might happen more quickly. But that hasn't happened so far, so it's probably not likely.'

There was not much more for me to say.

'Okay . . . I know this is not an easy thing to tell me, Grant, so thank you for your honesty.'

I accepted that I was probably going to die soon. Maybe very soon. But I would never give up. I would maintain my surrender. I never wanted to lose my will to live. No matter how certain the prognosis, I had to keep hope alive. It would help me have more time, more life. And life is, after all, the most precious thing we have got.

If you don't have cancer, cherish life. If you do, cherish it even more.

17

REPRIEVE

Out. Keep it for now. Out. Hmm, not sure – that can go on the 'maybe' pile.

I was sorting out clothes. Apparently, this was one of the most distressing experiences for relatives after the passing of a loved one. I thought I'd get in early and help save Sam some of the anguish later on.

Out. Out. Won't be needing those running shoes anymore. Everything went into a box on the front balcony for the Salvation Army, except the stuff that wasn't good enough, which went straight into the rubbish bin.

Earlier that day I had turned on my laptop and found myself stuck staring at the screensaver. It was a photograph of Matisse and me. We both looked so happy and healthy. Eventually, I'd had to look away and shut the computer down.

I just didn't know what to do, besides get everything ready in case there was not much time left. Normally, as November drew to a close, I would be lamenting how there were not enough days left before Christmas; this year I was mourning that there were simply not enough days left.

Everywhere I turned there was sorrow. Tiernan had asked Sam, 'Will Daddy still be here to see what Santa brings?'

These were the hardest days of my whole cancer journey. The cruellest. It felt like I was a dead man walking, just waiting for the guards to come into the room and lead me away. I didn't even know which day they would be coming. Would there be time for a last request, a final meal? We were down at our beach house in Rye and had organised for about sixty or so of our closest friends to come over for a barbecue that Sunday. I didn't know what to expect, but we were hoping to keep it an upbeat day. I saw it as a last chance to catch up with people, just in case things took a turn for the worse and there was no other time to say farewell.

The day before the barbecue, Sam and I headed out for breakfast at a café a couple of kilometres up the road in Blairgowrie; a few close friends – Hugh Ellis, Don McLardy and Trisha Silvers – joined us. The mood was palpably sombre as we did some last-minute planning for the barbecue. Don had a lined up a caterer who had done some corporate functions for him, and we considered whether to organise an acoustic guitarist to ensure there were no awkward silences.

We were running through a list of guests when Sam's phone rang. She glanced at the display panel. 'Grant McArthur,' she explained, leaning away from the table to take the call, a hand pressed to her other ear. The rest of us returned to breakfast, but after a minute or two Sam turned towards me, saying, 'Hang on, Grant, I'm not sure I can deal with this. You better talk to Jim.' She handed me the phone.

Struggling to hear Grant, I made my way outside the café. As I stood there, looking across Point Nepean Road and past the gnarled tea trees to the water glistening in Port Phillip Bay, I listened while he delivered the most remarkable and unexpected news. The tumour in my duodenum had halved in size, and the brain tumours looked to have receded to the extent that further surgery looked possible. Perhaps the PD-1 was having an effect after all. At least, it was buying me more time. We would need to reconvene in Melbourne the following week to discuss the next step, but it looked like brain surgery before Christmas was on the agenda.

After the call, I stood there for a moment, stunned. Then I burst back into the café with a beaming smile, my arms held out wide. 'I'm fookin' Lazarus!' I declared. A few startled faces snapped towards me, not least from our table. A ten-minute phone call had taken me from the deepest depths to feeling utterly energised – it really demonstrated the power of the mind.

One moment I was like a condemned man who been given a peek into the room containing the electric chair. The next moment the door was being unbolted so that they could hand me a stay of execution.

We started to hit the phones. The farewell barbecue was off and we began to hatch grander plans. I had to make the most of this reprieve. Hugh wondered if there was any prospect of me travelling. His catamaran was still moored in the Caribbean Sea.

Our weekend was turned on its head. We went from

planning finger food and napkins on Saturday morning to the logistics of island-hopping from Colombia to the Panama Canal by Sunday night.

All that had to be negotiated was medical approval and authorisation to travel with the various drugs I needed – that, and the small matter of more brain surgery.

I headed back to town ready to face the world again. I fronted the media at Melbourne training after publicly presenting our new recruit Mitch Clarke with the number eleven guernsey I had worn for most of my playing career. I did an interview with Martin Flanagan, the journalist who writes so beautifully and optimistically about the game. I went to an Eminem concert; it gave my swelling brain a massive headache but also a new-found respect for the guy. I loved the fact that he could emerge from periods of adversity in his life and pack out stadiums, all based on his drive and passion for hiphop.

And then I met the doctors and revealed the proposed Caribbean leg of my odyssey. Grant was not convinced about the merits of the trip. 'If you were talking about the Whitsundays, I'd have reservations but I'd say "go for it". But out in the open ocean . . .'

Professor Rosenfeld was similarly hesitant. 'Let's talk about it after the surgery,' he said. 'Even the flight would be a major risk. You could get an air bubble in your brain, which would kill you.'

The operation was booked for 9 December, which would

only give me two weeks to recover and convince everyone that I was healthy enough to undertake the journey. We were hoping to fly out on Christmas Day.

When Wayne drove me to the Alfred Hospital on the morning of the surgery, I was more nervous than I could ever recall having been. I sat in the passenger's seat, looking down, not sure that I wanted to move. 'Come on, mate, you'll be right,' Wayne offered, tapping me on the shoulder. I inhaled deeply, opened the car door and Sam and I headed inside for brain operation number six.

I woke up in a recovery room, with a nurse rubbing my shoulder and smiling. 'Hello, Jim,' she said. 'My name is Kate. How are you feeling?'

'All right,' I croaked.

'How's the pain?'

'All right. It's okay. But my head hurts.'

'If it's worrying you, you can push this button. Can you tell me where you are?'

'Hospital.'

'Yes, that's right. Which one?'

'Ah, I don't know.'

'Okay, is it the Epworth, the Alfred or Royal Melbourne?'

'Umm . . . Alfred.'

'Good. And do you know what month it is?'

I slowly recited the months to myself, at the same time counting them on my fingers. 'December?'

'Great, Jim, you're doing fine.'

I was alive. I reached up to feel my head. The back half had been shaved, and I could feel a lot of stitches. It was throbbing but the pain was dull. I tried opening my eyes and looking around, but my vision was blurry. I could make out someone sitting in a chair against the wall. Underneath the baseball cap was a big cheesy grin. Jules.

'How are you, big man?' he asked.

I gave him a thumbs-up. 'Good. How are you?'

He began laughing as I closed my eyes and went back to sleep.

'Where are you?'

Hospital. The whole post-op routine had begun again. This time I forgot that it was December, but Kate was still satisfied. Jules got to his feet. 'When you leave, Kate, we're going to cram,' he said. 'We want him to leave here with first-class honours.'

She chuckled and then turned to me. 'Now, remember, if you're struggling with the pain, push this button.'

I felt my head again. It only hurt when I lay on my back. Jules helped me to get comfortable.

'Need a drink of water?' he asked. 'Anything I can get you?' I leaned forward and had a sip through a straw. 'I know one thing,' he added. 'This is not the place to come for a hair-cut.' Apparently, they had only shaved the back half of my head, much to Jules's amusement. He took a couple of photographs with his iPhone and held them up for me to see, but my vision was not good enough to make out much more than a blurry head on the screen.

'I think the operation went all right,' I said.

'Apparently your surgeon is ecstatic,' Jules replied.

'Really? Did he drop by? How do you know?'

'I read it here,' Jules held up the phone. 'On the *Herald Sun* website. Do you want me to read it to you? This is bizarre. Three hours after you're out of surgery, and you get to find out how it went from a website. Hang on a minute, here we go.' He read out the article.

Risky surgery to remove a tumour from Jim Stynes' brain has been successful. Prof Rosenfeld told the Herald Sun *that Stynes, 45, continued to surprise medical staff. 'I don't know the exact number of operations I have carried out on him now, I have lost count,' Prof Rosenfeld said. 'Jim is an amazing stayer who just bounces back and a lot of people just don't bounce back like he does . . . The operation went well. Everything as planned, there were no surprises.' He said there was a 'good clearance' of the last tumour but couldn't guarantee it was removed completely. 'I would never say 100 per cent, you can never get that, but it looks good.'*

I leaned back on the pillow. 'That sounds good,' I said. 'But how would they know all of this?'

'I suppose they put out a statement,' Jules said. 'It says here that there was something posted on the Jimbo Super Muesli Facebook page: "A message with an update on Jim: 'All in all, it looks like a big success . . . Thanks to everyone for your well wishes and prayers. We all love you, big guy.'" Sounds like Hugh. Then, at the end of the article, sixty-seven people have left messages of support. Wait, no, sixty-four of them are messages from ex-girlfriends asking you to call them.'

Over the next few hours, Jules sat with me, cracking gags and keeping the nurses entertained whenever they came in to check on me.

Eventually, the next person on Sam's roster arrived for his shift: Garry Lyon. We talked for hours. We spoke about trivial stuff, like the merits of wine gums versus jubes. We reminisced, and reassured each other that we really were pretty decent footballers in our day.

I love to tell people about the first time Garry and I met, when we were both training with the Melbourne under-19s. He couldn't understand my Irish brogue, and I thought Garry's home town of Kyabram was somewhere in the outback and misunderstood his tan and his thick black hair; I went home that evening and, over dinner with the Caddy family, declared, 'I met my first Australian Aborigine today.' I had got a few laughs out of that story over the years.

Like a few of my closer mates, Garry and I had found it easier to open up in recent months. We could talk about our emotions, our fears, our insecurities and our passions.

One of those was the future of the Melbourne Football Club, and we discussed how the football department seemed to be getting back on track under our new coach, Mark Neeld. Garry believed the appointment of Neil Craig as director of sports performance would help prevent any more disconnections between the football department and the board. He mentioned that our former skipper Greg Healy might be in a position to step up and take on the role of football director. He also canvassed my opinion about appointing co-captains.

It was remarkable. This was the most alert I had ever felt after coming out of surgery. Was I kidding myself by daring to dream that there might yet be a miracle?

When I first learned that I had cancer, I always thought I would get the better of it, and that it would just be another part of my story. I can distinctly remember thinking to myself, *You'll beat cancer, leave it behind and then just sail off into the sunset.*

We flew out of Melbourne at 10.30 am on Christmas Day, and it was the greatest feeling of release. It seemed like we had left behind every stress life had to offer. I looked out the tiny window at the suburban blocks below and imagined all the families gathered around tinselled trees, opening their presents. It was that wonderful time of the day when kids were delighted and parents could sit back contentedly before things got manic and cars had to be loaded, lunches piled high and extended family politics negotiated. Instead, Sam and I reclined our chairs and accepted the offer from the stewardess of a sip of champagne.

On our last day before flying back to Melbourne, the girls wanted to check out the shopping district, so we headed to glitzy Rodeo Drive.

Everyone had been clucking over me the whole time we were away, but here, somehow, I found myself on my own in the Hugo Boss store. Heading downstairs, I looked a few metres across to see the other seven members of our party going upstairs.

'Jimbo!' Sam called out, pointing upwards. 'This way.' But I could hear Hugh telling her not to fuss, saying that some time on my own wouldn't do me any harm.

They spent an eternity up there, looking at the designer clothes, and to relieve the boredom I allowed a sales assistant to talk me into trying on a tuxedo. Just as the others came back downstairs, there I was, adjusting a bow tie and checking out the length of the sleeves.

Sam began laughing. 'I knew that if I left you alone for a moment you'd get up to all sorts of mischief!'

I spun on my heel and thrust out my arms, like a magician calling for applause. 'You have to admit, I do look sharp.'

Hugh wandered over, nodding. 'Just as a matter of interest,' he said, 'can you see yourself needing a new dinner suit any time soon?'

I smiled and shrugged my shoulders. 'Well, who knows? I'm trying to stay positive about the possibility. You have to live in hope.'

POSTSCRIPT

The Stynes family arrived back from their holiday on Thursday 19 January 2012. Jim felt blessed to have negotiated the twenty-five days of travel without a single health glitch. He was beaming at having spent some quality time with his beloved family. He hoped they would carry those carefree days with them through their lives.

The day after their return, however, he felt unwell. On the Sunday, he was admitted to hospital with stabbing pains in his stomach. Doctors discovered that the bile duct between his duodenum and liver was blocked. Scans also showed that there were new spots on his liver. After years of finding ways to take on cancer, it was time to acknowledge that he was not going to beat it. Now it was about managing his demise.

On 31 January, the day before the Melbourne Football Club's annual general meeting, Jim sat down with Sam at their kitchen table and prepared a statement to announce that he was stepping down as Melbourne's president. The next day, while Jim was at St Vincent's Hospital for surgery to put in a stent to unblock his bile duct, the Melbourne board met to accept his resignation and install Don McLardy as the club's new president.

Jim went home to spend time with his extraordinary wife and two children. Sam made a great effort for him to have some peaceful time with the family. After a very public life, it was time for some privacy.

His last public appearance was at the Melbourne Football Club's inaugural commencement dinner on 15 March 2012, at which Ron Barassi – the man who had handed Jim his first Sherrin football in Dublin – presented him with a club blazer.

Jim Stynes died five days later, a month shy of his forty-sixth birthday.

On Tuesday 27 March, a state funeral was held for Jim at St Paul's Cathedral, Melbourne, with thousands of people watching from across the road in Federation Square. In Dublin, mourners sang 'Waltzing Matilda' at a memorial service at his local Ballyroan parish church. That weekend, a minute's applause to celebrate his life was held at football matches at both Croke Park and the MCG.

Jim requested that his ashes be scattered in Ireland, beyond Hell Fire, at Sally Gap.

AFTERWORD

By Sam Stynes

Life with Jim was an amazing adventure – exhilarating, fun, relentless and exhausting. Often it was like being a passenger aboard an out-of-control high-speed train that somehow managed not to derail or crash. Yet if I had the choice of trading that experience for an easier marriage to a partner with whom I would reach old age, knowing we would die together peacefully in our rocking chairs, I wouldn't take it. I wouldn't change a single thing.

Jim and I challenged each other immensely. I believe that is what made our relationship so wonderful and exciting. Ultimately Jim and I shared a great love story as we continued to grow both as individuals and together. Yet, like many couples, we spent years fighting for autonomy and space.

When an Irishman and an Italian girl marry, it's a certainty that much passion, fire and spirit will follow. In the early days of our marriage, I felt frustrated when Jim would plan out his busy schedule barely consulting me. More often than not, I was literally left holding the baby. I wasn't brought up to believe that being a wife automatically meant that I would wait on my husband hand and foot, be it domestically, emotionally or logistically. There was huge pressure to share in Jim's very public life along with a fight to maintain my own identity.

On one particular occasion, pre-cancer, Jim shouted at me, passionately, 'Do you have any fookin' idea how difficult it is being married to a woman who never, in a stereotypical sense, views herself as a wife?' I yelled back, 'Do you know how horrible it is being married to a man whose sole purpose in life is to be there for people other than your immediate family?'

I struggled to accept the roles associated with being a WAG (Wife and Girlfriend of a footballer). The perception of WAGs being shallow, dumbed-down arm candy, there only to be ogled, judged and joked about, has always seemed to me like a modern form of stoning 'witches' in the town square. I struggled to accept the roles associated with marriage. I struggled to accept the roles associated with parenting our two children, Matisse and Tiernan. To be honest, I struggled to accept the roles associated with being the primary carer of my terminally ill cancer-ridden husband. Like a wild horse that always needed to be broken in, I kicked and I bucked against it all.

I'd always considered myself a generous person with a positive outlook on life – Mum had even nicknamed me Tinker Bell. But a dark part of me was thinking, *Why should*

I put myself in this role only to be ultimately let down, hurt and potentially destroyed? Will Jim even appreciate it? Hasn't Jim always forged ahead with his own life without consideration for my needs and me? Would he do it for me?

Then, one frosty winter's morning, Jim's friend and business partner asked me to go for a walk with him along the beach. As we sipped takeaway coffees, he pulled no punches. 'If you don't step up and take on that role, I will actually lose respect for you. Jim really needs you, Sam. Now more than ever.'

I will never forget those cutting words. They struck a chord with me. From the outset, I'd instinctively known that while Jim's life-expectancy could be challenged and extended, it would be highly unlikely that my husband would beat cancer. I'd had first hand experience of final-stage cancer, having lost my father to prostate cancer in 2005. I can't help but feel that it's no coincidence that Jim died on 20 March, my dad's birthday.

Jim had taught me the importance of stepping up to the plate and taking on challenges that really mattered to me, in order to keep growing both personally and professionally. Jim had taught me how to avoid being diffident and to apply myself by working hard to get the most out of life. Even if I didn't always reach the destination, it was the learning along the way that really counted.

I ended up taking on the role as Jim's carer unconditionally and with great gusto. It was the most rewarding thing I've ever done, regardless of the heartbreaking outcome. I didn't know that so much love, growth, inspiration, resilience and calmness could emerge from within.

I found it a privilege to be Jim's primary carer and support person, although it's fair to say that the learning curve was steep for both of us. I surprised myself as I found out what I was capable of. On a purely practical level, what I learned throughout Jim's cancer battle was varied and empowering, from how the human body works to advances in medical research, from acquiring nursing skills and how to manage medication to the logistics of managing a life overflowing with appointments with specialists, surgeons and doctors while simultaneously maintaining a positive and realistic frame of mind. Jokes were made about awarding me 'honorary nursing and doctor' status. It was a mindboggling and highly emotive experience.

The medical support Jim received was nothing short of remarkable. His medical team seemed to fight his cancer battle as if it were their own. After one of Jim's many surgeries, my dear friend Kirsty and I were in the ICU, surrounded by Jim's impressive team – surgeon, oncologist and specialist nurses. We quietly joked to each other that while there'd been times when we thought we were pretty good, we were actually the biggest underachievers in the room – perhaps we should have pursued careers that actually meant something, like helping to save people's lives!

Most importantly, I learned about self-sacrifice. Up until the diagnosis, I'd always worked with Jim under the conditions that I wouldn't compromise on my independence, lifestyle or dreams. It was refreshing to put Jim's welfare before my own wants and needs, and I succumbed to doing so with an extremely full heart. And it was only then that it came to the forefront of my mind that while I had accused Jim of being self-centered and selfish – and there's no doubt he often was – it was these very traits that enabled him to work for the greater good. Jim wasn't perfect, yet once I came to understand that these foundations of his being enabled him to achieve what he did, I realised that he was extraordinary.

It is not uncommon for relationships to crumble under the pressures of cancer. Not only does the cancer patient's life change dramatically, cancer also affects the lives of those closest to the patient. Normal life as any individual knows it swiftly flies out the window. It took courage and effort on both Jim's and my side to accept our new direction and go on the cancer journey together. Right up until the time Jim died, we worked as a team. We enjoyed the highs of the good news regarding Jim's health and shared the lows to do with the fears, sadness and disappointments that came our way too. When cancer cuts the patient some slack, it's referred to as 'a window of opportunity'. We rejoiced when any window of opportunity was opened, and simply lived life to the fullest. It didn't matter so much what we were doing, whether it was something extravagant like going on holiday or simply going out to dinner or to see a movie. Taking a walk in the park on a sunny day with a sandwich in hand was one of our favourite things to do.

While our relationship continued to go from strength to

strength throughout Jim's illness, it was during the last two months of Jim's life that our love truly flowed. Sure, we'd loved each other, but I'd never before experienced a feeling of love that just flowed effortlessly, free from disturbances, road-blocks, darkness and fear. We both knew that it was inevitable that Jim was going to die, and we no longer fought it. We were deeply saddened, heartbroken and disappointed by this real-ity, sometimes to the point where I felt as though I'd never recover. And yet we'd fought the good fight together. Our love story ended with us losing in the biggest way, yet it was loving regardless. The way we saw it, as a team, we'd actually won. We had both become better versions of ourselves.

Two weeks before Jim's death we discussed how ridicu-lous it seemed to have had to go through the gruelling cancer journey as patient and carer, in order to undergo such extreme personal growth and discover this blissful place.

The night before Jim slipped into a non-comprehensive state, we took one last stroll around the lovely leafy streets of St Kilda West, where we had built our wonderful life together. With Jim surrendered in a wheelchair, being pushed by his mate Hugh Ellis – by this stage I was too drained and emo-tional to do the pushing – we headed off to dinner in busy St Kilda. We giggled at how Jim still had me out and about living, even though I was incredibly worried that he was in such a bad way. That night, Jim enjoyed his very last meal – two courses no less, with several whiskeys and Coke!

Because of the depth of Jim's character and that of those surrounding him, there was much beauty in the lead-up to his death. The experience of helping someone you love to die, surrounded by dear family and friends, without the dramas that can so often accompany families in general, gave me great faith in the overriding goodness of the human spirit.

Jim's oncologist, Dr Grant McArthur, often used a mountain metaphor to explain where things were at with Jim's health, saying that he was sitting on the edge of a cliff, at times just holding on. He told us that if Jim started to slide down the slippery slope, things could go wrong very quickly. Together, along with the rock-solid support of our extended family and friends, Jim and I hiked up the seemingly endless super-steep mountain and eventually took in the view. Sights I'm certain that neither of us had ever thought we'd see took our breaths away.

Following Jim's death, I continue to draw strength from what I learned during our relationship. It's only since he died that I've come to realise how Jim had been craftily and cleverly grooming me to get out there and really live life to the fullest. As he did with so many others, Jim helped me to stretch my potential.

Jim tried everything in life without reservation. He wasn't always successful, but he always gave his all. His was a bold spirit with the least timorous of souls. He taught me that while we all have insecurities, apprehensions and fears within, the special bit of knowledge is that we can actually overcome them.

Everyone's common fate is mortality – we can postpone it but we can't avoid it. Jim died young and he suffered. He left me with the gift of our two beautiful children. Without reservation, I have eagerly accepted the roles associated with being a single working mother. I baulk at describing myself as a 'widow', though. It's such an old-fashioned tragic-sounding term, and Jim certainly wouldn't have approved. Some of his last words to me were, 'It will be really tough for a while, Sam, but you're strong and in time you'll go on and start a new life for yourself while continuing to provide a wonderful life for Matisse and Tiernan.'

Being Jim's wife, mother to his children and his primary carer has made me wise up and become more resilient. Jim gave me the tools to do so, and set the best possible example of getting the most out of every experience life throws your way.

PICTURE CREDITS

PAGE 1 Private collection

PAGE 2 Private collection

PAGE 3 (Top) Courtesy Melbourne FC
(Bottom) Jim Stynes in Melbourne rooms after a VFL match
in the 1980s. Courtesy Newspix

PAGE 4 (Top) 19 August 1987. Courtesy Newspix
(Bottom) 18 January 1988. Jim Stynes training.
Courtesy Fairfax Syndication / Jason Childs

PAGE 5 (Top left) Courtesy Newspix
(Top right) May 1996. Jim Stynes leads the Demons onto the MCG
before his record-breaking 205th consecutive match against Essendon.
Courtesy Newspix / Wayne Ludbey
(Bottom left) 1980s. Jim Stynes of the Melbourne Demons takes
a kick during a VFL match. Courtesy Newspix
(Bottom right) Courtesy Newspix

PAGE 6 22 June 1998. Jim Stynes in an 85-point hammering by
St Kilda at the MCG. Courtesy Fairfax Syndication / Joe Armao

PAGE 7 (Top) 23 September 1997. Courtesy Fairfax Syndication /
Pat Scala
(Bottom) Jim Stynes in the Australian jumper ahead of the
1998 All-Australian football tour to Ireland. Courtesy Newspix /
George Salpigtidis

PAGE 8 Private collection

PAGE 9 (Top) 2 July 2009. Courtesy Newspix / David Caird
(Bottom) James McDonald holds up Jim Stynes' jumper.
Courtesy AFL Photos / Sean Garnsworthy

PAGE 10 Private collection

PAGE 11 (Top) Private collection
(Bottom) 26 January 2010. Courtesy Newspix / Andrew Henshaw

PAGE 12 (Top) Private collection
(Bottom) 18 April 2010. Courtesy Newspix / Michael Klein

PAGE 13 (Top) Private collection
(Bottom) 21 March 2011. Jim Stynes shares a laugh with Prince William
after a wayward handball comes close to hitting a photographer during
the royal tour of Victoria's flood-affected areas. Courtesy Newspix /
David Caird

PAGE 14 Courtesy Mark Strachan / markstrachan.com

PAGE 15 Private collection

PAGE 16 Tuesday 27 March 2012. Courtesy Newspix / Nicole Garmston

ACKNOWLEDGEMENTS

Thanks to the numerous people who contributed in various ways to getting Jim's story right and making it into a book: Adam Ramanauskas, Andrea McNamara, Anita Simon, Brian Stynes Sr, Brian Stynes Jr, Bridget Maidment, Carolyn Trewin-Galbally, Ciarán Farrell, Don McLardy, Garry Lyon, Graeme Southwick, Grant McArthur, Hugh Ellis, Jules Lund, Julian Welch, Lance Armstrong, Mary Williamson, Matisse Stynes, Michael Scott, Paul Currie, Peter Day, Sam Stynes, Sharon Stynes, Teresa Stynes, Terri-Ann Stynes, Tiernan Stynes, Trish Silvers, Wayne Ludbey.

Special thanks to my family – Tif, Jock, Lex and Samantha – for giving me the time, space and support to help Jim tell his story.